Kate Conway-Turner, PhD
Suzanne Cherrin, PhD

Women, Families, and Feminist Politics
A Global Exploration

DISCARDED

D1462486

*Pre-publication
REVIEWS,
COMMENTARIES,
EVALUATIONS . . .*

"**T**his is t.. ook I've been waiting for– to use not only with the teachers in my classes, but also with the community literacy movement in which I'm involved. At last I have in my hands a book that presents reality about family life and economic and social issues from a global feminist perspective. The personal *is* political and these authors have done an admirable job of taking us to a deeper level of knowing that."

Sally Z. Hare, PhD
*Singleton Professor of Education,
Director, Center for Education
and Community,
Coastal Carolina College,
Myrtle Beach, SC*

More pre-publication
REVIEWS, COMMENTARIES, EVALUATIONS . . .

"**T**his text is a comprehensive and scholarly approach to issues of women's health, family, and development internationally. The strengths of the book are its interdisciplinarity and international scope plus its skillful synthesis of critical research reviews, personal observations, and women's voices from around the world. The strong introductory chapter presents the organizing concepts and frameworks. The authors courageously and honestly confront the challenges of and to a feminist framework and provide background for understanding this approach, making this book as valuable to the general public as to students and academics. This approach is woven throughout a book that addresses comprehensively all the aspects of women's lives that they themselves consider most important, from family and sexuality to work, health, and violence.

Women, Families, and Feminist Politics would be an invaluable text for women's studies, public policy courses, and international health and women's health courses in a variety of university departments. It is accessible to undergraduate students but scholarly enough to be valuable to graduate students and researchers. Hopefully it will be made available to nongovernmental women's organizations and official international bodies such as the World Health Organization and other UN agencies worldwide. It is an extremely important book!"

Jacquelyn C. Campbell
Anna Wolf Endowed Professor,
Johns Hopkins University
School of Nursing,
Baltimore, MD

Harrington Park Press
An Imprint of The Haworth Press, Inc.

Women, Families, and Feminist Politics
A Global Exploration

HAWORTH Innovations in Feminist Studies
J. Dianne Garner, DSW
Senior Editor

Women, Families, and Feminist Politics
A Global Exploration

Kate Conway-Turner, PhD
Suzanne Cherrin, PhD

Harrington Park Press
An Imprint of The Haworth Press, Inc.
New York • London

Published by

Harrington Park Press, an imprint of The Haworth Press, Inc., 10 Alice Street, Binghamton, NY 13904-1580

Cover design by Jennifer M. Gaska.

The Library of Congress has cataloged the hardcover edition of this book as:

Conway-Turner, Kate.
    Women, families, and feminist politics : a global exploration / Kate Conway-Turner, Suzanne Cherrin.
        p.   cm.
    Includes bibliographical references (p.   ) and index.
    ISBN 0-7890-0482-8 (alk. paper)
    1. Feminism. 2. Feminist theory. 3. Women—Social conditions. 4. Women—Political activity. 5. Women—Legal status, laws, etc. I. Cherrin, Suzanne. II. Title.
HV1154.C6526 1998
305.42—dc21
                                                                                            98-6096
                                                                                              CIP

ISBN 1-56023-935-2 (pbk.)

CONTENTS

Chapter 3. Population, Reproduction, Sexuality and Women's Status 69

Chapter 4. Women and Work Worldwide 105

ABOUT THE AUTHORS

Kate Conway-Turner, an applied social psychologist, is the immediate past Director of the Women's Studies program and a Professor in the Department of Individual and Family Studies and the Department of Psychology at the University of Delaware. Her areas of research include international women's health, women's intergenerational relationships, marital patterns, and the impact of race and culture on the lives of women and their families. She writes and lectures in areas that reflect these research interests. Dr. Conway-Turner was a 1990-1993 recipient of the Kellogg's National Leadership Grant and the recipient of an American Council on Education Fellowship (1996-1997). She participates in a wide variety of women's studies, family studies, and ethnic studies of professional organizations.

Suzanne Cherrin is an Assistant Professor of Women's Studies at the University of Delaware. She teaches and lectures on international women's issues, with an emphasis on how world inequality and militarism affect women's lives. She is a co-editor of *Women's Studies in Transition: Interdisciplinary and Identity* and the author of "Breast Cancer: A Critical Analysis of Advice to Women," within this text. In June 1998, Dr. Cherrin led a Women's Studies Mission to China under the sponsorship of the Citizen Ambassador Program of People to People International, with the support of the Women's Studies Institute of China and the All-China Women's Federation.

Introduction

This text is the result of our ongoing discussions concerning women worldwide. We brought to these discussions our collective interest and experiences through secondary analysis and primary investigations. We are both multidisciplinary scholars who bring the breadth and diversity of sociological inquiry and social-psychological interpretation to the explorations within this text. These perspectives inform a critical examination of community and family, health and reproduction, war and peace, and other central issues that impact the lives of women. We are guided by a feminist perspective and a critical understanding of how culture and ethnicity are essential to any serious exploration of women's lives.

The discussions and information in this text center on the lives of women, often within the context of family. In some cases, women's families are socially defined and accepted, and in other cases, women's families are self-defined through fictional family connections, self-definitions of family, and shifting views of whom women identify as family members. Our focus here is adult women representing varied cultures and parts of the world. Girls are discussed only when their young lives relate to issues facing adult women or when girls assume the role of adults, although they might still be considered children in some cultures (e.g., child marriage).

The status of women in virtually every country is subordinate to men, and yet women do exercise varying degrees of control of societal resources. Our observations are far from static, as we continue to witness change in the gendered landscape of the world's societies. We find ourselves sad, angry, empathetic, and sometimes bewildered by the various contours of female/male behavior and relationships. We ask ourselves which changes are good for women and which are not. Our motivation to write this book stems from the desire to share our questions and our findings about women worldwide. We begin with the powerful images that surfaced during our discussions. Two examples are:

In Otavalo Market, Ecuador (1990), dawn had scarcely broken when I witnessed hundreds of women, many with babies on their backs and small children following close by, descending from their homes. These women were carrying produce, candy, handicrafts, handmade clothing, and every other type of product imaginable to set up shop for another day. I was moved by the hard work of these Ecuadorian women and saddened by their poverty. Moreover, I wanted to know more about their lives, joys, and sorrows and how they perceived their own situation.

Lining a sidewalk in Bulaywo, Zimbabwe (1992), were young girls who appeared to be between the ages of twelve and fifteen. I asked my guide if these young girls were waiting to go to school and learned instead that they were the newest tragedy in Zimbabwe—young prostitutes. They were forced from their countryside homes to the city to earn money. The drought in Zimbabwe (November 1992) had been going on for two years, and hunger had driven these young girls to prostitution as a means of survival for both themselves and their families.

These examples are but two of many that we shared, and it became apparent that these events occur in many places, revealing many faces of despair, as women struggle with the obstacles within their lives.

WOMEN, CULTURAL CHANGE, AND CULTURAL DEBATE

Exploring women's lives in societies around the world is often like looking through a kaleidoscope, as the picture changes somewhat with each observation. Women and the families they are connected to are rarely isolated from the influences, cultures, and world systems that exist beyond the borders of their countries. Histories of colonizer-colonized, exploiter-exploited, and empowered-powerless relationships create a backdrop for the present lives of women across the globe. Most Western social scientists label the spread of cultural customs by the neutral term "cultural diffusion." Nationalist leaders refer to the same phenomenon as "cultural imperialism," emphasizing zero tolerance for the power politics of the First World.[1] Debates about cultural change and resistance to change often posit women's roles and gender relations as a central feature in the battle of maintaining a society's culture. Since women's roles are central to these discussions, all women should participate in the dialogue about the wide range of views concerning the meaning of women's equality, power, and success.

ETHNOCENTRISM, CULTURAL RELATIVISM, AND THE FEMINIST PERSPECTIVE

How much do Americans, especially American college students, know about women and gender relations in other countries? What is the best way to evaluate information about gendered customs different from our own? Is international travel creating a forum to understand other cultures?

International travel opportunities have grown for many U.S. citizens and other middle- and upper-middle-class citizens throughout the world. Travel represents a point of contact between two cultures, an opportunity to learn about the lives of others, a chance to develop cross-cultural friendships, and at times a forum to explore one's cultural self. Several circumstances interfere with attaining these goals: the gap in wealth, power, and prestige between travelers and most local residents prevents a truly equal exchange; the nature of much travel generated by the tourist industry is geared toward a specific experience, ranging from a jungle safari to a chance to relax and be catered to; tourists frequently resist any framework or analysis that facilitates an understanding of local or international processes which influence the roles and status of women worldwide.

A common reaction of Americans who have spent time in another country is that they now appreciate all the rights and privileges accorded to women in the United States. Many believe the customs in other countries are backward and need improvement. "Other" women are criticized for allowing themselves to live in such an oppressed state, and their traditional cultural resources are seldom recognized. Additionally, there is the tendency to dichotomize cross-cultural information; if women are suppressed or brutalized in the other culture, then they must be liberated in this country. When we ask American students to explore how the international economic system, which benefits many citizens in the United States, adversely affects women in many other countries, we find ourselves treading on sacred ground. Students do not wish to acknowledge the benefits American citizens receive from the oppression of others.

These beliefs are manifestations of "ethnocentrism," the tendency to judge other cultures by the standards of one's own or, typically, what we perceive as our standards. Most of us accept our own environment without question and consider our own culture's ideas of morality, beauty, relationships, family, and work as the standard against which to measure others. Ethnocentrism is more than just a learned attitude; it is an individual's link to and affirmation of his or her own cultural traditions. When shared agreement asserts that Western culture and Western countries offer the best opportunities for women, it promotes a sense of complacency about gender relations here and fosters misinterpretations of the conditions for women worldwide. Ethnocentrism is an inadequate beginning to the study of global women's issues. It is a form of prejudice that results in a judgmental and elitist approach and inhibits true cross-cultural understanding of women.

As we traverse the globe examining women's lives, we will fight the ethnocentric tendency and instead utilize aspects of cultural relativism to undergird our discussions. "Cultural relativism" is the recognition that one culture cannot be arbitrarily judged by the standards of another. Cultural practices can only be fully understood by investigating the norms and values of the corresponding society. This perspective is a better mechanism to view and interpret women's lives in various parts of the world for it demands a greater understanding of the cultural context surrounding behavior and attitudes, yet by itself, it remains inadequate. Although cultural relativism does not insist that the observer approve of all practices explored, neither does it aim to advance the position of women, as does feminism.

Feminism as a perspective in academic writing and study is guided by the belief that women are equal to men and that their experiences are as important as men's. This perspective seeks social change in the direction of equality between the sexes. Some feminists make the assumption that the sex/gender system is the blueprint upon which all other systems of power rest. These feminists believe that equality between the sexes signals a transformation in all other types of domination. Beyond these general statements, defining feminism becomes problematic. It is an umbrella term for both a set of political agendas and diverse ideas, theories, and solutions to women's oppression.

Multiple theoretical frameworks are identified as feminist. Liberal feminism, Marxist feminism, socialist feminism, and radical feminism represent major contemporary categories. The conflict among each of these perspectives, as well as other ideas about women's status, may be analyzed by determining their responses to two questions: (1) Does the theory hold that differences between women and men are minimal or maximal? This creates tension concerning social policy. Should women strive for "equal rights" or "special rights?" (2) Does the theory encompass a diversity of experiences among women and do its goals benefit all or most women?

The liberal feminist tradition emerged from the Western European "Age of Enlightenment," with its emphasis on individual rights, progress, and freedom. Strategies rely on legal reform to remove barriers to equal education and employment and the assumption that logic and reason can overcome obstacles. Liberal feminists tend to believe that women and men are more alike than different. Although the liberal philosophy encourages equal opportunity for all, it contains no real critique of national or world economic/political stratification. Therefore, it is criticized for the failure to recognize that the advancement of most of the world's women requires substantial shifts in power and structural reorganization. Today many goals of the liberal agenda have been met in developed countries. Some of these include the right to vote, reproductive rights, increased opportunities in education, and career equality.

Liberal and minimalist (sameness) feminism remains a force throughout the world, especially in the United States and Canada. Many Western European feminists and feminists from traditional societies have placed a greater philosophical emphasis on gender difference, celebrating "womanliness" and male/female complementarily rather than sameness. (This focus embodies aspects of radical feminism that extol feminine qualities and eschew the notion that women should imitate the masculine model.) In Europe and much of the developed world, philosophies borrowed from socialist feminism aim to secure social benefits and support structures for families and to assist underprivileged women by proposing governmentally subsidized social welfare policies and services, which include paid parental or maternity leave, free child care, and efforts to reduce the wage gap between women and men.

In many developing countries, feminist theory intertwines with the theoretical perspective of national liberation movements. This sometimes, but not always, employs a Marxist feminism that locates the source of women's (and others') oppression in world and local capitalism, promises that an equal distribution of goods and services will ensure equal decision making, and contends that all women, as all men, can share power and resources if they work for the revolution or nationalist movement. Feminist philosophy, Marxist or otherwise, is usually a consideration of nationalistic movements, but unfortunately, it usually fails to deliver its promise of equality to women.

Radical, socialist, and liberal feminist orientations offer us a broad understanding of women's lives; however, they fail to fully illuminate the diversity among women, the contradictions inherent when women hold multiple identities, and the hierarchical divisions among women. We will try to avoid Western/elite feminist hegemony and monolithic constructions of women by region, race, ethnicity, or socioeconomic status. As you read this book, you will find feminist and social science insights that best apply to each particular topic.

THE PROMISE OF GLOBAL FEMINISM

History might well assign 1975 as the year in which a global women's movement began to emerge. The United Nations designated 1975 as International Women's Year and convened a World Conference in Mexico City. Women leaders further proclaimed January 1976 through December 1985 as the United Nations Decade for Women, with the theme "Equality, Development, and Peace." However, the forces promoting feminist activity had begun long before.

Jessie Bernard (1987) believes that the industrial revolution, accompanied by increased female literacy and education, caused the separate worlds of women and men to slowly erode. She also observes that as women from all over have come into contact with one another and discovered commonalities, the costs as well as the rewards of this separation have come under scrutiny and given rise to a kind of global feminist consciousness.

Robin Morgan's impressive volume, *Sisterhood Is Global,* is subtitled *The International Women's Movement Anthology.* Morgan (1984) declares that women are disproportionately victims of worldwide patriarchy, but that they form a numerical majority and a world political force. She notes that in many third world countries, feminists are said to be outside agitators, but she defends this attack by asserting that an indigenous feminism has been present in every culture in the world and in every period of history since the suppression of women began.

The promise of global feminism is the formation of an extensive network of women working across the "artificial" boundaries of nation-states to liberate themselves, their sisters, and daughters from the restrictions of patriarchal control. Many global feminist activists predicate their position on the now famous quotation made by Virginia Woolf in her book, *Three Guineas:* " . . . as a woman, I have no country. As a woman I want no country. As a woman my country is the whole world" (1938, p. 109). Many believe that women are more compassionate, more humanitarian, and that global feminism may be the medium to save the planet from war, environmental destruction, poverty, and starvation. Bella Abzug, at the World Women's Conference in Copenhagen and Nairobi asked, "What if women ruled the world?" The conclusion was, if women ruled the world, they would allocate resources more equitably and find peaceful solutions to world conflict, thus ruling differently from men (Matson, 1985, p. 15).

CHALLENGES TO GLOBAL FEMINISM

Women's movements have emerged separately in many areas of the world. They have in common a concern for improving conditions for women in society. Many issues can be subsumed under the same headings: education, economic independence, family roles, freedom from violence, and improved health care. In explicating the source of the problems and the proposed solutions to them, each country's movement follows a distinctive course, and its agendas are shaped by local circumstances and influenced by international trends. Existing ideological, cultural, regional, and class differences pose numerous obstacles in trying to recast the many specific goals of women into one global feminist movement. The unity of feminism across international boundaries is threatened by political, economic, and cultural divisions.

The most serious worldwide women's political debate has centered on who will represent all the women of the world. Can and should Western women speak for non-Western women? It is of particular concern that many writers, particularly from the United States and Western Europe, see the U.S. women's movement as the movement others should emulate. We caution Western feminists to police themselves in several ways: they need to temper their enthusiasm to become liberators of the women of the world; they must be aware of the limitations of their own perspective; and white feminists must guard against their own racism and classism that stems from their relative historical and present advantage.

Political controversy is exacerbated by the economic disparity of women activists from advantaged countries (United States and Western Europe) compared with activists in economically exploited nations (Sub-Saharan Africa, Latin America, parts of the Middle East, and South and Central Asia). During the three conferences of the U.N. Decade for Women, and to some extent in the fourth world conference, representatives of non-Western nations challenged Western feminism to address macroeconomic issues: "Global issues such as the relationship of women's poverty to development and the global economy, and the importance of incorporating into feminist ideology an understanding of anti-imperialism and national liberation struggles were introduced by Third World women" (*Connexions*, 1985, pp. 17-18).

Cultural differences cannot be overestimated as a challenge to global feminism. Waldman and Waldman (1992) ask whether it is ever ethical to pass judgments (about local customs) without understanding their meaning within the cultural context. They warn us of two types of error in delineating a global feminist perspective. The first focuses mainly on common forms of oppression and fails to recognize cultural diversity. The second overemphasizes exotic forms of oppression, making them seem essentially different from the commonplace.

THE REALITIES OF WOMEN CONNECTING TO WOMEN

In 1915, over 1,000 women from thirteen countries, including Britain, Germany, Holland, Hungary, Belgium, and the United States met in The Hague in Holland to strategize ways to prevent the progression toward World War I. This convention gave birth to the Women's International League for Peace and Freedom (WILPF), an international organization of women dedicated to the establishment and preservation of peace and justice (Bussey and Tims, 1980). This is important in two regards. First, frustrated by the actions of male world leaders, but with no official authorization, these women were motivated to meet independently. They recommended resolutions designed to avoid bloodshed and ensure a lasting peace (unfortunately these recommendations went unheeded). The second significant aspect of this conference was that it foreshadowed a much larger and more diverse gathering of women sixty years later.

The first International Women's Conference occurred in Mexico City in 1975. The United Nations sponsored the official meetings. Delegates to the conference were sanctioned by their respective governments. The 1975 conference spawned the U.N. Decade for Women (1976 through 1985) and three subsequent conferences: one in Copenhagen, Denmark, in 1980; the end of the decade conference in Nairobi, Kenya, in 1985; and the final conference in Beijing, China, in 1995. Parallel to each U.N. conference was a nongovernmental (NGO) tribunal, in which women activists raised and discussed issues similar to those on the U.N. agenda. The ambitious goals established in Mexico City as themes for the decade were the eradication of underdevelopment, the quest for peace, and the pursuit of political, economic, and social equality for women worldwide.

Of all these conferences, the mid-decade conference in Copenhagen was the most "politicized." Many women from developed countries argued that discussions centering on the New International Economic Order, the Situation of Women in Palestine, or Women under Apartheid were not appropriate "women's issues." Further, many women from developing countries believed that feminists from developed countries took a "we know better" approach to issues such as female circumcision, population control, and how to define a family. "These tensions were left unresolved, and many came away from Copenhagen uncertain about the prospects of future international solidarity actions and concerned about moving beyond the divisiveness" (Cagatay, Grown, and Santiago, 1986, p. 403).

In contrast to Copenhagen, the end of the decade conference in Nairobi, Kenya, was dubbed by many to be a turning point. O'Barr's 1986 article, "Reflections on Forum '85 in Nairobi, Kenya" declared that "Nairobi ushered in a new and more complex appreciation of global feminism, of women's attempts to define the terms by which they participate in culture and society, and of the need to live with differences among women while building on the commonalities of the female experience" (p. 585). The November/ December 1985 issue of *Humanist* reflected an overwhelmingly positive appraisal of the Nairobi conference. Articles declared that this summit was the "Road to Victory," "A Window of Hope," and that, despite language barriers, women were "understanding each other" (Matson, 1985, p. 14). The NGO meeting of Forum '85 was the site of over 1,000 activities, including workshops and panels, a film festival, a Tech 'n' Tools Appropriate Technology Fair, and the now famous Peace Tent. There were 13,500 participants at this conference. Because most women attending came from developing countries, this conference was more representative of the world's women than the previous conferences. Also about one-half of the 2,500 women from the United States were women of color, thus representing diversity among developed countries. Most of the women were determined to make this last conference work and to turn their differences into creative energy.

Women from the developed north (i.e., United States, Canada, European countries) focused on acid rain, pesticide use, nuclear power, and out-of-control technology, while women from the developing south (i.e., South Asia, Latin America, African countries) expressed concern about available land for crops and houses and the desire for increased technology to reduce the drudgery of women's lives. Further, women from the developing regions generally expressed a greater preference for a feminism that incorporates support for family obligations. Women at the official U.N. Conference of Forum '85 worked long hours to hammer out differences and voted to adopt the main text of the document "Forward-Looking Strategies." This manuscript made recommendations for the progress of women from 1986 until the year 2000. The fourth conference held in Beijing, China, in September 1995, gathered momentum from the U.N. general world conferences of the 1990s, all of which accorded women a central role: the Conference on Environment and Development (Rio de Janeiro, 1992), the World Conference on Human Rights (Vienna, 1993), the International Conference on Population and Development (Cairo, 1994), and the World Summit for Social Development (Copenhagen, 1995). The Fourth World Conference on Women was the largest U.N. conference ever held. Almost 17,000 people were registered for the official U.N. conference and approximately 30,000 attended the overlapping NGO conference in Huairou, China (UNIFEM, 1996).

The Beijing Conference was marked by widespread media publicity, notable women speakers,[2] and much attention to repressive tactics and human rights violations by the Chinese government. Complaints of attendees ranged from room searches and confiscation of tapes to propaganda warning the Chinese people that radicals were coming and that some of them might be infected by the AIDS virus (Morgan, 1984).

Despite much hoopla and real problems in Beijing, there was a unanimous endorsement for the Platform for Action. This document identified twelve areas of concern, with nonbinding recommendation for local action. Perhaps the most important aspect of the Platform for Action is that it gives women's issues new visibility and can serve as a template for national policies and legislation.

OVERVIEW OF CHAPTERS

Women's lives are orchestrated within the confines of family, community, and societal structures. These structures are part of, and connect to, the larger culture and the world community. It is the institution of the family that best explains women's lives. It is here that she orchestrates internal and external work, although internal family work (often called domestic) remains hidden, unpaid, and undervalued for most women. Women are the channel for the life force as they reproduce new family members through childbirth. This reproduction incorporates the contradiction of the stresses of increased workload and health concerns with the possibility of extreme joy resulting from this procreative act. Many joys and concerns women face evolve from family relationships. Women and their roles within their families as wives, mothers, workers, sisters, children, and much more frame the choices, concerns, and issues they face.

Globally, the choices available to women vary depending upon the cultural structure of family. In general, women in developed countries articulate a greater level of freedom from family responsibilities than women in developing countries. However, the difference in women's family obligations is one of degree rather than substance.

In this text, we recognize the differences in the opportunities that women in highly developed regions have available to them in comparison to their sisters in developing countries. These differences exist along a continuum, with the choices of ethnic and poor women in developed countries sharing greater commonality with the majority of women in developing countries.

The six chapters following this introduction provide information and insight into the lives of women across the globe. Within the contents of these chapters, we furnish extensive information concerning the topic under discussion and, when possible, case studies and primary data to further illustrate the material under investigation. The information cuts across disciplinary boundaries and explores critical issues and concerns that affect women around the globe. Chapters 1 and 2 examine information concerning women and family structure.

Chapter 1, "Marriage and Family Formation," focuses on cultural diversity in monogamous heterosexual marital relationships. In this section, we address the meaning of marriage within various societies. Additionally, we discuss the use of culturally specific marriage traditions and their relationship to gender roles. We investigate how bride-prices and dowries affect the treatment of women in the family. We analyze numerous cultural examples of the clash between traditional customs and modern methods. Worldwide trends in divorce are discussed, including the impact of the legality of divorce, the societal climate surrounding divorce, and the effect of separation and divorce on women and families.

Chapter 2 addresses the "Diversity Within Family Formation" that is manifested throughout the world. The differential place of women within nonnuclear, monogamous relationships is considered. This section examines a variety of alternative family forms, ranging from those that vary by size (extended versus nuclear) to those with monogamous female/male configurations (polygamy to polyandry) to those families break cultural taboos (lesbian families, mixed religions, mixed races).

Chapter 3 addresses issues of reproduction and sexual standards for women worldwide. This chapter begins with a discussion of the status of world population, examining the consequences of overpopulation in terms of human misery, environmental damage, and women's status. The next section turns to challenges in reducing birth rates. Here, we review structural barriers such as pronatalist or antinatalist government policy, education, poverty, and access to contraceptive and abortion technology. We also discuss normative considerations such as religion, sexual practices, beliefs about contraception, and cultural values regarding family size. Case studies illustrate successful attempts to develop family planning programs and the subsequent benefits to women, their families, and their communities.

Chapter 4 addresses gender equity in work. It begins with an exploration of how governments define work. For instance, it is estimated that 828 million women were economically active in 1990 (United Nations, 1991b), but the number fails to reflect the fact that almost all women work. This chapter analyzes the intersection of gender, class, and race in producing job stratification worldwide. Within this connection, we explore domestic work, the global assembly line in multinational corporations, and programs for women in global development. Further, we discuss women in nontraditional occupations and professions as we examine the future trends for working women.

Chapter 5 addresses the critical issues of "Women and Health Care." This chapter begins with an elaboration of health care concerns for women and then provides three case studies. The countries of Zimbabwe, Norway, and Cuba were chosen, not as representative of all countries, but because of their vast distinctions. They represent different cultures, varied political philosophies, and extreme differences in resources, and they have emerged to develop health policies that endeavor to meet the needs of their populations, although each has strikingly different historical influences. Each is moving in different directions as they wrestle with critical societal issues. Their differing characteristics create the backdrop for understanding the presenting need and the potential resolutions for meeting those needs.

Chapter 6 examines "Women and Violence." In this chapter, we carefully examine the multiple situations that women find both unsafe and violent. This chapter addresses violence on the societal level and explores the impact of national and international conflict on the lives of women worldwide. It also describes several consequences of war and revolution, including war rapes and women as refugees. Concerns here range from structural examples of violence, such as footbinding, female circumcision, and dowry burning, to examples of battery, sexual harassment, and rape. Each instance is discussed within the cultural framework of the occurrence.

The conclusion of this book revisits the importance of understanding the complexity of women worldwide and the demands women face. Here we address the ways that global women face similarities and differences, experience resistance and backlash to feminist views, and move toward a future based on the realities of their lives.

KEY WORDS

Cultural diffusion

Cultural imperialism

Cultural relativism

Ethnocentrism

Feminism

Globalization

Liberal feminism

Marxist feminism

Maximalist perspective

Minimalist perspective

Radical feminism

Socialist feminism

Chapter 1

Marriage and Family Formation

Global marriage and family issues involve many concerns that guide a discussion in this area. Concerns often center on the definition and formation of families. Feminist scholars representing liberal, radical, and socialist views have critiqued the traditional Western view of family and the imposition of this view throughout the world.[1] In *Rethinking the Family* (Thorne and Yalom, 1992), scholars challenge the reader to see families in broader terms. Families are not monolithic. Although individual families are socialized to see a specific cultural norm to be the appropriate defining nature of a family, it is imperative for researchers and policymakers to view the broad array of families. Feminist scholars challenge research concerning families to address the importance of gender in understanding family issues. Understanding women's place within families illuminates an examination of women's lives and broadens our understanding of the experiences of diverse women.

Most women throughout the world are a part of monogamous, heterosexual family systems. This chapter explores these women and how critical issues of family formation, maintenance, and dissolution impact the lives of women worldwide.

Women across the globe are socialized to adhere to a role significantly defined by their gender. Socialization is the process of acquiring the behavioral and social skills needed to become a social being and a functioning member of your existing society. This process is limited by the ascribed roles of women and men within the existing society. The molding of girls to fit a cultural norm is a central function of families. Within the context of family life, young persons are first introduced to definitions of femaleness and maleness. In all societies the family serves as an agent in the process of socialization.

Psychological theory has sought to explain the socialization of individuals. Diverse theories explain successful processes that ensure socialization. Instrumental conditioning can assist our understanding of how women learn as girls to perform in ways defined as feminine. Within this framework, girls learn to make certain responses by the consequences of those responses. Behaviors that result in rewards occur more frequently, establishing responses that become socialized, and those behaviors that result in punishment diminish in frequency and finally are extinguished.[2] The family is central in delivering consequences for specific behavior. In this way, girls throughout the world are commonly reinforced for assuming nurturing roles and exhibiting conforming behavior, and are often punished for assertive and individual aspirations.

In sharp contrast to an instrumental conditioning frame of reference are psychoanalytic perspectives. Within these perspectives, the importance of biological drives and unconscious processes are stressed. The life experiences that occur within the early stages of human development are intricately linked with one's biological sex, thus shaping individual patterns throughout life. Therefore, girls are destined biologically to behave in what is defined as feminine and less capable ways. Feminist psychoanalytic researchers, however, have challenged the emphasis on biological determinism and the view of women's socialization as a deficit model. Revisions of psychoanalytic theory argue that explanations that focus on "penis envy" or biological inferiority of women neglect the obvious and pervasive discrimination that girls and women face.[3] Thus, feminist psychoanalytically oriented writers seek to understand the process of socialization by exploring both unconscious processes and the social conditions that subjugate and surround women.

Psychological exploration informs discussion on how women see their place within families and how families shape that place. Women conditioned to view themselves as self-sacrificing and less deserving enter relationships ready to accept that cultural norm. The roles women are socialized to accept guide their roles within marriage.

DO "MASCULINE" AND "FEMININE" ROLES CREATE INEQUALITY WITHIN MARRIAGE RELATIONSHIPS?

Traditional views of masculinity and femininity place men and women into separate but interacting spheres. These views cast women's development as inferior to men's and assign them an unalterable position of subordination, according to Williams (1993, pp. 27-62). Notions of maleness and femaleness develop within an androcentric arena nourished by a global patriarchal context. Definitions of masculinity and femininity emerge from these perspectives. Definitions of masculinity and femininity dichotomize the central essence of men and women. These definitions classically imply distinct traits to males and females. Masculinity consists of traits viewed as positive within many parts of the world; to be masculine means to be highly rational, autonomous, and capable of self-determination. Femininity, however, implies very different traits, such as highly emotional and irrational, nurturing of others, and deferential to males. Notions of such gendered traits as masculinity and femininity sustain the view of women's subordination to men as a "natural" phenomenon, based on the psychobiological differences between men and women. Many feminist researchers, including Eichenbaum and Orbach (1983), Lerner (1988), and Williams (1993), have critiqued such notions of natural gender subordination. The central basis of these critiques maintains that the acceptance of biologically determined masculine and feminine traits and behaviors denies the importance of patriarchy and societal views in shaping gender roles.

Feminist scholars challenge analyses that view masculinity-femininity as a dichotomous trait. Current research supports the multiple ways that socialization patterns, cultures, and family patterns reinforce traditions of masculinity and femininity. Cross-cultural feminist researchers have also criticized the dichotimization of female and male traits. Researchers such as Baca Zinn (1994) and Comas-Diaz (1994) challenge the universal assumption of established masculine and feminine roles that result in the subordination of women. These diverse viewpoints necessitate a closer look at cultural orientation and gender roles as they affect the lives of women.

The cultural beliefs of the individuals involved predicates the reality of their marital lives. Cultural expectations define notions of masculinity and femininity, acceptable forms of marriage, and much of the life experience of the marital partners. Societies that hold highly restrictive and inflexible notions concerning female and male roles constrain women's lives to a segment defined by gender.

Shifting tides within each community also shape the culturally defined roles that women and men play within the family. The machismo ideal that men of Mexican descent have traditionally adhered to is an example. Here, the machismo male is entitled by his male status to a superior position. This macho ideal is equated with authority, strength, and sexual virility. The man is seen as the patriarch who rules in all manner over females. According to Williams (1990) this traditional belief is not as ingrained as in previous decades, although it remains as an influential determinant in the relationships of wives and husbands.

These gender scripts are not only seen within Mexico, but also delineate the relationships of women and men throughout many parts of the world. The manifestations of superiority of the masculine role reach across the globe, affecting the treatment of women and the roles assigned to them.

Analyzing women in Nepal, Bennett (1983) describes how culture and custom influence the lives of Hindu women as brides and wives:

> Clearly, female children grow up with a strong awareness that their stay in the maita (family home) is transient and that their existence is peripheral to that of their natal patriline. While sons of the family remain members of the consanguineous group, daughters become identified with the affinal group and its patriline. For it is there, in her husband's house, that a woman will fulfill her most important structural roles in the dominant patrifocal model—as wife and mother. (p. 169)

Nepalese wives experience less significance within their families of orientation and procreation. These women serve as links between generations within their husband's family, not as important and significant individuals in their own right. In *Dangerous Wives and Sacred Sisters* (Bennett, 1983), women speak of feelings of both isolation and harassment caused by their family of procreation. Particularly, these women often feel that they are sent away from the maita (family home) to work in the "house of demanding strangers" where they are "critically watched and controlled." Typically, until they have had one or more children, fulfilling their "true" feminine role and bonding them to their families of procreation, Nepalese brides are targets of distrust.

Marital relationships vary in the equality of the marriage partners, how partners are chosen, under what conditions the marriage takes place, the ritual customs surrounding the marriage, the cultural experiences that shape the reality of the marriage, and of course, the long-term outcome of the marriage. Marital roles that prescribe women a feminine role equated with a subordinate position while equating masculinity with authority create the conditions for female oppression within the family.

THE IMPACT OF AGE ON MARITAL PATTERNS

Most women marry at some point during their life span, with most marriages occurring in the young adult years. The age of first marriage and the reality of marriage for women varies across cultures. This variability in age of first marriage exists, but does age at first marriage make a significant difference in the reality of marital life? In many African countries, nearly 50 percent of the women marry by age eighteen, and 40 percent of Asian women marry by eighteen as well (United Nations, 1991b). In contrast, in the United States, only 5.2 percent of women marry between ages fifteen and nineteen years; in the Netherlands, 1.2 percent; and in Hungary, 10.8 percent. These figures underscore the age differences seen in first marriages across the world, but do not fully represent regional and cultural differences seen in early marriages. An extreme and rare form of early marriage today is child marriage. Beatty describes this phenomenon in Nias in Southeast Asia:

> Child marriage is now rare. The groom in such cases is called solaya ono ("one who entertains/feasts the child/bride"). A girl of about ten is taken home by the groom (who may be an adult) or his father, following the payment of a substantial portion of bride wealth. In the local idiom, she is "carried home on his back" like a daughter. She is already called a wife (though, formerly, to satisfy Dutch government and missionary objections, she might be called a helper). She lives as a member of the groom's household until she becomes sexually mature. Then the remainder of the bride wealth is paid, the wedding feast can go ahead and the marriage is consummated. (1992, p. 175)

In all countries, men enter marriage at an older age than women. When this phenomenon is coupled with statistics across nations of women who enter marriage at an early age, a significant age-related difference is found throughout the lives of married men and women. Early marriage reveals a profound impact on women's lives.

This marital age gap can have serious consequences on the power wielded by married women. Since women are generally younger, and sometimes significantly so, they come into a marital relationship with less life experience than the male spouse. This can contribute to dependence on the male partner, particularly when the young woman has married early due to economic necessity. The high rate of early-age marriages for women strongly correlates with the poverty facing developing countries. In a system that accords women less importance than the men within the family, marriage is often the only recourse for daughters of a family living in poverty. By custom, young girls become engaged or marry early, thus transferring the young girl to another family through marriage. The option of choice is to marry the daughter to a man who will provide for her. For example, a young woman in Bangladesh typically marries a male who is seven years older than she; 73 percent of young Bangladesh women marry by age fifteen (United Nations, 1991b). Despite the contribution that she makes to the household or to the economic resources of the family, the age differential combined with customary patriarchal beliefs and views concerning masculinity and femininity place her in an assumed position of less knowledge, less experience, and less power within the family system.

The age of marriage also correlates to the inability to finish secondary education. These young married women typically interrupt education for marriage or face early removal from school to prepare for the marriage pool. For those who attempt to complete their education, early childbearing and household responsibilities make it difficult or sometimes impossible to complete school. An eighteen-year-old mother in southern rural Mexico stated, "School is not important for me; I have to work, take care of my daughter, work in the fields, prepare food for all, . . . help my family every day."[4] This situation is a common reality throughout the world for young married women, particularly those in sub-Saharan Africa, southern Asia, and other developing areas. However, in the same areas of the world, only 5 percent of young men marry under nineteen years of age (United Nations, 1991a). Therefore, young men seldom face the same familial responsibilities that many young women encounter. Additionally, an early marriage means early motherhood. Early motherhood, coupled with serial births, creates additional health consequences for women in many parts of the world (see Chapter 5).

The age of entering marriage relates to the lifelong pattern of marriage for women. Women are disproportionately widowed across all age categories (Schmittroth, 1991). This fact is partially the consequence of the worldwide tendency for young women to marry older men. Women also outlive men by four to eight years in most parts of the world. Women's longer life expectancy and female-male difference in age of marriage contribute to women's higher rates of widowhood. The removal of the male's contribution to family resources, the stress and concerns of bereavement, the forced remarriage in some cultures, or the stigma of widowhood are among the experiences that women will face. In describing the widowed women of Nias in Southeast Asia, Beatty states:

> Widows are objects of sympathy, though not charity, and are nominally under the care of the village. In reality they receive little or no help from anyone, and several live alone or with a grandchild for company, in remote huts, barely surviving in great poverty. Others live with their sons, but are not much better off. They are denied all but the necessities and continue working virtually until they die. (1992, p. 161)

This loss of a spouse through death can create financial and psychological burdens for women who are ill-prepared to handle them. These women frequently face poverty, decreased status, and loss of companionship. According to Kimmel (1990), twice as many widowed women over sixty-five in the United States live below the poverty line than do younger women. The early age at which women marry contributes to negative consequences throughout the life course of the marriage.

HOW ARE BRIDE-PRICES/WEALTH AND DOWRIES RELATED TO WOMEN'S MARITAL EXPERIENCE?

In many countries, a price is paid or a gift is given to the family of the prospective bride by the man she is marrying prior to the marriage. These gifts are referred to as bride-prices or bride wealth. The form of this price or gift has changed over the years with the changing social and cultural environment but has persisted throughout many parts of the world. Bride-prices are common throughout many societies and not restricted to only one economic status.

The lobola is such a marriage custom within the southern parts of Africa. This is a payment to the father or sometimes the parents of the woman entering marriage. The form of this lobola has changed over the years and presently consists of both a cash portion and a material gift.[6] The lobola, according to Batezat and Mwato (1989), may not have been greatly oppressive in precapitalist days but has since grown to oppress women, as the amount of the lobola has increased under capitalism.

During the colonial era, a combination of African custom and Western law set the conditions for marriage and dissolution of marriage within Zimbabwe. During this period, customary law created rigid boundaries that enforced a male-preferred situation. Women held minority status within marriages, had no contractual rites, remained under the guardianship of their spouses, and faced disastrous consequences on the dissolution of their marriages, whether by divorce or death (Batezat and Mwato, 1989). Whether divorced or widowed, women lost their entitlement to an inheritance or an equitable portion of the family's accumulated wealth. Women left the relationship with "mavoko property," consisting of the contents within the kitchen and any materials that she specifically made with her own hands. This system treats the woman as something bought and paid for by the payment of the lobola.

There were also consequences for children. With the payment of the lobola, the custom was that the male's family held the rights to any children created from this union; thus if separation or divorce occurred, the children were "his" as paid for by the lobola. Under customary law, women could be given custody of children under seven years of age, but the father remained the guardian of all children. Later, when a female child married, the lobola would go to the father. Many women resisted these kinds of customary laws and practices; however, before independence in 1980, little could be done.

In 1981 postindependence, women in Zimbabwe fought to add their voices to the cries for immediate change. They strongly verbalized their resistance to customary laws that upheld sexist marital statutes and practices. The struggle of women and their supporters in Zimbabwe culminated in the Ministry of Community Development and Women's Affairs.[7] A primary goal of this ministry was to remove the customary social, economic, and legal restraints that inhibited women's full participation in the development of the newly independent country. During the last sixteen years since independence, Zimbabwe has passed new laws and repealed others to provide greater legal marital equity between women and men. In particular, the Matrimonial Causes Act counters injustices seen within marital contracts. This act recognizes on paper the important role that women play within marriage. Additionally, it gives courts the power to supersede customary laws by equally dividing property postmarital dissolution. Other changes within the legal arena have given women the right to own property, the right to be guardians of their own children, and the right to contract in marriage without the permission of their fathers.

These legal changes affect the lives of Zimbabwean women in several ways, with a greater impact commonly occurring in urban environments where populations are more familiar with the court systems and judiciary manner. However, in the countryside, customary laws usually prevail. In 1993, a young woman receiving treatment for bruises and cuts in a Bulaywo hospital responded to questions regarding her injuries:

> My husband whipped me; it's not unusual; it happens a lot in my village. . . . No, I couldn't leave him; I'd go away with nothing; I'd lose everything I have. My children need me; I couldn't leave them. . . . Yes, I'd have to leave them with him; that's our way here.[8]

This illustrates the contradiction between the law and reality—a contradiction that is observed worldwide.

Kuper (1982) examines the traditional practices and the contemporary transformations of bride-prices within southern Africa. His discussion centers on "cattle in exchange for wives." In this analysis, several key factors are relevant. To understand the diversity seen within bride-prices and marital patterns, it is necessary to understand the relative importance of pastoralism and agriculture to the local economies. Due to women's heavy role within the agricultural economy of southern Africa, women in agriculturally based communities receive larger bride-prices. The marital kinship patterns also relate to the observed marital patterns. The preference of cousins as marital partners, as in the custom of Tswana aristocratic families choosing the "father's younger brother's daughter" as the marriage partner, indicates the importance of understanding the customary patterns of marriage between kin relations, thus keeping bride-price profit within the extended family system. Finally, it is important to understand the political stratification within the communities. In some Bantu societies, family alliance or belonging to certain ethnic groups may either prevent or facilitate a marital union. Also, marrying women with certain attributes (more status, education, etc.) calls for greater bride-prices. In these cases, calculating bride-prices involves an intricate weighing of the attributes of the woman sought for marriage and the relative value of women within the economy.

In the examples discussed here, women, as wives, are valuable commodities. They are valuable because of their characteristics and family connections and because they are expected to have and care for children and to work long and hard for the remainder of their lives. Several factors determine the value of the prospective bride: her perceived contributions to the man or his family (many children, hard work); determinations made by the customs and culture of the society (is she a true woman according to her culture's values); or her status, given her personal or family characteristics. In many cultures, women are a commodity to be given, bought, or won, not individuals and equal participants within marriage. The relative inequality varies from country to country, but a consistent feature is that marital roles and relationships are not equal and are frequently cemented with an exchange of goods or money. These differences persist despite geographical regions, cultural distinctions, economic systems, or religious differences.

Dowries or quasi-dowries are also evident in many places throughout the world and across numerous historical periods, including contemporary times. But, do these systems oppress women? Dowries are sums of money and property brought to the marriage by females in exchange for perceived valued characteristics of the male or his family. These gifts often extend over the first few years of the marriage and can result in negative consequences for the bride, according to Kumari (1989), particularly if the promised dowry is not forthcoming. Dowries are not class bound; they are found among the wealthiest families and among those who are extremely poor. The hardship created by a dowry relates to family resources and the negative repercussions of possible nonpayment. Harsh financial consequences are more frequently visited on the poor and financially marginal family.

In the United States, the custom of the bride's family paying for the wedding is a quasi-dowry convention. In this custom, the woman's family of orientation is paying the price for the woman to marry into a potentially valuable relationship. The newly married couple often receives large gifts, reminiscent of the dowry gifts that family members throughout the world provide to the husband or his family.

Dowries have historical acceptance in many sectors of the world, with dowries, bride-prices, and bride gifts coexisting during early historical periods.[9] Marriages have traditionally had little if any relationship with love, but they have had a strong association with the forging of family alliance or the increase of status within a particular family (Kaplan, 1985). The existence of dowries within European countries is well documented, as well as a transformation from dowries to trousseau to nothing (Kaplan, 1985). Documenters report that the decline of dotal marriages in many parts of the world occurred slowly over many years. Nazzari (1991) examined this decline in Brazil. Across all class groupings, 90 percent of the reported marriages in the seventeenth century were dotal, 80 percent in the eighteenth century, and 27 percent within the nineteenth century. They have totally disappeared within contemporary Brazil.

In Greco-Roman society, a well-developed dotal marriage system proved quite profitable to men.[10] Owen Hughes (1985) describes accounts in which men greedily sought substantial dowries from prospective wives to enhance their financial standing or their status in life. These dotal marriages, although extremely common during the past, exist less frequently within contemporary societies. Presently, extensive dowry systems exist in India, Italy, Spain, Portugal, Malta, Greece, Tunisia, and Lebanon.[11]

Comaroff (1980) argues that the existence of dowries in modern Greece has two major functions—both the economic and the social status enhancement documented in earlier times. Women bringing in large dowries increase the economic base of newly formed families. Supporters of the modern existence of dowries argue that its existence increases women's chances of marriage and enhances their roles within families. However, Kaplan (1985) suggests that even if marriage is the ultimate goal, dowry decreases one's chances of marriage by creating a system of needed resources that are difficult for most families to acquire. Presently in Greece, a woman with few financial resources may put off marriage for years while she works at a wage to save money for her dowry. This in effect reduces the marital pool (number of potential partners) and destroys freedom of choice of a marriage partner. Although a dowry was in some societies a woman's portion of her inheritance, a weighty dowry places a burden on her family that can create interfamilial conflict (Kaplan, 1985). This conflict often heightens within impoverished families, which are unlikely to be able to deliver large dowries.

India, clearly, has a very elaborate and well-documented custom of dowries. In describing the meaning of dowries in contemporary India, Kumari states:

> The practice of giving dowry was meant to assist a newlywed couple to start their life together with ease. However, now it has degenerated into a sordid commercial transaction in which monetary considerations receive priority over the merits of the bride. Never before have the demands for dowry been so exorbitant and so widespread as today. (1989, p. 1)

Documentation supports extreme repercussions for new brides upon failure to meet the demanded dowry. Estimates in Delhi suggest that a wife is beaten to death every twelve hours. Frequently, these deaths relate to the lack of meeting the demanded dowry or a man's desire to rid himself of an unwanted wife. Physical and emotional abuse, murder disguised as accidents, or suicides are all recorded as consequences of unmet or unpaid dowries (Kumari, 1989).

Despite the passage of laws that, on paper, inhibit the mistreatment of women entering marital union or during marital dissolution, continued male dominance has sustained dowry abuse. Investigators such as Kumari (1989) and Bennett (1983) document that the dowry abuse and burnings seen in India occur across educational and economic lines and across religions.

Many scholars have speculated on the cause of the decline and disappearance of dowries in some societies and the continuance within others.[12] Industrialization has an impact; as many societies become more industrialized and rely less on alliances between families for success, dotal marriages are less frequently observed. Other contributors to the decline of dowries are the increased educational standard for women and women's greater involvement in the workforce. In both these factors, women are bringing greater potential individual resources that mirror the valued qualities of the male mate. The weakening of the family as matchmaker is another important factor. In societies and times when upward mobility depended on alliances between families, family members, particularly the elders, played a key role in deciding who was the appropriate mate for each child. In this case, the appropriate mate was an individual who would advance the family. The increased value of individual achievement in comparison to inherited wealth is also important. Less control over potential mate selection appears when inheritance or the enhancement of the inheritance fortune is not the sole motivation. Finally, dotal marriages decrease as societies, through a variety of external and internal factors, begin to recognize the role of women as far greater than wife and mother. Therefore, in societies and communities in which the dowry is widespread, the above factors are not dominant.

MEETING MR. RIGHT

SWM, tall, attr., single parent. Blue collar, late thirties, is in search of SWF, avg. body and looks, someone who doesn't need a six-pack or pills to make it a night. We have a family here with lots of love when the right one comes along.

(Source: Classified Ads, *News Journal,* December 1994)

The way women meet their spouses and partners varies significantly from culture to culture, but what factors influence today's mate selection? In the section above, we discussed how families play a significant part in choosing a marriage partner among societies exchanging dowries or bride-prices. However, in many parts of the world, families play a less obvious role. In societies where women have access to education and personal freedom in mate selection, meeting Mr. Right occurs in varied and individual ways. Through personal interactions, educational settings, workforce participation, or social/cultural activities, women are thrown together with potential marital prospects. The more open the marriage system, the less restrictive the marriage selection process, and the greater the choice. Perhaps a woman reads and answers an advertisement similar to the one beginning this section. Throughout many parts of the world, you can open the classified section and read ads for women or men seeking mates. These advertisements may solicit dating partners or marriage partners.

The greater the control the society places on the marital relationship (closed marital system), the smaller the potential marital pool. In such closed systems, families (particularly parents) have the greatest control over whom their daughters marry, with personal choice becoming nearly meaningless. As illustrated in Table 1.1, Indian women and men often have marital partners sought for them. These advertisements, placed through family members and kin, carefully screen potential additions to the family. In societies that maintain control over the formation of marriage, advertisement does not mean open choice. From the parental choice in mate seen in Asia, to the elder choice in

TABLE 1.1. Advertising for Mates
Examples from India

(A young woman seeks a mate)	(Parents seek a mate for their daughter)
Professional (PhD Student), intelligent, beautiful, and down-to-earth, 28 years young woman, Gujarati, right combination of Indian and Western values. Highly educated family background. Sincerely seeking a life partner, 29-35 with some education, broad-minded, and independent. No bar. Please write directly to XXXXXX.	Punjabi Brahmin parents seek MDs, medical students, professionals, 23/28; for Canadian-born, very beautiful, slim, athletic, 22/5'7", highly cultured daughter. Pursuing profession in teaching. Photo/biodata please.
(A parent seeks a life partner for a daughter)	(A brother seeks a mate for his sister)
Alliance invited from prof. for Punjabi Hindu daughter, 3rd Med student, 24/5'7", fair, slim, serious inquiries only. Photo/biodata a must. No bar.	Brother invites alliance from Brahmin boys for 29/5', intelligent, beautiful girl, MSc (Maths) presently employed in Semi-Govt. establishment in Kanpu, India.

Adapted from *India Abroad*, November 11, 1994.

many parts of Africa, to the parental influence in India, and subtle family persuasion in many countries, women have varied amounts of choice in their marital partners. Even in countries where personal choice is perceived as high, the segregated educational institutions, living environments, and leisure activities created by race, class, and religion narrow the potential mating pool.

MARRIAGE RITES AND CEREMONIES

Most people in the world master the complexity of mate selection and begin a marital relationship. The rituals and ceremonies that acknowledge a person's marriage reflect the customary traditions of the society and the recent transformations within the fabric of specific communities worldwide. Are marital ceremonies universal in meaning? Each centers on a public display of the marital union and a focus on, almost an inspection of, the woman. The display of the bride on her wedding day is traditional in most cultures. This varies from the marriage ceremonies of the West, characterized by full white bridal gowns, to the ceremonial dress and dancing of the Nubians, to the customary viewing of the Hindu bride (Schwartz and Scott, 1994).[13]

The Japanese wedding ceremony evolved from a traditional Shinto ceremony to an elaborate multifaceted and highly commercialized event (Edwards, 1989). Often the ceremony consists of a cast of characters that includes priests, the bride, the groom, their families, a nakodo (a male who operates as a host at the festivities), and guests. The couple go through a series of highly orchestrated and formalized behaviors:

> The ceremony consists of practices shared with other shinto rituals (purification, prayer, invocation, and offering), mixed with customs whose presence makes it distinctly a wedding (the ring exchange, the recitation of wedding vows, and the sharing of sake cups). (Edwards, 1989, p. 16)

Following this part of the wedding is a formal reception, speeches by key individuals, specific ceremonies (cake cutting, candle lighting, flower arrangement, etc.), congratulatory speeches, entertainment, and closing activities. These activities center on a couple's formal initiation into the marital life of the Japanese community. The elaborate nature of this marital ceremony stands in contrast to the customary marriages within the Mandinka villages of West Africa. In these communities, after a brief negotiation with the woman's family and with far less fanfare, a young woman finds herself married:

> If a man wants to marry a girl he sends kola nuts to her family saying he wants to marry a particular woman. If they keep the kola nuts, it means they agree to the marriage. The two families quickly negotiate the bride-price and when it is paid the girl's family breaks the kola nuts and sends them back to the man with a message that he can now steal her away. He comes and takes her with him to his family's units and they're married.[14]

The marriage custom of Northern Nigeria has similar features. The negotiation of the bride-price and the interactions of elders in this marriage agreement are salient features. However, sometimes an alternate route toward marriage provides an interesting setting for negotiations. As described during an interview, Petsalis reports:

> One way of not paying the bride-price, and if the girl agrees, you can get her pregnant. Your in-laws will not like this. It's an insult to them. They are forced to accept it. When the girl gets pregnant before marriage, her father will throw her out. She will come to you. Later, when you have money, you can return to her father's house, pay the money, and apologize. One of the elders will go forward and tell them you want to settle. Some fathers will continue refusing because the daughter has shamed them and because she will not be respected in her new house. We are proud of our traditions and we want everything to be done by them. (1990, p. 39)

The marriage day, regardless of the length of the ceremony (ranging from several days, for the Nubian brides of Egypt, to a few hours for the Western bride), is a special and memorable event for families around the world. Although the reality of marital life varies, most brides come into their marriages with the hope of a good life. What this good life means and how she negotiates her marital years remains compromised by the cultural patterns, the expectations placed on women in a given society, and the financial resources that are available to her newly formed family of procreation. The universal custom is the perceived specialness of the event, as it marks launching into a new life. Commonly, this means the passage of the woman from parental authority to husband authority. The reality of this new life is constructed within the contemporary views of marital roles within the particular society. The ceremony also is symbolic of an indoctrination into domestic duties. The cooking for the family, the feeding of special foods to the husband, and the mutual feeding of the cake (with the wife feeding the husband first) are all examples of the new role the woman has as wife. (See Examples 1.1, 1.2, and 1.3 for examples of global weddings.)

EXAMPLE 1.1. Marriage Brief I

A Korean Marriage

C. P., married sixteen years, remembers her marriage ceremony this way:

I met my husband right after we finished college. We met through a mutual friend. We dated for two and a half years before we decided that we wanted to get married. We didn't meet each others' families until we decided to get married because, in Korea, dating is not accepted. To date means that you are going to get married . . . we were lucky, our parents agreed that we were a good match and a few months later we were married.

Our marriage was like all marriages; we had a two-part ceremony. The first part is like a community gathering with hundreds of people there. The host for the wedding was one of my husband's professors. That is quite common to have a highly respected person host that part. We exchanged our message of marriage and signed papers. The second part is very traditional. We changed into our traditional clothing. I wore a joktoori (traditional hat) and a daerabook hanbook (wedding dress). Only my husband's family are allowed in this portion of the wedding with us.[15] I bowed three times to each relative and received a blessing from them. Each set of three bows for each relative—I remember how my back hurt.

EXAMPLE 1.2. Marriage Brief II

An American Wedding

Tamara remembers her marriage, August 20, 1993:

The chapel was beautifully decorated with bows on every other pew and ribbon looping from pew to pew on both sides of the aisle. Big bouquets were also on each side of the altar, and the railing in front of the altar stage was decorated with ribbon, bows, and wreaths.

The chaplain appeared and greeted the guests, then looked to the back to signal the bridal party to begin their processional, and the violins began playing *Canon in D Major* by Pachelbel. Each bridesmaid wore an iridescent, emerald green, long gown with matching emerald earrings, carrying a bouquet of white flowers with lots of green leaves.

When all fourteen men and women (seven men/seven women) lined up at the altar, the two ushers marched up to the front to pull the aisle runner down for the flower girl to begin her march. Once she got about halfway, my uncle and I began our walk. Chaplain King gave the invocation, followed by the singing of *Ave Maria*. One of the bridesmaids stepped out of line to read the Scripture of 1 Corinthians 13; the chaplain asked, "Who gives this woman?" and I had asked my mother to stand and say she does, since she did not walk down the aisle with me. Once that was finished, my uncle kissed me and sat down.

Next, we exchanged our vows, and the rings were given to the chaplain for his blessing, and we exchanged rings for the ring ceremony. The chaplain said, "Those whom God has joined together, let no one separate. Amen." At our Consecration prayer, the chaplain began singing "The Lord's Prayer."

After the song, we rose and the chaplain gave his Benediction, and then he said, "Vincent, you may kiss your bride." We then kissed as husband and wife, and my new husband kept kissing; the church broke into laughter. Chaplain King said to the church to "Please stand, ladies and gentlemen, for the exit of Tamara and Vincent Johnson." We turned around with a white rose for each of us to give to our mothers when we left the altar. But first, we gracefully jumped the broom,[16] while our two ushers held it.

EXAMPLE 1.3. Marriage Brief III

A Bengali Wedding

A Bengali wedding is recalled:

In our community, a wedding is not merely a marriage between two individuals. It is the coming together of two families. Relatives and friends arrive from near and far, days ahead of the wedding. The atmosphere is one of a large, celebratory picnic. The actual wedding ceremony may continue for two consecutive days—not counting the various rituals that precede and follow, both in the groom's family as well as in the bride's. The bride and the groom have very little control over the events that overtake them. As a matter of fact, it is considered unseemly for the main protagonists to take an active interest or participatory role in their own wedding.

In Hindu weddings, the bride and the groom are supposed to fast all day before the ceremony and are allowed to eat only after all rites and rituals have been completed. Next came the ritual bathing with turmeric. This, too, purifies the bride before the wedding. Also, this helps to tint the skin a golden yellow, and in Indian eyes, obsessed with fairness of skin, makes the bride look prettier. This was followed by a visit to the temple of the deity, Kali Mother. Prayers were offered and the all-important white and red shell bangles were eased over my hands onto my wrists. These bangles signified that I was soon to be married, and their presence on my wrists would declare forever after that I was a married woman. I would also have to be careful about them all my life, and ensure that they did not break, for these bangles were symbolic of the life and well-being of my husband and any damage to them might well portend harm to his life.

The religious ceremony was preceded by a civil ceremony, where a marriage registrar officiated. By Indian standards, we had a short wedding. Our wedding consisted of the exchange of vows in front of the sacrificial fire, with the Fire God acting as the witness and priests from both sides officiating. Later there was an exchange of garlands made of flowers and then my newly married husband put a streak of vermillion in the parting of my hair. This signified that I henceforth belonged to him and his family. The vermillion mark, like the shell bangles, is once again supposed to protect the husband's life — and no wife worth her salt is supposed to ever go without it.

The groom spends the wedding night in the bride's house. But the next day, the bride must leave with her husband for her new home. Everyone weeps, and the bride usually breaks down completely, leaving the groom feeling extremely embarrassed and guilty. The same happened in my case, too. Perhaps more so because I was an only child and the eldest daughter of the family. The bride and the groom are expected to sleep apart on this night. (This stems from ancient folklore in which the groom was killed by a snake bite on the second night of the wedding, while the bride slept on. Since then, it is considered inauspicious for husbands to share the room with the wives on that particular night.)

The next day, the new bride is expected to serve lunch to all members of her new family. This is the formal indoctrination into the ways of the household, especially the kitchen. In the evening, the groom's family holds a reception for their friends and relatives. The bride's family is there too, and festivities continue late into the night. The two families exchange gifts and indeed become one large extended family.[17]

WHAT DOES LOVE HAVE TO DO WITH IT?

The question of love is one that many Western scholars and romantics discuss in relationship to marriage. For those women who live their lives in societies that carefully and consciously monitor marital units, love is not an issue. In many places throughout the world, it is the family that decides who a woman marries, with or without the consent of a woman; she marries the man of her family's choice. Women, married without a say, often find themselves continually adjusting to the unequal status of women within the patriarchal family. This is a pattern that persists in the face of the issue of love and choice in marriage partners seen in some societies. So what does love have to do with marriage? In the minds of many in developed countries, it has everything to do with marriage; in the minds of others, it may or may not play a part in the marital decision. In cases where love is the major motivation for marriage, women still find themselves perceived as unequal players on the marriage field. Thus, love may be the central reason a couple marries, but it is often only part of the story behind the marriage.

Arranged marriages and marriages for alliance purposes continue to exist. These marriages involve two individuals, united for life (sometimes), with little exposure to each other before the wedding day. Marriage for love unites a couple for life also, at least that has been the assumption in the past.

Despite the specialness of the wedding day, marriage is a process cemented in the reality of the cultural context. Women wield differential negotiation power within various societies, but in most societies, there are instances where these publicly acknowledged lifelong commitments dissolve through divorce. Throughout the world, divorce has greater negative impact on the women leaving the marital union than on the male partners.

MARITAL DISSOLUTION: HAS LIBERAL DIVORCE LEGISLATION HELPED OR HARMED WOMEN?

The numbers of marital dissolutions (commonly termed divorces) seen within societies relate to the social forces governing marital dissolutions throughout the world.[18] Although it is interesting to examine worldwide trends of divorce, these rates reflect the social forces driving marital relationships and the legal structures guarding such behavior. Extremely low or high rates cannot be interpreted in isolation from the reality of the local customs observed, the religious beliefs in place within each community, and the laws that reinforce the social norms.

Clearly, divorce occurs throughout much of the world, although its rates vary dramatically. The marital dissolution rate seen within the United States leads the world (see Table 1.2). The differences within the marital dissolution rates throughout the world underscore the necessity to explore carefully the reality of specific societies as related to marriage and divorce.

The divorce rates within the United States have risen dramatically since the 1950s. In 1950, 10.3 per 1,000 marriages ended in divorce, climbing to a high of 23 per 1,000 in 1980 and maintaining nearly that rate today (Parkman, 1992) (see Table 1.2). The initial growth in divorce rates occurred in the late 1950s and continued until the early

TABLE 1.2. Divorce Rates: Selected Countries 1980/1990

Divorce Rates per 1,000 Married Women

Country	1980	1990
Canada	11	13
Denmark	11	14
France	06	08
Germany	06	09
Italy	01	02
Japan	05	05
Netherlands	08	08
Sweden	11	12
United Kingdom	12	N/A
United States	23	21

Source: U.S. Bureau of Labor Statistics, *Monthly Labor Review,* March 1990; and unpublished data.

1980s. These differences reflect changes in the norms of relationships, changes in views toward women, and women's expanded
entrance into the economic arena. Although many factors contribute
to the rise in divorce rates, most scholars agree that the institution of
no-fault divorce had an impact on the continuing trend.

In the United States, the California Family Law of 1969 laid the
foundation for the global trend toward no-fault divorce and set the
standard for statutes enacted in other states and many countries. This
change from fault-based divorce to those where no fault assignment
was necessary was seen in other developed countries within the early
1970s.[19]

The creation of no-fault divorce responded to the extremely adver-
sarial nature of divorce law that needed to establish fault to grant
divorce and to establish a basis for the division of matrimonial property. No-fault divorce allowed for divorce based on "irretrievable
breakdown of marriage" or "irreconcilable differences." No-fault
divorces removed much of the acrimony attached to divorce and
lowered the cost; however, a multitude of concerns became apparent
in societies instituting no-fault divorce. Among these concerns was
the impact of divorce on the lives of women and their children.
Although women found it easier to get out of a poor marriage, they
frequently plummeted into poverty or near-poverty as a result of
no-fault divorce.[20]

In addition to worldwide changes in divorce law, other facts influence increasing divorce rates. As women throughout the world, particularly married women, have steadily moved into the workforce,
divorce rates have climbed.[21] Women who felt financially constrained
to stay in abusive or unsatisfying marriages have, with some financial resources, begun to see divorce as an option. Also, decreases in
family size due to planning, contraception, and abortion have created
a greater focus on the conjugal bond. Marriage over the last thirty
years has undergone greater scrutiny by couples.

In previous years, women raising large families had less time to
focus on the viability of their marriages and options to staying
within intolerable marriages. In many cultures, today's environment
represents an "era of realization" in which couples anticipate and
seek a high degree of emotional and intimate fulfillment. As couples have a greater focus worldwide on the conjugal bond and a

greater expectation of a good marriage, they become less tolerant of unsatisfying relationships. Finally, increases in life expectancy for women and men throughout much of the world greatly extends their years with a spouse, thus increasing in length their struggles with the predictable or not so predictable issues of marital relationships, marital conflict, and unequal roles within marriage. The presence of these factors, together with the greater availability of divorce in some countries, creates situations in which many women have divorce as an option, and thus encounter the psychological and economic consequences of such a decision.

Divorce has serious repercussions on women's resources. The differential earning power of women and the failure of courts to award—and ex-husbands to pay—alimony and child support are key factors in this downward mobility of divorced women and, consequently, their children (Parkman, 1992). Women in the United States and Canada are worse off than women of previous eras in terms of property settlement.[22] When husbands were found at fault, the courts provided mandates awarding larger settlements to the wronged wife. Although the present increased accessibility of no-fault divorce creates a greater likelihood that women can be liberated from intolerable marriages, it has not effectively created a system that allows women to reap their equitable portion of matrimonial property.

For example, the need to establish fault to receive divorce was changed in England and Wales in 1971. Prior to this ruling, women and men struggled to remove the stigma of divorce and increase the ability for women and men to escape unbearable situations. A 1966 commission instituted by the Church of England laid the groundwork for this decision. After lengthy discussion, this commission recommended that divorce should be allowed when marriage breakdown occurred (Phillips, 1988). Before that time, as in many other developed countries, it was necessary to establish blame based on the presence of adultery, inappropriate behavior, desertion, or a marital separation of two to five years before the courts granted a divorce (Gibson, 1994). The use of irreconcilable differences as a basis for divorce increased from 17 percent in 1971 to 39 percent in 1990. Unreasonable behavior has also gained acceptance within the court systems of England and Wales and represents the primary reason women petition for divorce.

In contrast to the rest of Europe, Ireland, in November 1995, finally removed its constitutional ban on divorce and remarriage, passing the legislation by a narrow margin of 50.3 percent to 49.7 percent. Why was the institution of divorce such a difficult battle in Ireland? This can be partly understood by the impact of Catholic teachings and religious philosophy on the lives of Irish citizens. Divorce is clearly against the religious teachings of the Catholic Church (Dillon, 1993). Earlier attempts evoked a swift response from the Church that seemed to turn the tide away from divorce. Some feel that the public support of Ireland's president, Mary Robinson, was pivotal in the 1995 vote to legalize divorce.[23]

During each of the previous attempts to legalize divorce, antidivorce forces campaigned with a self-defined pro-woman platform. They appealed to women to help themselves by opposing divorce. They argued that divorce would hinder, not help, the conditions of women. They suggested that women would be discarded and left with nothing if men had the right to divorce at will. They pointed to the poverty statistics of other women in developed countries to support the claim that it was especially pro-woman to oppose divorce. One widely quoted woman stated, "A woman voting for divorce is like a turkey voting for Christmas." This framing of women as victims is not only seen in Ireland, but has been widely used to support antiabortion forces, those against the equal rights amendment, and backers of other controversial legislature for women around the world.[24]

Others debated the economic consequences of divorce for Ireland. Beliefs that divorce begets economic instability and increases unemployment fed the antidivorce sentiment. Finally, great tension centered on the philosophy of marriage as a lifelong commitment.[25]

The constitutional ban on divorce did not prevent marital breakdown within Ireland; approximately 6 percent of the population is separated (Dillon, 1993). Separation,[26] foreign divorce,[27] civil annulment,[28] and ecclesiastical annulments,[29] are all used as ways to manage serious marital discord among women and men. As one Irish participant in the Global Summit for Women expressed:

It is hard to get on with your life, raise a family, and live with your world when you can never legally marry again and start your life again.[30]

According to 1997 estimates by the Irish government, over 80,000 people were legally bound in broken marriages when the law was passed (Clarity, 1997). This continues to have serious consequences in the lives of women throughout their lifetimes, and the world will watch carefully how this law is implemented and how the courts resolve the interconnected issues of longtime separation, property distribution, and the rights of both parties and their common children.

Marital breakdown ending in divorce is also seen within developing regions of the world. Most developing countries reflected a moderately constant level or a small increase in the 1980s. For example, Singapore's crude divorce rate was 2,028 in 1984, rising slowly each year with a rate of 2,708 in 1987. The repercussions of divorce for women and their children are quite serious. The customs in many cultures provide ownership of matrimonial property and guardianship of the children to the man. Divorce can leave women with little or nothing, including a mandatory loss of claim to their children. The impact of these customs is particularly salient in countries in Africa and Asia.

In Nias, Beatty (1992) reports the rarity of divorce. However, it is the wife in these rare occurrences who is usually the one divorced. Divorce can occur if "she was lazy" or "she was suspected of committing adultery." However, few divorce cases are documented because of the regimentation of marriage rules. For instance, since sexual relationships outside marriage are strictly forbidden, it is rare to see adultery as a reason for divorce. In past times, extramarital relationships when discovered would be dealt with harshly. The couple would be tied together and thrown in the river to die. Presently, a fine would be paid to the woman's family if such illicit relationships occurred. Beatty describes a fine for extramarital relationships:

Ama X married his agnate's widow after their liaison was discovered. His first wife wanted to go back to her family, but was persuaded to accept the new wife. A fine was added to the widow's bride wealth. This settlement involved the minimum of disturbance in alliance relations. (1992, p. 177)

In Egypt, separation of couples expressing marital problems is uncommon; divorce is considered extreme by Egyptian norms. Women face the need to overcome many obstacles to dissolve a marriage. Egyptian women find that the society requires demanding criteria for women who wish to acquire a divorce:

> To be specific, a Muslim husband may, if he will, dissolve a marriage contract without the intervention of a court simply by repudiating his wife three times (talaq). The right of divorce by this means can be delegated to the wife by her husband when it is so designated in the marriage contract. (Rugh, 1984, p. 176)

Christian marriages, a small minority within Egypt (6.3 percent), are even more difficult to dissolve. It is very rare for Christian families to be dissolved by means other than death (Rugh, 1984). Women face strong pressure against separation or divorce despite the magnitude of the problems they bear within their families.

In some countries, bride-price may impede the divorce process for women. As seen in Nigeria, a woman who wishes to petition for a divorce must repay her bride-price. In some cases, the inability to repay the equivalent of the bride-price forces a Nigerian woman to remain within a marriage she wishes to dissolve (Petsalis, 1990).

Worldwide consequences for women involved in divorce are attached to the stigma of a divorced woman, her psychological adjustment to the divorce process, the economic repercussions, and the limitations placed on the mother-child relationship. Societal customs and practices toward divorce prescribe women's experiences in the divorce process.

REMARRIAGE

Approximately 35 percent of all marriages are remarriages (L. Stone, 1990). For these widowed and divorced women, the customs of their communities guide their remarriages. As stated earlier, women tend to marry older men; therefore, women seeking remarriage are more likely to find partners of choice during their younger years.

Some societies mandate that the widow, no matter what her age, marry relatives of her deceased husband. This is often the case in polygamous societies, where the widowed woman becomes a wife among several wives.[31] This trend persists within several African and South Asian countries and has been historically documented in many societies.

In Zimbabwe, divorced or widowed women make less valuable marriage partners. These women face fewer opportunities to marry despite their specific personal qualities and their ability to contribute to the family and to bear additional children. "If she is married a second time the loss of her virginity impairs her value even if she is able to bear children" (Batezat and Mwalo, 1989, p. 53). Although remarriage occurs for both divorced and widowed women, the cultural norms held by some societies place these women in a continually devalued position. In eastern Nigeria, a widowed woman married by customary law must pay her bride-price back to her husband's family if she wishes to remarry (Petsalis, 1990). Again, economic hardships create obstacles to a potential choice of marriage.

Petsalis documents the complexity of the remarriage customs in contemporary Nigeria. The conflict between traditions and newly infused ideas and laws intensifies this conflict. A recent widow, who is presently a businesswoman, recalls her experiences after the death of her husband:

> The custom is that you can be taken over by the husband's brother. When an uncle died, my twenty-two-year-old aunt was taken by her brother-in-law. It was a family decision. The idea is that the woman is the property of the family to be kept there and to be protected. She must be looked after. So she is acquired by a brother, unless she refuses.
>
> In my case, there was no proposal. I was too independent, too strong. I had offers, but I refused. So they were bitter toward me. There was also another problem. When a rich husband dies young, there is always a suspicion the wife may have done away with him to obtain inheritance, especially if he had married by a statutory marriage as I had. The suspi-

cions were there. His family tried to take away the business. But I know my rights. My statutory marriage protected me and I had my brothers to advise me. (1990, p. 74)

India practices the cultural tradition of marrying widowed women to male relatives of the deceased, as observed among the Chuhras of northern India. In these societies, it is most appropriate for a woman of childbearing age to remarry her husband's brother after the appropriate waiting period (typically a year). However, for older women (those with grown children or who are postmenopausal), the expectation is for them to remain unmarried with a pledge of celibacy (Kolenda, 1985).

In the United States, the remarriage rate is quite high, but it varies by age of the woman. In this case, most women remarrying are divorced, unlike the larger numbers of widowed women remarrying throughout much of the world. In the United States, three out of four divorced women remarry by age thirty; however, only one out of four women aged forty or older remarry (Levitan, Belous, and Gallo, 1988). In either case, remarriage is less likely as women grow older, reinforcing a worldwide devaluation based on lost virginity and lower ability to bear children and a standard of beauty based on youth. Cultural patterns determine the factors that play the most significant part in societies.

SUMMARY

Studies reveal that marriage is an expectation for women worldwide. The reality of this relationship is influenced by culturally accepted views of masculinity and femininity. Marriage has several significant similarities throughout the world: women enter the process of marriage with great ceremony, live marital lives that may not always meet their expectations, and in increasing numbers, turn to divorce or separation in unbearable situations as a choice to redirect their lives. This chapter has focused on heterosexual, monogamous marriage customs. In the next chapter, we discuss diverse family forms seen throughout the world and women's place within those families.

KEY WORDS
Bride-price/Bride wealth
Dowry
Family of orientation
Family of procreation
Femininity
Lobola
Machismo
Marriage pool (marital pool)
Masculinity
No-fault divorce
Patriarchy

Chapter 2

Diversity Within Family Formation

Feminist thought broadens our notions of family to include the experiences of women from varied cultures, classes, and conditions. The language and much of the discourse concerning families has, until recently, reflected the view that monogamous, heterosexual, and nationalistic family formations are the only valid family forms. This perspective serves to negate the diverse reality of women worldwide. Many feminist writers have challenged this view and struggled to demystify the ideology of the monolithic family.[1] This demystification has taken many forms as feminist scholars grapple with the diversity of women and the realities women face nationally and internationally. Some feminist theorists, however, are criticized for failing to centrally include women of color within analyses and for having a superficial understanding of the lives and families of women of color.[2] Although the perspectives of contemporary feminist scholars include a recognition of the diversity of women's lives worldwide, some scholars challenge the depth of this knowledge. This chapter will explore the often neglected diversity among women's families and relationships across the globe.

DEFINING FAMILIES

Most women throughout the world regard themselves as part of a family recognized by their community or peers. The forms these families take vary both within and between communities. In most communities, distinctly different family forms coexist. This chapter will explore the realities of family forms that women find themselves a part of around the globe. This discussion will not capture the intricacies of all families' alternative structures but will highlight those most commonly observed and examine how these forms explicate the realities of women's lives.

Families are defined here as a group of persons who consider themselves a stable unit and are related to one another by blood, marriage, adoption, or a consensual decision to live together and who provide acknowledged emotional and financial support for members. The family forms under discussion are grouped within two broad categories: those that exist within simple households and those that exist within multiple-family households. Those described within simple households include cohabiting heterosexuals with or without children, women living (primarily) alone with or without children, and lesbian couples with or without children present. Those described within multiple-family households include polygamous families (both polygynous and polyandrous); vertically complex families, consisting of several generations within the same household (sometimes called coresidential extended families); and laterally or horizontally complex families consisting of siblings, friends or fictive kin, with or without children, living within the same household. Issues of the impact of mixed races, mixed religious backgrounds, or intercultural mingling are discussed as they relate to some family forms. The additional blending of norms and expectations found among mixed races and religions further complicates the lives of women and their families as they manage their existence within their families and communities.

The similarity among the women discussed in this chapter is that they differ from the majority experience of assumed monogamous, heterosexual unions bound by a legal marriage. A distinct difference for these women is the degree of society's acceptance of their family forms and the ramifications they face resulting from any lack of acceptance from their communities or those outside their communities.

SIMPLE HOUSEHOLDS

Although most scholars agree that monogamous, heterosexual, marital union is the preferred family configuration for most women, some women prefer and form other family ties through remaining single, cohabitation, or developing romantic/family ties with other women. With these choices, women have redefined the normative view of family and formed families along lines that have not always been as visible.

Single Women

There is an increasing trend for women to remain unmarried longer and for women to choose a family not based on wedlock. In many parts of the world, the number of households that consist of "one person" has revealed a dramatic increase. In Canada, one-person households increased from 9 percent of the total number of households in 1960 to 20 percent by 1980; in the Netherlands, from 12 percent in 1960 to 22 percent by 1980; and in the United States, from 13 percent of the total number of households in 1960 to 23 percent in 1980, indicating significant increases within developed countries of never-married and single individuals.[3] As women in these countries see broader worldwide possibilities beyond early marriage and childbearing, they begin to extend their singlehood to pursue educational endeavors and to explore life's adventures in ways that previously were available only to men.

For many single women, the family of orientation maintains a central focus within their life. Others have developed complex systems of family through friendship ties. Stack (1974) describes non-blood-related family members as fictive kin, who serve to provide many of the same behaviors as blood kin. Thus, female friends become similar to sisters and male friends similar to brothers, enlarging family networks. Although this phenomenon is well documented in African-American families, it exists within many other single- and two-parent households (Thorne and Yalom, 1992).

Mirroring the increase in one-person households are the increases observed within single-parent families. The number of households with single parents (typically mothers) and children has increased in most countries. The percent of women heading households has continued to increase throughout most of the world. In Argentina, 19 percent of women head households; in Costa Rica, 19 percent; in France, 22 percent; in Guyana, 24 percent; in Indonesia, 14 percent; in Switzerland, 25 percent; in Thailand, 16 percent; and within the United States, 31 percent (United Nations, 1990). Although great variation exists, a significant portion of single women head house-

holds throughout the world. These female heads of households represent a large group of women who view family in terms of themselves, their offspring, and possible extended family members,
fictive kin, and close relationships.

Does being single have a consequence on the quality of life of
women worldwide? Many women around the globe, regardless of
their marital status, are living in poverty. In all cases, households
headed by women are overrepresented among those in poverty.
When comparing women's wages to those of men, the worldwide
trend shows that women earn less than men in all regions. The
percentages range from women earning a low of 50 percent of men's
wages in Korea and 52 percent in Japan, to 73 percent in the United
States, to a high of 90 percent of men's wages in Iceland.

In many countries, women's wages as a percent of men's average in
the 70 percentile, including countries reporting significant increases in
women's positions within the labor market.[4] As more women head
households with fewer resources in hand, they encounter challenges in
their attempts to provide the necessities for themselves and their children. (See Chapter 4 for a more detailed discussion of work-related
issues.)

Although singlehood may be a temporary or uncommon situation
for some adult women, other regions report high levels of single-parent, simple households. In many Caribbean countries, the majority of
households are headed by females. Female-headed households (consisting of women with children) range from 40 to 75 percent of all
households within this part of the world. The lower rate of 40 percent
is observed within St. Vincent, whereas Jamaica leads Caribbean
countries with 75 percent of their households headed by women.[5]
Countries that have a significant East Indian population (e.g., Guyana and Trinidad) reveal higher marriage rates, as does Belize with
its greater concentration of Amerindian population. Even in countries where marriage rates are low, women regard marriage as desirable, and often an ideal that is unlikely to become a reality. Senior
(1991) describes a progression of relationships for Jamaican women
who, in their early years (twenty-five years and younger), "visit"
with significant males within their lives and, in many cases, have
children with these partners. Later, in the late twenties to late thirties,
they settle down in cohabitation with a chosen mate, usually the

biological father of their children. Then finally, in the late thirties to middle forties, the typical pattern is for women to marry the mate they have bonded with during the years of cohabitation.

Although this pattern is common within Jamaican culture, there are many women who depart from this model. Women from the middle and upper classes tend to depart from these norms and marry earlier before having children. Also, those representing other than Afro-Caribbean ethnicity (particularly Chinese or East Indian) follow an earlier pattern of marriage with a postponement of child-bearing until after marriage. Although extended single parenting is a common family pattern, there is diversity within the experience of Caribbean women concerning marriage patterns.[6]

Further, single life is a documented personal or familial choice among some cultures. Women may have very specific reasons for never marrying. In Tibet, women may adopt this lifestyle because of a desire to be celibate. Among Tibetan Buddhists, 8 percent of all females over fifteen years of age become religious celibates and develop a life that does not define family through conjugal ties (Schuler, 1987). Religious celibacy is a custom within some families in this part of the world and is not a personal inclination but a familial responsibility. Also, in areas where polyandry exists, never-married women are common.[7] The Chumik in Southeast Asia is such a region. The smaller pool of available males, given the existence of fraternal polyandry, makes family life without marriage a reality for many women. Among Chumiks with a tradition of religious celibacy, communities have developed strategies to prevent daughters from pursuing marriage. As seen in many parts of the world, unmarried daughters are valuable caregivers for the family. It is, therefore, an unmarried daughter who cares for the family if the mother dies or is ill. In this case, a daughter remains to provide domestic services if her brothers are too young to marry. She provides these duties until they become of age and take wives. Occasionally the aged members of the family barter property inheritance with a daughter if she does not marry or postpones marriage (sometimes indefinitely) to provide caretaking services (Schuler, 1987). Daughters remaining single and acting as caregivers to aging parents are seen worldwide.[8] This is a responsibility that is observed in widely different cultures and in both developed and developing regions. In either case, a woman's decision rests on a negotiation between the needs of the family and her personal wishes.

Women in Cohabitation Relationships

The majority of women in most parts of the world marry or enter cohabitation by their middle twenties (United Nations, 1991b). Cohabitation is a choice in many countries, particularly when the cultural norms do not either forbid such a union or evoke extreme negative sanctions on the couple making this choice. Although some countries have legal recognition of such relationships, few ensure women's rights either within or after the relationship. In some cases, efforts have been made to develop or preserve parental inheritance or maintenance rights (child support) for children born during cohabitation. However, given the difficulty worldwide of divorced women receiving child support, children born of cohabitating parents fare less well. In 1981, Barbados gave legal status to partners in common-law marriage if the couple had been together longer than five years. This law further ensured inheritance rights for children born during these cohabitation relationships.[9] This move to ensure a legal recognition of cohabitation is atypical for a Caribbean nation, but despite the worldwide status regarding this issue, inability to gain support even if ordered is the typical pattern.[10]

Sweden leads the world in its integration of cohabitation relationships as legal family systems. How has Sweden been so successful in normalizing cohabitation? All references to illegitimacy of children were dropped from Swedish law in 1917, followed by lengthy legal reform to create equal benefits throughout society. The legal equity of such relationships has created a long-standing norm of acceptance of cohabitation. Presently, greater than 25 percent of all relationships are cohabitators and many present marriages were initially cohabitation relationships. The acceptability and equal legal status make this option a viable and positive reality for Swedish women and men (Eshleman, 1997). Sweden's ability to remove the stigma that many couples experience worldwide is due to the early liberalization of laws, followed by vigilant adherence to the legal mandate. Together these have set up the community standard of acceptance that we observe today.

The possibility of palimony, widely publicized in the United States, is another example of individuals attempting to gain rights for cohabitators. Occasionally, a member of a cohabitation relationship successfully litigates for palimony (monetary awards after the dissolution of a cohabitation relationship) based on the woman's economic and emotional support provided during the relationship.[11] Palimony cases throughout the world meet with greater opposition than success, when women attempt to garner any portion of what is considered "male property" after a cohabitation relationship ends. Thus, the lack of rules associated with cohabitation as a family form places women in a vulnerable situation both during and on dissolution of the relationship.

Lesbian Relationships

Romantic and loving relationships between women have been documented in many countries around the world. Do these relationships differ from heterosexual cohabitation?[12] The form that these romantic ties take depends on the norms of the community and the wishes of the women within these relationships. On a global level, the common issues and concerns confronted by lesbian women came to light in 1981 at the International Lesbian Information Conference in Amsterdam. During this conference and a subsequent one in Italy the same year, lesbian women representing different countries gathered to discuss various questions: What does it mean to love another woman? What issues do lesbian mothers encounter? What is a lesbian lifestyle? What is the impact of racism and classism on lesbianism? (*Connexions*, 1981a, 1981b). This began a global dialogue among lesbians that forced communities in many parts of the world to address the concerns of this subpopulation.

Issues concerning marriage and lifelong partnerships are central to discussions about lesbian families. Denmark and Sweden recognize marriage between women (or men).[13] However, women desiring a declaration of their commitment find varied ways to acknowledge their union. The institution of marriage holds a central conflict within the lesbian community. For some, the custom of marriage is connected to women as extensions of men, and such unions hold negative and patriarchal meanings. Others insist that marriage within one's belief or religious traditions validates the sanctity of the lesbian union. Some argue that until the legalization of same-sex marriages occurs, there will be no true recognition of lesbian rights (Butler, 1990). It is within this conflict that lesbian couples world-wide, with various views concerning marriage, attempt to gain public recognition of their relationships.

Lesbian relationships are documented in many parts of the world. These women report that despite their experiences with acts of oppression, they continue to create lesbian families. As shown in Table 2.1, lesbian relationships, as documented by linguistic tags, exist in many sectors of the world.

In *Ceremonies of the Heart*, Becky Butler documents the cere-monies of twenty-seven lesbian couples who developed ways to celebrate their union representing their cultures and traditions. A New Zealand couple wrote:

> In March 1986, after having lived together for three years, Noreen and I had a trysting ceremony at Noreen's beach prop-erty. This ceremony was, in Noreen's view, about two and half long years overdue, but for me it was an experience involving considerable conflict. On the one hand, the ceremony felt like an insult to our relationship (our commitment to each other did not require "proper validation" through social ceremonies—it was already valid); like a return to quasi-patriarchal institutions (trysting = wedding = overtones of patriarchy); and even like something of a hollow game, because I had no real commitment to Goddess ritual at that time. But on the other hand, I felt as though I was a dreadful heel for having denied Noreen her trysting for so long, especially as it was obviously so important to her. (1990, p. 92)

In this excerpt describing their ceremony, the conflict between the meaning of the ceremony as viewed by society and the wishes of the couple are apparent. In communities that stigmatize lesbian relationships, it becomes necessary to weigh the importance of the ceremony against the "traditional" meaning of a marriage cere-mony. The importance of creating alternative ceremonies that honor lesbian unions becomes a crucial issue.

Other lesbian couples highlight the internal struggles they faced before coming to the decision to have a ceremony uniting them as a

TABLE 2.1. Examples of Languages Referring to Lesbians or Lesbianism

English	lesbian, dyke
French	lesbienne, gouine (slang), goudou (slang)
German	lesbierin, lesbe (slang)
Italian	lesbica
Japanese	daiku (dyke)
Portuguese	lesbica
Quechua	mamaku (mannish woman), qharincha (tomboy)
Spanish	lesbiana, marimacha (slang), tortillera (slang), tortilla (slang)
Swiss	warmi (slang)
Swedish	lesbisk

Adapted from *Connexions: An International Women's Quarterly,* Global Lesbianism, January 1982, p. 3.

couple. In some cases the struggle may take years, and other times it is relatively short. An Australian couple describe how they came to their union as a lesbian couple in 1988:

Marion and I decided to have a ceremony for a number of reasons. For Marion, it was because she had hidden away, denied even, her sexuality for over twenty years. After much soul-searching, she had reached a point of being able to rest in the knowledge that she was still worthy, lovable, and precious in the eyes of God. Having come out, she felt good and whole about being who she was, and she wanted to make a public declaration of this fact. Second, we both wanted to share our deep joy and happiness with others. We also wanted to ask our friends to be willing to help us should we ever get into strife and need counseling or deep caring and understanding.

I felt an inner certainty that this relationship would be long-term, hopefully, "till death do us part." By making a public statement of my love and commitment to Marion, I was saying to others, and perhaps more important, to myself, that this was no flash-in-the-pan, short-term affair . . . We courted for twelve

months and had the ceremony on the anniversary of our coming together as lovers. (Butler, 1990, p. 151)

These couples reflect the desire to express deep and hopefully
long-term commitment to each other; they formally acknowledge
their love and caring with a ceremony. However, the lack of legal
recognition of these unions precludes these women from the privileges and benefits that members of heterosexual couples receive
throughout the world. In addition to documented inequalities within
heterosexual marriages and lesbian relationships, women within lesbian marriagelike relationships are further disadvantaged by their
unrecognized status in most parts of the world. In most countries,
these women are denied inheritance rights associated with marriage
and health and insurance benefits and confront discrimination regarding custody decisions.

S. Stone explains the precarious position of lesbians within Canada. In the case of Anderson versus Luoma, the author describes
two lesbians who lived together and shared their assets for several
years. However, when the relationship dissolved, the courts had
difficulty seeing the women as a spousal unit:

> When they dissolved their relationship, one applied to the court
> for maintenance for herself, support for the children, and for an
> order for equal division of the assets of the union. Dohm, J. [the
> judge hearing the case] held that the plaintiff could not rely on
> the Family Relations Act to support her position, for the Act did
> not "purport to affect the legal responsibility which homosexu-
> als may have to each other or to children born to one of them as
> a result of insemination." (1990, p. 110)

Other lesbians speak of a great isolation and invisibility. In these
cases, women cannot make a public commitment due to fear of
persecution. Cuba does not theoretically discriminate against lesbians; however, practice suggests institutional discrimination. One
example is the allocation of housing to Cuban families where families are defined as married couples. Others must live with parents or
family members. Thus, equal access to housing is denied lesbians. In
principle, memberships to groups are not based on sexual orientation, but in reality, lesbians (if known) would be excluded from

participation in organizations central to Cuban way of life.[14] Lesbians in Cuba, as in many parts of the world, live a hidden existence so as to prevent negative sanctions and are not able to live independently as easily as heterosexual married couples.

In many parts of the world, lesbians report jailing and intimidation, and lesbians in Asia and Africa often feel invisible. As a Japanese lesbian describes:

> Being a lesbian in Japan in completely different from being a lesbian here [in the United States]. Lesbianism gets no visibility in Japan. Even if you are living with a woman, no one imagines that you might be a lesbian. You live in the closet all the time and it's really hard. When I talk to my mother, she asks me when I'll get married. I tell her I'm not getting married, that I don't like men. She doesn't think I might be a lesbian. But here people would begin to wonder. (*Connexions,* 1981b, p. 16)

Little documentation exists of contemporary non-Western romantic ties between women. Swidler (1993) describes a ritual seen among the Azande in the Sudan called the baghuru ritual. This ritual began when two women within the same polygynous marriage (co-wives) loved each other and wanted to form an alliance. With the permission of the husband, the two women exchanged small gifts. In the early 1900s, it was common for each to cement the relationship by planting seeds from the same maize cob. This exchange is similar to the exchange of blood in African brotherhood rites. A sexual dimension of baghuru sometimes developed but without the knowledge of the husband. Although the baghuru love tie was acceptable, the addition of a sexual dimension, if discovered, would be considered adultery and would have been punishable by beating or death. Suppressed in the 1930s, this tradition is only rarely seen today. However, researchers speculate on similar egalitarian relationships between contemporary polygynous co-wives. This type of bonding was not unlike bonding between Native American women in the nineteenth century (Butler, 1990).

Although acknowledging that same-sex marital or romantic relationships are rare within Africa, one such relationship is documented. In *Homosexuality and World Religions* (1993), Swidler explains that the Nzema of Lesotho occasionally engage in same-sex relationships in which women have intimate ties with younger girls. These relationships replace puberty rites that were originally a part of the culture. Within traditional Nzema culture, young girls participated in group spiritual and sexual instruction to increase the passion of marriage. Christianity and labor migration disrupted traditional patterns, and this new form of woman-woman relationship between older and younger women provides for some features of original puberty rites. These older women care for the younger women, instructing and advising them in manners concerning heterosexual relationships, school, and community matters. Intimate and sexual relations are a part of this relationship, and in many ways, the older women operate as patrons to the younger. These transgenerational relationships last for several years and typically dissolve as the young woman develops a permanent relationship with a man. These relationships, although intimate and significant, are typically not permanent.

Although lesbian relationships continue to exist throughout the world, the cultural and legal prohibitions against such relationships have not allowed complete documentation. Women around the world continue to be jailed, lose custody of their children, and face harassment because of their sexual preference.[15] Courts typically scrutinize the conduct of lesbian mothers and maintain they are unfit parents due solely to their sexual orientation. Despite these negative sanctions, many lesbians continue to find ways to combat the prejudice of worldwide court systems. Groups such as LMDF (Lesbian Mothers Defense Fund), founded in the 1980s in Toronto, continue to support women in fighting obstacles faced by lesbians (S. Stone, 1990). Lesbian couples in greater numbers are deciding to live their lives openly as women loving women; however, some continue to hide behind veils of heterosexuality, cross-dress for acceptability, or live in isolation. These women face the same discrimination as cohabitating couples but face additional discrimination based on the homophobia of communities and legal systems.

INTERCULTURAL, INTERRACIAL, AND INTERRELIGIOUS COUPLING

The cultural norms of every society regulate the formation of relationships that will develop into family unions. We have described here how many cultures develop both marriage ties (Chapter 1) and a variety of alternative simple households. Frequently, individuals of relative similarity (similarity in background, religion, race, economic status, and educational aspirations) form families.

However, some women have broken this selection sameness in mates and have developed lasting relationships with individuals who are not a part of their marriage or relationship pool. These women have decided to develop families with individuals that differ from themselves by race, culture, religion, or ways that stand in contrast to their social norms. The formation of families that cut across cultural, religious, and racial lines relates to the amount of control exercised by the gatekeepers of the family. In societies that tightly monitor relationships, there is little opportunity for cross-cultural or other blending to occur.

Blending is most centrally an issue within societies where women and men enjoy a significant amount of freedom in choice of relationship partner. Thus, open marriage systems, those characterized by a significant amount of individual choice in marriage partners, allow for a greater pool of possible partners. In an open marriage or relationship system, affectual ties are a primary focus, and relationships are seen as arising out of interpersonal attraction and compatibility that can transcend issues of diversity. In these cases, family members attempt various strategies to influence mate selection, and these strategies are often informal in nature. A family may voice disapproval of a cross-racial or other blending, but an absolute veto carries little concrete weight for adults entering temporary or marital relationships.

In contrast, closed marriage and relationship systems exercise a great deal of control over individuals in order for the interests of the wider domestic group to be satisfied. These closed systems regulate control by relegating that coupling authority be placed in the hands of kin members. These marriages are often connected with significant exchanges of property. In systems where kin are matchmakers, individuals exercise minimum authority over their choice of partner. Therefore, only in open systems of family formation does real blending of diverse cultures, races, or religions become a significant issue.

Much of the scholarship exploring cultural, racial, or religious intermarriage is directed at issues of selection and is underscored with a pathology model.[16] Scholars often capture the reality of those choosing such relationships by exploring unmet needs, rebellious periods, or escapist tendencies.[17] Despite the assigned reasons for marrying and developing relationships outside a woman's primary cultural context, whether it is seen as truly the ability to move beyond narrow ethnocentric behavior or the product of psychological deficit, the reality is that such unions are increasing worldwide where open marriage and relationship systems exist.[18]

Interreligious marriages in Northern Ireland are an example of such blending. The Catholic-Protestant conflict, which has received worldwide scrutiny since 1969, has not eradicated the religious mingling through marriage of these two factions. The rate of interreligious marriages is considered inaccurate due to both the underreporting, for fear of reprisal, and the impetus to emigrate among couples who have crossed the religious line (Lee, 1994). It is estimated that at least 2 percent of the couples marrying in Northern Ireland are interreligious, although survey research suggests that families voice their disapproval of these relationships and state that they would be "angry" if a mixed marriage occurred between Protestants and Catholics. Families further state that such a mixed marriage brings dishonor and humiliation to the family (McFarlane, 1979).

No major denomination actually prohibits the out-marriage of its members, but it is discouraged in many places, including Northern Ireland. In particular, the Catholic Church's restrictions serve to discourage such coupling; these stipulations center on the fact that a priest must marry a couple for the marital union to be recognized. Also, the couple must promise that any children from such a marriage will be raised as Catholics.

The general religious segregation within schools, social groups, churches, and the workforce prevent the contact between individuals that is a precondition for developing relationships. Interreligious couples in Northern Ireland typically meet accidentally, not within the typical religiously segregated events that shape most of their lives. How do these couples handle this interreligious conflict? Lee (1994) discussed the variability in the marital experience of a group of interreligious couples in Northern Ireland. They vary from those who avoid any discussion that would center on religious conflict or a United

Ireland, to those who find arguing to be central to their relationship, to those who report much harmony within their relationship.

One woman, representing this latter group, spoke of the harmony within her marriage and felt it was related to shared Christian views:

> In terms of our Christianity, our Christian views are almost the same. We come from different theological backgrounds so we have got to work out how different—how the differences we have work into this. We recognized there are certain points of view which are different but on the whole we actually agree a lot about our religion, our belief in God, the way it affects our lives, these sorts of things. (Lee, 1994, p. 54)

These women and their chosen mates usually face only moderate disapproval from family members *after* the marriage, but face open disapproval from the larger community. However, they make individual decisions to cross the barrier of religion within a climate of religious battling for the love and companionship of a chosen person. Although families attempt to dissuade such relationships, they continue to exist within Northern Ireland.

So what does love have to do with these relationships? Couples who make commitments that are not sanctioned express feelings of love and commitment. They defy the social norms due to these feelings of love. Despite the multiple reasons that push these blended couples together, communities often see them as outsiders. They are commonly viewed as odd, deviant, or nonnormative.

MULTIPLE-FAMILY HOUSEHOLDS

Polygamy

Polygamous families (plural marriages) exist in several parts of the world. Polygamy exists in families where one male marries more than one female (polygyny) or in families in which one woman is married to more than one male (polyandry). Each type of polygamous family creates a complex household that situates each individual woman within an intricate matrix of relationships. (See Example 2.1.)

EXAMPLE 2.1. The United States Experiment with Polygamy: The Case of the Church of Jesus Christ of Latter-Day Saints

In the 1830s, Joseph Smith, leader of the Church of Latter-Day Saints reported he received a visitation from God that directed men within his faith to take multiple wives (polygamy). Although many Mormons had much difficulty embracing this philosophy initially, it eventually became a practice that was both preached and encouraged by church leaders. During the years 1852 to 1890, thousands of Mormons entered and lived their lives within polygynous marriages. Beginning in the 1850s, opposition grew against United States' polygamy from outside the Mormon community. The Merrill Act of 1862 prohibited plural marriage, disincorporated the church, and restricted the church's ownership of property. Further antipolygamy tactics in the 1880s included fines, disqualification from jury service, inability to vote, and ownership restrictions. During the late 1800s and early 1900s, some Mormon men developed polygamous relationships in Canada or Mexico to elude such restrictions. The practice has slowly died out, with some plural wives continuing to live with their husbands throughout the 1970s. A radical segment of Mormons continues this polygamous tradition in isolation and closed communities in the western United States today.[19]

Polygyny

Polygynous marriages are the most common polygamous family. This family form has existed since recorded time and continues to be an alternate form in some areas (Maillu, 1988). Polygynous families are seen within many African and South Asian countries and recently in other parts of the world.[20,21] Polygynous families typically exist in communities that also exhibit monogamous marriage patterns. Polygyny is rarely the dominant or sole form of marriage but coexists as a viable alternative. In Nigeria, polygyny is practiced by the Yoruban. However, only a portion of the males can afford the bride-price necessary to have more than one wife or to afford the maintenance of contributing to a family of multiple wives and their children (Bascom, 1969).

Muslim law allows for a man to marry four wives if he can provide for them. Consequently, polygyny is commonly seen within the Muslim world. Egypt represents an example of this philosophy. However, the reality and the meaning of being able to care for a multiple household is left up to the conscience of each man.

Women marrying into polygynous relationships marry individually within the custom of the community. Once a co-wife, a woman develops a relationship within the household between herself and the shared husband, other wives, relatives, and children. The first wife operates in a monogamous relationship until other wives are brought within the family, creating a polygamous union. Then, the first wife will generally hold a position of higher status in relationship with subsequent wives. However, other factors can create "favor" for a certain wife; such factors as increased fertility, birthing of sons, or a special attachment/affectional tie to the husband may elevate a given co-wife's status.

Usually, individual wives become productive units that contribute economically to the overall polygynous family. Sometimes, this is shared agricultural production, and in other cases, women become entrepreneurs. In both cases, although men initially provide for wives' basic needs, the expectation is for wives to enhance the greater family's economic standing.[22]

Coexisting with polygynous marriages are women who vocally disagree with this family form, speaking out against such relationships and focusing on problematic issues facing polygamy (Rugh, 1984). Some opponents believe polygamous households unite women in backbreaking labor to assist in the support of their families. Critics of polygyny point to the lack of value placed on individual women, which is demonstrated by a particular woman's ability to be replaced with yet another wife. Other women (Global Forum of Women, 1992) speak of the passing of AIDS within multiple households, increasing the likelihood that entire multiple subfamily systems can be wiped out by AIDS. The marrying of young, uneducated women is also a concern, thus not affording these women an informed choice in life. The Mormon experience with polygyny in nineteenth-century America precipitated a great deal of debate and governmental sanctions for those practicing polygyny (see Example 2.1). Contemporary polygyny does not coexist as easily worldwide as it has in past times. However, polygyny continues, with the support of many men and women, in the face of critical views that challenge its value in this historical era.

Polyandry

Polyandrous families are less frequently seen but do exist within some sectors. Levine (1988) explored polyandrous families among the Nyinba of northwestern Nepal. Within this community, the most common marital form is fraternal polyandry, in which brothers marry one woman in common. In Levine's research, the largest Nyinba household encountered contained eighteen men and women representing three generations. This family consisted of the following membership:

> The most senior generation included three polyandrously married brothers, who ranged in age from fifty-two to sixty, and their common wife, who was fifty-nine at the time. Living with them were five of their sons, aged twenty to forty, and their sons' wife, who then was thirty-five. The other household members included one unmarried teenaged daughter, three grandsons, and four granddaughters. (1988, p. 152)

This type of family indicates a great deal of complexity due to its size, the generations present, and the varied subsystems within the family. Wives' participation with their multiple husbands, their shared lineage children, and the various generations create a highly complex matrix of family relationships. These relationships defy the territorial features of monogamous and nuclear family relationships.

In some polyandrous families, particularly when several brothers are comarried, additional wives are brought into the system. A conjoint marriage occurs when brothers marry another second common wife. This type of marriage seems most successful when the women are related by blood. For instance, marrying a second sister is considered the most successful possibility. If within a fraternal polyandrous marriage no children are born, brothers generally marry another common wife. Sometimes, a dissatisfied brother might lobby his brothers for another wife if he feels his relationship with the common wife is unsatisfying. Thus, polyandry and polygyny can exist within the same family.

Nyinban women report that they find fraternal polyandry advantageous because, with more than one husband, there is a sense of security that the wife will never be widowed. It is possible that these women also might be advantaged by greater personal, intimate, and sexual attention (Levine, 1988).

Family leadership is also a part of this multiple-family system. Within these families, there is a male head and a female head who hold the greatest authority within the family. The male head is the oldest male in the system and typically succeeded by his oldest son. The female head is usually the common wife of the family head. This head woman controls the assignment of women's work and the allocation of food and sleeping space.

Levine (1988) documents greater disharmony between women within polyandrous households than the men. These men are all blood related (brothers, father, sons, grandsons), whereas the adult women within the household are unrelated by blood (generational wives of brothers). The primary obligation of the different generational women is to their separate sets of children, thus they appear less committed to the entire Nyinban family network. Levine notes that when disagreements occur between men they are often reframed to be the fault of the head woman. So, in many ways, women marrying into polyandrous situations remain marginal throughout their lifetimes.

Many outsiders find the existence of polygamy hard to understand. However, historically, these forms have existed throughout the world. The basis for these relationships is a strong cultural premise that polygamy is a viable option. Industrialization moves families in the direction of simple households and makes multiple and complex households more difficult to maintain. Polygamy today is most likely seen within agriculturally based and remote areas. Some critics of polygamy point to women's decreased authority, choice, and ability to move into the workforce as real problems for women within polygamous relationships. Whether "the man takes many wives or the brothers take a wife" does not allow individual women much choice in their destiny. However, women within such relationships see a life similar to women before them (their mothers, sisters, and grandmothers). So in many ways, the existence of polygamy is yet another example of an old tradition that remains culturally valuable, but it is faced with critics who are looking for a new place for women within their societies.

VERTICAL AND HORIZONTAL COMPLEXITY WITHIN FAMILY LIFE

Many families worldwide situate women within large sprawling systems of relatives, kinlike relationships, and friends that add to the complexity of life. Vertical complexity indicates multiple generations within the same household. This type of complexity crosses the globe but is more frequently observed within non-Western families. Characterizing this type of extended family are adults, children, grandparents, and possibly great-grandparents living together and interacting in regular and significant ways. These vertically complex families survive despite the monogamous or polygamous nature of the adult relationships. The cultural norms of families and their economic needs determine their vertical complexity (Eshleman, 1997).

These vertically complex families not only exist in developing regions but within subpopulations throughout such areas as Europe, the United States, and Canada. In these areas, domestic ethnic groups and newly immigrated families often cluster within intergenerational households. This pattern is predicated on both cultural norms of intergenerational families and the economic reality for these units. African-American families and Mexican-American families are more likely to manifest such patterns within the United States.[23]

Sometimes coexisting with such vertical complexity is horizontal complexity, where a family household may contain several individuals within the same generation. Several siblings may live together or generations of siblings might coreside. This develops a family matrix containing a wide array of relatives (cousins, aunts, uncles, great-aunts, etc.).

These types of relationships characterize many polygynous and polyandrous families described previously, but are also a feature within some monogamous systems. The addition of each family member or kinlike relationship increases the complexity of the family system, increases the efforts needed for the establishment of communication lines, and complicates the duties and responsibilities of the families. Women find themselves at center stage when negotiating the inner workings of family systems, whether complex or more comparably simple.

SUMMARY

Feminist scholarship addresses diversity within families. Issues of diversity necessitate an exploration of the impact of cultural norms and expectations on family formation and family life concerns. This chapter examines simple households including cohabitating heterosexuals, women living primarily alone, and lesbian couples; these families may sometimes live with their children. Additionally, multiple-family households are investigated, including polygamous families and those that are either vertically or horizontally complex.

Varied structure, forms, and complexity characterize families world-wide. Women, as the "kin keepers" of the family, find themselves central in maintaining, developing, and orchestrating behaviors within the family. This is further complicated when women are marginalized by society (by developing relationships not sanctioned in their communities).

Feminist scholars argue that an understanding of the diversity of women's experiences within families is central to understanding family experiences. Family life is not one monolithic experience; it varies based on the realities of women's lives.

KEY WORDS
Conjoint marriage
Fictive kin
Fraternal polyandry
Horizontally complex families
Palimony
Polyandry
Polygamy
Polygyny
Vertically complex family

Chapter 3

Population, Reproduction, Sexuality, and Women's Status

No woman can call herself free until she can choose consciously whether she will or will not be a mother.[1]

A woman's control over her own fertility has been called the freedom from which other freedoms flow.[2]

HOW ARE WOMEN'S LIVES CONNECTED TO THE POPULATION EXPLOSION?

The World Population Conference in Cairo, in 1994, championed the notion that furthering women's educational, political, and economic opportunities is the best way to curb future population growth. The World Women's Conference, held in Beijing in 1995, supported the principles that the number of children each woman has must be her choice and that women's ability to limit family size is a necessary precondition to personal freedom and public power. This chapter argues that when each woman in the world can control her own reproductive life, both she and the world will benefit.

Worldwide demographic variables reveal much about the status of women within social groups and among nations. Population growth or decline in any given society is a function of birthrate (the annual number of births per 1,000), death rate (the annual number of deaths per 1,000), and migration rate (the annual number of emigrants and immigrants per 1,000). On a worldwide basis, population fluctuation can be calculated solely by knowing annual births and deaths. The demographic terms fecundity and fertility make a closer connection between population increase or decrease and women as the people who bear children. Fecundity represents the number of children a woman is capable of having, which may be as high as twenty to twenty-five. Fertility, always less than fecundity, is the actual number of children a woman bears. Knowing the number of women in their childbearing years (roughly ages fifteen to forty-nine), combined with knowledge of fertility, facilitates population projections. Whether a woman has 7.1 children (the 1991 average in Jordan) or 1.8 children (the 1991 average in England) significantly affects her life choices and activities (Weeks, 1992).

For most of the history of the world, human population grew very slowly. It did not reach one billion until around 1820, but by 1930, it had doubled to two billion. In 1950, there were 2.5 billion people in the world; by 1994, there were approximately 5.6 billion, and demographers predict 7.9 billion by 2020. Estimates indicate that ninety-five million people are added to the population each year, resulting in an ever larger base number.

The unprecedented size of the world population alarms most scientists, environmentalists, economists, and politicians.[3] Despite the fact that very rapid population growth is slower due to decreased fertility rates, there are more women of childbearing age, and therefore, world population continues to increase (see Table 3.1). Demographers report that 90 percent of the growth predicted into the next century will occur in "developing" countries.[4] In developed countries, the highest population growth rate usually occurs within the poorest segments of the population. Controversy has arisen concerning the unequal distribution of resources and which countries are being asked to control their populations. Those leaders who advocate population control (antinatalists) are often facing national, religious, or popular spokespersons who favor large families, disapprove of contraceptives, and/or equate numbers with strength (pronatalists). Women's bodies are the battleground of this debate, but too often, discussion about the desirable number of children for women to bear proceeds without input from women themselves.

TABLE 3.1. Slower Growth (Total Lifetime Births per Woman)

	1980-1985	1990-1995
Africa	6.3	5.7
Latin America	3.8	2.9
Asia	3.7	2.8
Developed Regions	1.8	1.7
World	3.6	3.0

Adapted from United Nations *Report on the World Social Situation*, 1997, p. 18.

WHAT ARE THE CONSEQUENCES OF UNCHECKED POPULATION?

High fertility and overpopulation results in human misery, environmental destruction, and the continued subordination of women. Thomas Malthus, writing in 1789, was one of the first to warn of the potential for humans to multiply to an incalculable number, thus outdistancing the food supply. Malthus advocated moral restraint rather than birth control; he did not espouse sex equality, nor did he deal with class inequities. He did, however, posit that poverty and starvation would be the result of overpopulation. Malthusians today see the world's population growth as potentially catastrophic, with human misery, environmental destruction, and pollution as consequences of too many people and burgeoning consumption. Paul and Anne Ehrlich state:

> We shouldn't delude ourselves: the population explosion will come to an end before very long. The only remaining question is whether it will be halted through the humane method of birth control, or by nature wiping out the surplus. (Ehrlich and Ehrlich, 1990, p. 17)

Developing countries have witnessed the most extreme cases of poverty, famine, and malnutrition. African countries lead the so-called "misery index" as containing the most indebted nations of the world—those with the lowest measures of human development (life expectancy, literacy) and the lowest average daily calorie supply. Over one million people died of starvation in the African famines of the 1980s. Mozambique, followed by Somalia, Ethiopia, Sierra Leone, and Chad were ranked most critical according to the agency for International Development's "Food Security Index," issued in 1991 (*Misery Index,* 1992). Population pressure contributes to the bloodshed over territory and scarce resources. Crowded, impoverished conditions led to fighting and further food shortages in Ethiopia during the mid-1980s and in Somalia and Rwanda in the early 1990s. Many speculate that the growth rate of developing countries will decrease with modernization and the concomitant achievement of a higher standard of living. Others believe this optimism is extremely ethnocentric, as developed countries do not signify the answer; they represent another version of the problem.

Countries such as the United States, Canada, England, France, and Japan, although their population growth is slower, have a large responsibility for the environmental crises that worsen with increasing population. The prevailing attitude of industrialized societies is to equate development and "progress" with the domination of natural resources. As perceived "needs" increase, the capacity for exploitation expands. A high standard of living and high consumptions levels place unsustainable demands on the earth's resources and environment. Each person in an affluent nation uses many times more of the world's resources and generates much more pollution than does the addition of one person in a developing nation. Thus, even the relatively small population growth of the United States has a global impact. One average North American (from the United States and Canada) equals approximately 385 average Ethiopians in energy consumption and 370 average Bengalis in grain consumption. Americans, with about 5 percent of the world's population, use one-quarter of the world's energy. Further, Americans generate more than twice the waste per person as typical Europeans and far more than people living in the third world (Saperstein and Stutsman, 1989).

Bearing and raising larger numbers of children thwarts women's progress toward education, economic independence, and political equality. For example, in 1989, the average Rwandan woman had over eight children, the highest birth rate in the world. Women in this country work the land, fetch wood and water, and cook and clean. Local norms grant women status for larger families, but most are overburdened by the combination of repeated pregnancies and the work involved. More than one-half of all women in Rwanda are illiterate. An early education would supply the know-how to prevent unwanted pregnancies, as well as better ability to care for wanted children. Once large families and the resulting workload become part of a woman's life, she has little opportunity to attain educational advancement (Perlez, 1992).

CULTURAL NORMS, GENDER ROLES, AND FERTILITY

The pressure to "be fruitful and multiply" exists, in varying degrees, in the vast majority of cultures today. That societies differ so greatly in total fertility rate indicates a cultural difference affecting individual behavior and reproductive patterns. Human motivation to procreate and/or to control births is strongly affected by cultural norms, beliefs, and myths.

Women and men may or may not internalize cultural dictates in the same way. There is growing evidence to suggest that they regard family size differently and that, if women were empowered, they would choose to have fewer children. Demographers speculate that a primary reason for reproduction is the need to replenish society. In areas of high mortality, particularly high child and infant mortality, the desire to bear many children stems from fear of the loss of one's children. In Senegal, as with most sub-Saharan African countries, both birthrates and death rates are high. Population indicators for 1991 showed life expectancy of forty-nine, annual infant mortality of eighty per 1,000, and a fertility rate of 6.2. To put this in perspective, the U.S. figures for 1991 were: life expectancy, seventy-six; annual infant mortality, eight per 1,000; fertility rate, 1.9 (Sadik, 1991, p. 42).

In societies such as Senegal, where survival is tenuous, having six children increases the chances that some of them will make it to adulthood. Families in high fertility societies may desire many children because they are needed for labor. A large family is often an economic advantage in a low-tech, agricultural economy where even young children can perform productive tasks. Later they serve as a personal insurance policy, as they will take care of their aged parents.

Gender values that foster personal prestige for men through fatherhood and for women through motherhood affect the number of children a woman desires or feels pressured to have. In Latin America, gender roles are greatly influenced by the concepts of machismo and marianisma. These cultural constructions, stemming from a Spanish colonial and Catholic heritage, define separate spheres for each sex. Machismo embodies the ideals of aggression, courage, sexual prowess, and virility for men. Marianisma is the complementary expression of an appropriate gender configuration for women, stressing obedience, moral superiority, stoicism, and the glorification of motherhood. Within this framework, the birth of children augments the status of both men and women. For a man, becoming a father provides evidence that he is virile; for those men who provide protection and financial support for a large family, additional honor is conferred. A woman receives respect when she becomes a mother by fulfilling a time-honored role as lifegiver and nurturer. This theme of status enhancement through bearing children exists with customary variations throughout the world.

In many cultures, there is not only the pressure to produce children, but there is a distinct preference for sons. This desire is most pronounced in Asian societies, yet it is also revealed in survey tabulations in the United States.[5] In societies such as India and China, there are traditional cultural practices revolving around the obligations and privileges of sons, such as burying parents and inheritance going to the eldest male heir. The convention of the family name being carried on through one's son, suggestive of lengthened mortality or immortality, is common in many developed nations. Male dominance alone provides sufficient reason for parents to value sons over daughters.

The World Fertility Survey (WFS) found the desire for sons to be a factor in high fertility. In Korea, of women who already had two boys, 77 percent said they wanted no more children, but for those having two girls, only 36 percent said they wanted no more children. In Pakistan, if a woman had six daughters, there was a 46 percent chance that she would want another child, but if a woman had six sons, there was only a 4 percent chance that she would want to have another child (reported in Weeks, 1992). Barbara Miller (1993) reports that the pressure to bear sons in India results in female infanticide, female child neglect, and now, selective abortions. "Strong preference for sons which results in life-endangering deprivation of daughters is culturally acceptable in much of rural North India with its patriarchal foundation (p. 432).

In some countries, girls are less likely to be taken to the hospital when ill. In Bangladesh, for example, girls have a 70 percent higher mortality rate than boys (United Nations, 1991a, p. 39). Practices that favor survival of male children produce a lopsided sex ratio in select areas worldwide. Reports from areas of China and India reveal a stark shortage of women of marriageable age, with one result being many lonely young men. In some regions of China, by age thirty, men outnumber women by as much as ten to one. The question of how the shortage of women affects women's status remains unanswered for now. Interestingly, some see young women finding themselves more valued, treated with a new respect, and able to pick and choose from a number of prospective mates as a consequence of this situation (Shenon, 1994).

In 1991, Jordan had an annual growth rate of 4.1 percent and one of the highest total fertility rates at 7.1 children. Researchers who interviewed Jordanian husbands highlight the importance of culture-specific husband control in determining the use of contraceptives. A 1985 survey of Jordanian husbands reports that over 50 percent said family size decisions were "up to God," and over 40 percent did not believe in practicing birth control. In general, those husbands who lived in urban areas, who had more education, and who were younger were less likely to hold this fatalistic attitude and were also more likely to share decision making with their wives. However, "those husbands who do not believe in contraceptive use feel no need to discuss the issue with their wives (ninety-five percent state 'No')" (Warren et al., 1990, p. 37).

Carole Browner used participant observation and interviews to investigate reproductive attitudes and practices in an indigenous community in the state of Oaxaca, Mexico, in the 1980s. She found that most of the women did not value high fertility. Historically, they used medicinal plants to control births. Currently, they had less access to modern contraceptives, yet their fertility remained high due to community pressure. The ostensible reasons given for reproduction as a cultural contribution were high infant mortality and the future expected need of "manpower" for military purposes, labor, and political representation. The community labeled women with small families as "selfish," and they were "repeatedly criticized for causing miscarriage or using contraceptives," and suspected of "marital infidelity," with the result that most succumbed to the pressure to have large families (1993, p. 391).

WHAT IS THE RELATIONSHIP BETWEEN WOMEN'S STATUS AND FERTILITY?

Women's equality, measured in real life choices, education and employment attainment, health care, and equal decision making from the home to the highest level of government, is the single most important factor in low fertility. The ability of women to control their own reproduction is the necessary freedom that creates other freedoms. Low fertility increases women's ability to gain status in other areas, and the enhancement of women's status leads to low fertility.

Education is a prime component in this equation. Educated women are more likely to be decision makers in the size of their families and the spacing of their children. They are more knowledgeable about contraception and about health care for their children. When other conditions are equal, women have greater assurance that the children they do have will survive to adulthood and have less motivation to bear large families. The United Nations reports that women with seven years or more of education tend to marry on average four years later and have 2.2 fewer children statistically than women with no schooling (Sadik, 1991). Table 3.2 further illustrates the correlation between a female education index (based on a ratio of girls to boys enrolled in primary and secondary education) and infant mortality and fertility rates.

In addition to the importance of female education, employment patterns and income are closely linked with fertility. David Shapiro and B. Oleko Tambashe (1994) collected data on 2,399 women of reproductive age in Kinshasa, Zaire (now Congo), and found that women who are better educated and employed in the formal sector are most likely to use contraceptives. These women desire fewer

TABLE 3.2. Maternal Education Correlates with Lower Infant Mortality and Lower Fertility

Selected Nations	Female Education Index	Infant Mortality (deaths/ 1,000 births)	Fertility Rate (children/ woman)
Japan	95.8	05	1.6
France	99.7	07	1.8
United States	97.7	09	1.9
Thailand	66.5	27	2.5
China	67.0	29	2.5
Zimbabwe	66.2	49	4.9
Kenya	57.0	67	6.5
India	50.4	92	4.0
Namibia	72.2	100	5.9
Rwanda	50.2	120	8.3

Source: United Nations, reported in: Shapiro, D. and Tambashe, B.O. "The Impact of Women's Employment and Education on Contraceptive Use and Abortion in Kinshasa, Zaire." *The New York Times* (April 13, 1994): A12.

children, and because of the absence of reliable contraception, they also have a greater incidence of induced abortions. Researchers report that higher incomes correlate with lower fertility. Employment enables women to afford the costs of contraception and grants access to better health care for the entire family. This better health care reduces infant and child mortality and lends security of child survival, thus lowering the need to have large families (Shapiro and Tambashe, 1994).

THE DIVERSITY AND CONTROVERSY OF SEXUAL NORMS

Religion is very strong. If a girl has premarital sex, she will not talk about it. Religion prohibits sexual relations before marriage . . . lots of girls marry young, maybe around eighteen, in order to have sex.[6]

Premarital sex is completely normal. There is especially a lot of education in school about AIDS and protection. There are magazines for young people (ages thirteen to fifteen), showing how to use a condom, and the pill is most common. Abortion is legal up to three months.[7]

Sex is [was considered] very sinful. Boys and girls cannot [were not expected to] fall in love with each other. Sex education would be embarrassing. If a girl was caught having sex, she would probably commit suicide.[8]

As we can see from these quotes, people hold very different views on sexuality. These differences are no accident. They reflect the respective influence of traditional culture and religion and the entry of newer, more open views of appropriate sexual conduct. The blend of traditional and modern also affects the relative acceptance of a "sexual double standard," with restrictive rules for women and lenient ones for men.

Worldwide, cultural lines between permissive and restrictive sexual norms are far from clear-cut. We often assume that developed areas of the world, such as North America and Europe, are bastions of sexual freedom, yet there are vast regional and subcultural differences. Market-driven sexuality (e.g., pornography and prostitution), often originating in developed countries, exists in virtually all large cities on every continent. However, many feminists believe this version of sexual freedom merely gives men permission to explore their sexuality and transforms women into sex objects. "Sexual rights" were debated at the Fourth World Women's Conference (September, 1995). The final document approved various aspects of women's "sexual rights," from the belief that women should have the right to say "no" to sex to the notion that it should be a woman's decision as to whether she has children and how many.[9]

SEXUAL SCRIPTS CROSS-CULTURALLY

Ruth Dixon-Mueller challenges demographic researchers to confront broader aspects of sexuality, including ideologies of male entitlement that threaten women's sexual and reproductive health. She believes demographers err when they assume that (1) the sexual experience is the same for women and men and (2) sexual involvement is voluntary on the woman's part. Unequal gender power often means that the woman has not consented to, or has not the option to consent to, sexual intercourse; the woman may not have a choice in mate selection; the woman may not experience sexual satisfaction; and, she may not be able to decide whether to practice contraception or to determine the type she prefers (Dixon-Mueller, 1993a).

When Alex Chika Ezeh investigated the influence of spouses over each other's contraceptive attitudes in Ghana, the data revealed that rather than being mutual or reciprocal, the influence is an exclusive right exercised only by the husband (Ezeh, 1993). In the process of investigation, men and women were questioned on a variety of issues designed to elicit information on gender power. Answers revealed that partner selection was a male prerogative. If a woman directly indicates that she favors a particular man, she risks the reputation of "morally weak" or "bad character" and may be the object of "mockery." Both sexes told researchers that the husband had the final say in family planning. For example:

> In my estimation, the woman has no legitimate right. For since it is God who grants children, the woman has no right choice in the number she prefers since it is you the man who decides when to have sex with her. The other point to note here involves the feeding and education of the children, which all rest on you, the man.[10]

This attitude of male privilege is not unique to Ghana, and it is often resented by the women of a given society. Dixon-Mueller summarizes several studies to report that women in Peru, the Philippines, and Sri Lanka complain that it is difficult to practice NFP (natural fertility planning) when their husbands have been drinking or become aggressive and cannot wait for sex. Women in a Mexican study revealed humiliation and physical dissatisfaction due to their husbands' treatment of them during sexual relations (Dixon-Mueller, 1993a).

When intercourse begins at too young an age, girls/young women are less likely to be able to prevent pregnancy and the transmission of sexually transmitted diseases. Teenagers in most countries are misinformed about sexuality and contraception and how to obtain family planning services. Gender roles make early sexual experiences very different for boys and girls. Boys are often taught about sex and goaded into initiating sex and viewing it as a conquest. Girls are usually expected to learn how to resist sex, yet circumstances often make this expectation impossible. A higher percentage of girls than boys report their first sexual experience to be nonvoluntary (Moore, Nord, and Peterson, 1989).

The United Nations Convention on Consent to Marriage (1962) attempted to obtain national cooperation in stopping the practice of forced and arranged early marriage of girls to older men. Although many countries have officially complied with the international standard, more than thirty countries permit girls to marry before the age of fifteen. This is especially prevalent in sub-Saharan Africa and in South Asia, but there are marked contrasts by region. Over half of women interviewed at a health clinic in Ethiopia stated that they had intercourse with their husbands before they menstruated for the first time (Duncan et al., 1990). The timing of marriage for girls severely affects their power in the relationship and their sexual and reproductive freedom. Early marriage is associated with a more limited knowledge of and access to contraceptives. Women who marry before age nineteen have two to four times more children than women who marry after twenty-five (Dixon-Mueller, 1993a).

Girls and women in industrialized countries are also vulnerable to a sexual double standard, but within the past several decades, the combined impact of the "sexual revolution" and the feminist movement eased the stigma attached to females who engage in premarital heterosexual relationships (see Example 3.1). Premarital female sexuality and unmarried motherhood is now a fact in much of the world. In the United States, studies conducted over the last thirty years reveal that an increasing number of young people are engaging in premarital coitus and that the proportion of women reporting coital activity has increased most rapidly, now reaching parity with men (Hofferth, Rahn, and Baldwin, 1987).

Research indicates that initiation into sex is rarely planned and that, while most adolescent girls do not want to get pregnant, a large proportion fail to use, or fail to insist that their partners use, birth control (Eshleman, 1997). Despite the fact that the pill and other forms of contraception, as well as abortion, have become increas-

EXAMPLE 3.1. One Woman's Life Reflects a World in Flux

Vera Garcia, born in 1970, in Ojinaga, Mexico, grew up in times when sexuality and pregnancy were not discussed, not even in the family. But the norms of her community were changing. Young women were having sex; they just weren't talking about it. Their reputations were at stake. Birth control was unavailable and abortion was, and still is, illegal. Young men did talk about their sexuality. For them sexual conquests represented status and the lack of sexual experience brought them shame. Vera and her boyfriend began having sex when she was sixteen. By the time she was seventeen, she was pregnant, although at first she was too naive to know what was wrong with her. When she finally figured it out and told her boyfriend, he replied, "That's your problem." But when her parents found out, they arranged a hasty wedding—a marriage that never really had a chance. After the marriage broke up, Vera joined a growing number of independent Mexican women and came to the United States looking for something better for herself and her daughter. When she travels back to Ojinaga to visit friends and family, she notes a change. Sex education is taught in schools; family planning clinics disseminate contraceptive education and devices. The birth control pill is sold in the drugstore. But the attitudes, says Vera, have not changed sufficiently. Young women are still pressured to have sex early, and the responsibility to prevent pregnancy still belongs to them.[11]

ingly available since the 1960s, and despite the fact that the overall birthrate has declined, the rate of births to unmarried women in the United States shows a dramatic increase:

> There has been a 620 percent increase in such births since 1950, and unwed births as a percentage of all births has increased from four percent in 1950 to 23.4 percent by 1986. (Eshleman, 1997)

Which countries are the most sexually liberated? Is this liberation good or bad for women? Many would answer the Scandinavian countries, particularly Sweden. These countries are also regarded as comparatively progressive for women. Swedish policy has encouraged both men and women to express their sexuality freely, but responsibly. Most young people have intercourse before marriage, and women who become pregnant before marriage are neither penalized nor forced into marriage. In fact, almost half of all births in Sweden are out-of-wedlock births, but the government plays an active role in supporting these families. Sex education in Sweden informs young people about all aspects of sexuality, including sexually transmitted disease, homosexuality, and contraception. Such education transmits ethical values such as "the use of psychological pressure and physical force in any context is a violation of the personal freedom of others" and "men and women must be subject to identical standards of sexual morality" (Eshleman, 1991, p. 304).

Although the institutional structure in Sweden is one of the most supportive in the world, we should not think that women are equal to men, nor is everyone satisfied with current arrangements. During the 1980s, Swedish sex clubs and pornography were curtailed following the protests of women's groups and the formation of a conservative "pro-family" coalition (Schmidt, 1992). One aspect of a change toward more cautious sexual behavior in Sweden and elsewhere is the current worldwide presence of the fatal sexually transmitted HIV virus.[12]

ARE PRIVATE CHOICES ABOUT SEXUALITY AND FERTILITY AFFECTED BY RELIGIOUS IDEALS?

Major religions throughout the world define sexuality as a moral province. A broad review of Judeo-Christian and Muslim traditions lends insight into the various beliefs about sex and women that still constitute a source of disagreement and continue to present a dilemma to any unified course of action designed to give women the choice to limit births. Ancient Judeo-Christian precepts left lingering ideas that sex is only appropriate in marriage and that its chief function is procreation rather than pleasure. Sexual expression in any other context is a sin. Socially, the mixed messages surrounding sexuality apply most strongly to women and women's bodies.

The idea that women be chaste, pure virgins at marriage has crossed time and cultures. In the nineteenth and into the twentieth century of Western culture, a woman's decency and worth were equated with her sexual reputation. Victorians believed that good women had no sexual desire, hence if a woman enjoyed sex, she was aberrant—"bad." If not a "tart" or "harlot," then the other alternative in the court of public opinion was that the woman in an unsanctioned relationship must be weak. Here, sex must be the result of surrender by the female and conquest by the male. Sexual experience elevates men and degrades women. These ideas persist.

ISLAM: A CASE STUDY

Muslim beliefs about sexuality and gender direct social policy in many Islamic countries (Koss, Heise, and Russo, 1997). In Pakistan, women suspected or found guilty of illicit sex are frequently imprisoned. Notions that neither males nor females have much self-control, coupled with the supreme importance of keeping sexual activity within marriage, create a need for elaborate social/legal restrictions. Counsel from the Qua'ran tells men to marry if possible because it "keeps you from looking with lust at women and preserves you from promiscuity" (Omran, 1992, p. 18). In contrast to Judeo-Christian concepts, Islamic thought holds that women are sexually aggressive by nature and that it is socially necessary to prevent them from having sex with abandon. The custom of purdah, male/female separation in many aspects of daily activity, helps women and men avoid sexual temptation. A large part of this practice is wearing the veil, increasingly mandated in Islamic nations. Female circumcision (see Chapter 6), although not exclusive to the Muslim religion, is widely practiced in Islamic Middle Eastern, North African, and sub-Saharan African countries. This surgical alteration of female genital organs prevents sexual pleasure and has the potential to prevent willful promiscuity. In principle, polygyny is sanctioned by Islamic law and allows men up to four wives (usually this practice is limited to a small percentage in the population). Women cannot take additional husbands; their role as wife requires strict marital fidelity.

Many Islamic countries have legislated against the influences of "Western sexual immorality," while others are facing an internal struggle between fundamentalists, who want to return to the basics of traditional religious doctrine, and those who favor a more liberal interpretation of the scriptures. The two Islams are split on the question of family planning. Maulana Maudoudi, a religious leader from Pakistan, attacks "birth control" for the following reasons:

The birth control movement is a plot against Islam. To import birth control into developing countries would be tantamount to ushering a moral malaise ranging from the breakdown of the family to sexual promiscuity and sexually transmitted diseases.

Women would feel free to join the labor force and abandon their traditional roles. (Omran, 1992, p. 206)

What do we know of women's reactions to the strict Islamic laws? Almost everywhere in the Islamic world, a debate is raging. Fundamentalist clerics condemn women whose writings publicly criticize antifeminist cultural interpretations of the Qua'ran. Nawaal El-Saadawi is a physician and champion of women's liberation from Egypt. She is the author of more than twenty-four books, many of which are banned in Egypt and other Islamic countries. After her 1972 publication of *Women and Sex*, she was fired from her position in the Ministry of Health and imprisoned. Nevertheless, El-Sadaawi asserts that Islam is not the problem for women, rather it is how those in power interpret Islamic principles (Lerner, 1992).

Taslima Nasreen, a feminist Bangladeshi writer, attacked Islamic gender codes in her novel *Lajja* (Shame). In 1994, Bengali Islamic militants retaliated by issuing a death threat against Nasreen, who they say advocates the liberation of women through sexual license, adultery, and the dismantling of the family. Nasreen won the attention of the Western media and the sympathy of many Western feminists. However, many Indian and Bengali spokeswomen assert that women in her own country believe that Nasreen is too confrontational and that she has hurt their cause more than helped it (Wright, 1994).

The question of overall influence of religious doctrine on women's sexual and reproductive lives depends on many factors. From all evidence, women hold a range of attitudes toward the propriety of rigid sex segregation and subservient behavior toward men. In many countries, such as Saudi Arabia, Iran, the Sudan, Kuwait, and Taliban-controlled Afghanistan, women have little choice but to conform to religious-backed gender norms (see Example 3.2).

SEXUALITY, FEMINISM, AND REPRODUCTIVE TECHNOLOGY: HISTORICAL ROOTS

Nineteenth-century Western feminists held a range of attitudes on sexuality and the effect of contraception on woman's control of her own sexuality. Bourgeois British feminists during the Victorian era opposed artificial contraception. Instead of believing it to be a

EXAMPLE 3.2. In Kandahar, Afghanistan, the Taliban Religious Movement
Punishes Sexual Transgressions

The condemned woman, Nurbibi, age forty, was dressed in a sky-blue burqa, the
head-to-toe shroud with a gauze panel for the eyes that the Taliban require all women
to wear outside their homes. They lowered her into a pit where only her chest and
head were above ground. The cleric evoked relevant provisions in the Sharia (the
ancient Muslim legal code) for stoning adulterers. With that, the all-male crowd began
throwing stones until Nurbibi and her lover (also her stepson) were dead.

The Taliban became an active fighting force in Afghanistan's eighteen-year-old civil
war. With backing from Pakistan and rumors of American support, the Taliban seized
control of major areas in Afghanistan by late 1996. They immediately imposed harsh
rules of sexual segregation, closing girl's schools and forcing many women out of the
workforce. When women fail to conform to the extremely modest dress required, they
are beaten on the spot. Taliban practices comprise the extreme of Islamic fundamentalism, condemned by more moderate factions in the Islamic world.[13]

means to female emancipation, they saw it as causing greater subordination to men's sexual desires. They feared that it would
weaken women's ability to regulate sexual activity, as fear of pregnancy could no longer be used to protest having intercourse. They
also worried that birth control technology would encourage husbands' unfaithfulness because men could take other women without
the risk of impregnating them. Idealistic and class-based, these
feminists advised that, instead of artificial contraception, marriage
partners should unite in a system of "cooperative self-denial,"
using withdrawal or abstinence.

Despite some who continued to distrust contraceptives as instruments of male pleasure, the theme of sexual autonomy and the goal
of women having ultimate control over their sexual and reproductive lives emerged in the twentieth century, with various degrees of
specificity. Emma Goldman, socialist, anarchist, and activist, disagreed with other socialists over the issue of birth control. She
recommended birth control as a means of "opposing male tyranny
and liberating female sexuality."[14]

Marie Stopes was the leader of the birth control movement in
England; when she wrote *Married Love* in 1918, British publishers
refused to print it because of its graphic descriptions and its insis-
tence that women have sexual desires and that both partners should
have satisfaction in marriage. The book was eventually published in
New York. The early twentieth century witnessed several global

spokeswomen and activists in the quest for women's reproductive rights. For example, in Australia in 1916, three feminists, Jessie Street, Annie Golding, and Kate Dwyer, formed a Social Hygiene Association to eliminate venereal disease and prostitution and to provide sex education. They encountered difficulty expanding the operation due to sexual prudishness (Siedlecky and Wyndham, 1990). Without a doubt, the most famous crusader for birth control was Margaret Sanger, who was snubbed by male scientists at the First World Population Conference but eventually became co-president of the International Planned Parenthood Association, along with Lady Rao of India, in 1952 (Dixon-Mueller, 1993b).

In opposition to anti-obscenity laws and moralists, Sanger published a sixteen-page pamphlet titled "Family Limitation" in New York in 1914. The document was very explicit, intending to inform and empower American women, especially working-class women, on douching, the use of the condom, the French pessary, sponges, and vaginal suppositories. Sanger offers a perspective on everything from sexuality to the connection between women's choice to limit the number of children they have and the most serious problems of the world. In sexual relations, she argues against coitus interruptus, saying it deprives a woman of sexual satisfaction. In world problems, she tends to blame women for their role, while imploring them to act toward change:

> War, famine, poverty, and oppression of the workers will continue while woman makes life cheap. They will cease only when she limits her reproductivity and human life is no longer a thing to be wasted. (Sanger, 1995, p. 508)

Sanger's prominence in the birth control movement spanned five decades and was international in scope. She traveled to Japan, China, England, Switzerland, Russia, and India to participate in population conferences. Her view that "no woman can call herself free until she can choose consciously whether she will or will not call herself a mother" continues to be echoed by feminists today (Sanger, 1995, p. 508).

The forces that have dominated the population control crusade throughout most of the twentieth century have been uncomfortable with the linkages between contraception and women's rights, sexual equality in particular. Stella Browne, British feminist and communist, shattered the front of respectability in the male-dominated 1922 Fifth International Neo-Malthusian and Birth Control Conference when she articulated that birth control means women's "social and sexual freedom" (Dixon-Mueller, 1993b). The change from the name "birth control" to either "planned parenthood" or "family planning" represents an ideological shift focusing on the well-being of the family unit rather than on emancipating women, married or unmarried, to determine their own sexual and reproductive roles. International conferences continue to witness tension between what constitutes women's rights and family/community duties.

THE EVOLUTION OF INTERNATIONAL POPULATION CONFERENCES

Those concerned with population growth began cross-national meetings as far back as the late 1800s, when neo-Malthusians from England, Holland, Germany, and France came together to promote the use of birth control. During the first half of the twentieth century, international conferences on population and/or birth control were convened by private, nongovernmental organizations. Two scientific world conferences were sponsored by the United Nations; the first was held in Rome in 1954 and the second in Belgrade in 1965. The 1974 World Conference held in Bucharest, initiated by developed countries (particularly the United States), was the first to include government representatives in their official capacities.

The Bucharest conference created a world population "Plan of Action," with the basic theme that both population control and development were needed to improve the quality of life of the world's people. The principles formulated at this conference identified the family as the basic unit of society and the target agent for change. The status of women within their family unit was mentioned in six of the conference's recommendations. For example, governments were encouraged "to remove barriers to women's education, training, employment, and access to health care." The wording of the resulting document was cautious, reiterating the rights of parents and encouraging governments to provide education on "sex and family life" and hardly mentioning the abortion issue. The purpose of the 1984 International Conference on population, held in Mexico City, was to review the impact of the Plan of Action adopted ten years earlier and to draft recommendations for population initiatives into the next decade.

By 1984, many developing countries believed in the necessity of controlling their national birthrates and were anxious for help in the implementation of programs. At this time, the world was still adding seventy-eight million people per year, which indicated it would double within thirty-five years. The annual growth rate, however, had decreased from 1.9 to 1.7, illustrating that the Plan of Action was having some impact. The first world women's conference (Mexico City, 1975) reported that women in developing countries were saying they desired fewer children but that they still wanted between three and five on an average. This conference gave considerable attention to the status of women, despite the U.S. policy statement that ignored the subject.[15] It was not until the 1994 World Conference on Population and Development in Cairo that the status of women was recognized as one of the most important factors in regulating population growth.

THE 1994 CONFERENCE

An Overview

The 1994 International Conference on Population and Development offers more promise to improve the status of women worldwide than all other conferences combined. Population conferences have historically been male-dominated events in which population planners (often led by those from developed countries) discuss how to keep the world's poorest women from having babies. Their solutions often centered around establishing quotas and funding modern birth control technology, including sterilization, IUDs, and birth control pills. Official delegates to the 1994 Conference (held in Cairo, Egypt, from September 5 to 13) were largely male. However, Dr. Nafis Sadik, Executive Director of the United Nations Population Fund and the Conference's Secretary General, is a woman, and women worldwide monitored the proceedings.[16] Dr. Sadik was one of many recommending a new approach, one based on the recognition that women's status is a powerful predictor of lower fertility. This new plan concentrates funds on women's education and offers contraceptive services as part of a total health package, including such things as AIDS counseling and child immunizations. The plan further promotes gender equity by asking men to take responsibility for preventing pregnancies and sexually transmitted disease.

Despite the myriad of voices at the Conference, delegates reached compromise with a viable plan. Those who endorsed the more comprehensive plan of advancing women's rights to reduce the birthrate sparred with traditional family planning advocates who wanted to continue the current methods of supplying contraceptive technology. Traditionalists doubt that the more encompassing but more circuitous path to population control will be as effective. They fear that the costs of the endeavor will be unmanageable. The most conservative contingent was loosely composed of the Vatican, many Latin American countries, and traditionalist governments, which oppose abortion and contraceptive dissemination (especially to unmarried women), and Muslim fundamentalists, who are especially suspicious of women's rights.

Ellen Goodman writes:

> In an unholy alliance of holy men, the Vatican took up with some of the fundamentalist Muslims who together tried to turn a conference on population and development into a forum on abortion and sexuality. They tried to turn the debate from the methods to the morality of limiting population. To turn attention from a joint effort of the world to a clash of cultures. (Goodman, 1994, A7)

Islamic fundamentalists accused delegates to the Cairo conference of trampling morals, promoting promiscuity, and supporting premarital and extramarital sex. Both this faction and representatives from the Vatican expressed opposition to offering confidential sexuality counseling to teenagers and to any proposal which indicated that abortion is a woman's right. The Vatican hammered away at this single issue of abortion for five days of conference deliberations, finally agreeing to suspend protests to the final statement on abortion.[17]

Despite disagreement, and not to understate the challenges that continue to exist, the perspectives and goals of the Cairo Conference, if implemented, will be extremely beneficial to the world's women. A report published by the International Institute for Sustainable Development (ISD) states that, "Many delegates and NGO representatives have commented that the language in the Programme of Action on the empowerment of women goes much further than the text prepared for the Beijing Women's Conference" (*Earth Negotiations Bulletin*, 1994, p. 10). The Cairo plan calls for women's full involvement in policy and decision making. All countries are urged to provide girls access to primary education. Women's autonomy in reproduction was the focus of the section on the "rights of the individual," and although there was resistance from Islamic and Catholic governments, the final document granted individuals the right to decide on the number and the spacing and timing of their children and to do this free of violence and coercion.

An enormous step exists between hammering out doctrine and policy on paper and implementing the designated concepts into the lives of people in diverse cultures with unequal resources. One international women's rights group, the Women's Environment and Development Organization (WEDO), wants to change sexist attitudes that blame women for population growth and concentrate instead on empowering women to fight together for a healthy environment (Abzug, 1995). Some efforts win support globally, but they must be mediated through national and local governments and the philosophies that these governments represent.

NATIONAL POPULATION POLICIES AND WOMEN'S LIVES

Most nations of the world decide (and sometimes redecide) whether their collective interest would be best served by establishing policies to facilitate population decline or to promote population growth in their countries. The resulting propaganda, laws, and structure have considerable impact on citizens' private lives and human rights, particularly women's rights. Both pronatalist and antinatalist policies have the potential to interfere with women's choices and opportunities in life.

Pronatalist Measures

There are two very different types of countries that believe their populations are too low. The first is trying to combat a declining birthrate and may also wish to offset immigrant population growth. Most European countries are included in this category. The second type of pronatalist country has high birthrates and a growing population but maintains that more people are necessary to meet national, often military, objectives. Iraq has one of the world's highest fertility rates and yet wants to maintain a growing population.

The Rumanian government took a strongly pronatalist stand to reverse the downward trend in the birthrate. In 1966, with a fertility rate of 1.9, they changed their liberal abortion policy and made abortion illegal except in extreme circumstances. They made contraceptives unavailable, except for medical justification, and set about blockading the importation of birth control devices made in other countries. Policy transformations were accompanied by a network of spy operations in which pregnant women, who wanted an abortion, were not sure who they could trust.

A West German women's newsletter reported in 1988 that both women in search of birth control and abortion information and women offering counsel were wary of discussing the matter because government discovery could result in punishment and death. Women were monitored through workplace examinations, which were supposedly given for cancer screening but which served to identify pregnant women and track them so they would carry the child to term. The secret police in Rumania had "interrogation specialists," disguised as doctors, working at women's clinics. If women had a botched abortion, they were required to confess methods and accomplices before they could receive treatment (*Connexions*, 1989). The birthrate rose from fourteen per 1,000 in 1966, to twenty-seven per 1,000 in 1967. It did not remain this high, however, since women resorted to other means of birth control (such as the rhythm method and withdrawal) and clandestine abortion (Weeks, 1992). The maternal mortality rate soared due to these unsafe illegal abortions. In 1989, Rumanians overthrew and executed longtime Communist Dictator Nicolae Ceauşescu. One of the first acts of the new government was to again legalize abortion.

Before the demise of the Soviet Union, eastern block countries had a decades-long, easy-access-to-abortion policy. It was a common method of birth control. Now with low birthrates and religion as a growing political force, abortion policies may be revised. In Poland, 1993, a new law made abortion illegal except to save the mother's life, in cases of rape or incest, or because of irreversible malformation of the fetus. The American media reports on the anguish of one Polish woman whose illegal abortion had been uncovered and who was then coerced to name the physician who performed it. If found guilty, the doctor will face up to two years in prison and lose his medical license for up to ten years (Perlez, 1995).

While several countries experiment with the repressive politics of desperation to increase the birthrate, many others use economic incentives for having babies. Mothers and/or couples in Sweden receive family leave, a child allowance, and free day care (Sidel, 1987).

Antinatalist Measures

In 1949, Communist factions won control of China's government. They confronted the long-standing patriarchal traditions to officially establish sex equality. They outlawed polygyny, selling daughters, and female infanticide. At the same time, they gave women access to contraceptives and abortion and actively encouraged paid employment. Marxist philosophy viewed overpopulation as the product of unequal wealth, and originally they expected their own high birthrate to go down as the new system took effect. When this didn't happen, China resorted to a series of interventions. Today, China's one-child policy represents the most antinatalist one in the world.

There was a family planning component to the Great Leap Forward (1958-1959) and the Cultural Revolution (1966-1969) in China, but these efforts did little to reduce fertility. Issues of hunger, housing, and human services motivated the government to take more decisive action (Croll, Davine, and Kane, 1985). The early 1970s introduced the slogan "late, spaced, and few." The model called for late marriage, "at about twenty-seven and twenty-five years of age respectively for men and women in the cities, and twenty-five and twenty-three in the countryside," a recommended spacing of "at least four years between births," and fewer children. Another slogan advised "one's not too few, two will do, and three are too many for you" (Ibid.). During this era, a network of family planning committees were established and a wide variety of fertility control measures became available within the delivery of basic health care. Local clinics kept records of women's fertility histories, cycles, contraception, and future birth plans. Birth control pills were brought daily to women working in the fields, and IUD, barrier methods, abortion, and sterilization were provided without charge (Ibid.).

A series of economic incentives and disincentives were established to facilitate compliance with the one-child policy. One-child certificates offer such things as monthly allowances, better housing, more land (proportionately) for cultivation, and a variety of preferences for the child—schooling, a better occupation, and even larger retirement benefits. Although second children are permitted in some locations and/or under some circumstances, parents who have two or more children without permission must repay child allowances, pay for medical costs, and pay a tax for additional children. In some cases, the penalties are severe. The policy operates through small group peer pressure and sanctions—"work units" in the more urban areas and community cadres in the countryside. These local leaders, in charge of enforcing target births per family (directed from the government), have been besieged with conflicting messages: control population "no matter what," but do not alienate the masses (Aird, 1990).

Many Chinese couples do not like to be limited to one child, especially when, in about half the families, that child would be a daughter who would marry, move away with her husband, and not be able to look after parents in their old age. The practice of female infanticide, common in China before 1949, has resurfaced in some areas. Chinese orphanages overwhelmingly house infant girls. The Chinese media reports lopsided sex ratios:

> The 1982 census data on births during 1981 indicated 112.45 male births per 100 female for Anhui Province, the highest provincial birth sex ratio in the country; the national average was 108.47. County figures as high as 139 male births per 100 female births, commune figures of up to 175 males per 100 females, and brigade ratios as high as 800 males per 100 females were reported from several areas. (Aird, 1990, p. 28)

In China, women can certainly obtain contraceptives and abortions when they want to, but their rights are restricted because they are required to use these measures even when they do not want to. In many localities, officials coerce women with one child, often under the penalty of fines, to have an IUD inserted; couples with two or more children are forced to be sterilized; women pregnant with an "unauthorized" child have to submit to an abortion (Aird, 1990).

The Chinese policies have rather dramatically reduced the birth rate in the last thirty years. In the mid-1960s, the fertility rate (TFR) was 6.7, and as of 1990, it was 2.2 (Weeks, 1992). Despite this reduction, China is experiencing an annual 1.4 percent rate of natural increase, and because of the high base population, this adds approximately sixteen million people yearly to the country's population (Ibid.). In addition to concerns that government failure to meet target population control figures will result in mass starvation, the coercive practices have been condemned by the international community, and the United States has boycotted funds for family planning in China because of the practice of forced abortions. (See Example 3.3 for a glimpse into how Japan's pronatalist movement affects that country.)

EXAMPLE 3.3. Focus on Japan

With crowded commuter trains and cramped housing, it is surprising to many that there is a strong pronatalist movement in Japan. The total fertility rate for Japan hovers around 1.4 and has dipped to 1.1 in Tokyo. Politicians, mostly male, worry about the long-term consequences of a declining birthrate and wonder what they can do to induce Japanese women to have more babies. Several years ago, Prime Minister Ryutaro Hashimoto, when he was finance minister, suggested that keeping women out of college would increase fertility. Both this remark and repeated local and national proposals that women who have three or four children receive a bonus anger women's groups in Japan. Some complain that men's help with home and children would go a longer way than money. Japanese women, who defy any simplistic Western stereotypes, are marrying later (sometimes not at all) and are more ready to divorce when disappointed with the marriage. In short, they prize their freedom.

Japan is one of a small number of countries where the birth control pill is still illegal. Surveys show that women are leery of its health side effects. Many women don't use any contraception and resort to abortion, technically difficult to obtain but, in practice, readily available. Condoms are the most popular form of protection: they safeguard against AIDS and can be easily obtained in vending machines. Sexuality is casual in Japan; there's considerable tolerance of pornography, image clubs, night clubs, and prostitutes. Some Japanese women believe liberal sexual mores foster their personal freedom, while others worry that this freedom is too male-defined.[18]

The United States and International Population Policy

The official position of the United States has been satisfaction with current levels of fertility and support for individual freedom of choice through the availability of contraceptives, voluntary sterilization, and legal abortion. Surrounding this stance, however, there is much disagreement concerning population objectives, sexuality, women's status, and abortion.[19] The balance of power of selected interests in the United States affects not only U.S. domestic policy, but also U.S. international policy. This is of major importance because since 1965 the United States has contributed more to foreign population control programs than all other countries combined (Kasun, 1988).

In 1961, the United States established the Agency for International Development (AID), and assistance for family planning programs soon came to be recognized as a key factor in foreign development. The population control funds from AID are often disseminated to other countries through international organizations such as the United Nations Fund for Population Activities (UNFPA) and the International Planned Parenthood Federation (IPPF). The conservative mood of the 1980s prompted vocal opposition to the U.S. domestic policy of legal abortion and called for a change in foreign policy. In 1985, the Reagan administration, using the coercive Chinese policy as justification, cut off U.S. government funding to agencies disseminating monies to programs in China and other countries that practice abortion (Weeks, 1992). President Clinton reversed the Reagan policy as one of his first acts after assuming office. The Clinton administration sent a U.S. delegation to the Cairo Population and Development Conference with a broad-based strategy—one that stresses the rights and needs of women.

Various factions, such as nationalists, religious leaders, and some scholars view U.S.-funded family planning efforts in developing nations with suspicion. For example, if a woman in an Indonesian village volunteered for an IUD, she received a community food bonus. Critics claim that if three-fourths of Indian villagers submitted to vasectomies, the entire village profited. In Thailand, motivational efforts "in the labor rooms of hospitals" have resulted in coerced sterilizations. In a scathing criticism of international family planning policy and technology, feminist Betsy Hartmann confronts the health risks of hormonal birth control methods (the pill, Norplant, Depo-Provera), the IUD, and sterilization (1995).[20] Prior to the 1979 fundamentalist revolution in Iran, all methods of birth control and abortion were legal. Kasun states that, "Upon seizing power, the new government threw out the family planning apparatus, threw out the law allowing abortion and sterilization, and in short order, threw out the United States" (1988, p. 89).

PROVIDING EFFECTIVE FAMILY PLANNING PROGRAMS

The United Nations reports that fertility is declining in all major regions of the world. They further report that now, more than ever before, many developing countries are interested in decreasing their birthrates. Sadik notes another hopeful sign:

> [C]ompared with any previous generation, women are saying that they want fewer children; although actual fertility is much higher than desired fertility in many developing countries, the overall rate is now falling in all regions of the developing world. (1991, p. 1)

The cornerstone of the 1994 population conference was the recently acknowledged partnership between overall development and family planning. Most responsible planners believe that incentive schemes and coercive sterilizations are not effective for the long term. The best programs take place in an environment dedicated to human development and in conjunction with measures designed to improve maternal and infant health, provide a variety of contraceptive methods, and offer information and instruction about their use. When women begin to share equality of rights and opportunities and have informed access to birth control choices, the real birth rate will start to parallel the ideal family size. All programs introduced into a culture must be sensitive to the unique needs and norms of the community.

Using the Mass Media for Family Planning Education

The mass media, in the form of radio, television, video, films, newspapers, magazines, billboards, and posters, is an effective educational tool. According to the UNFPA, "there is now one TV for every twelve people in the developing world," and video parlors are "spreading through Africa and Asia" (Sadik, 1991, p. 22).

The U.N.-based Population Communications International produces the majority of motivational television and radio programming addressing the three top reasons that women do not use contraceptives: (1) lack of knowledge, (2) fear of side effects, and (3) opposition from husbands (Ryerson, 1994). PCI reports success in popular response from Latin America, Africa, and South and East Asia. Five family planning serial dramas in Mexico aired between 1977 and 1986, correlated with the 34 percent decline in the growth rate and increased contraceptive use during the same period. In Kenya, between 1987 and 1989, a family planning radio and television series attracted the largest audience in the history of both these media. During this period, there was a "58 percent increase in contraceptive usage and a decline in desired family size from 6.3 to 4.4 children per woman" (Ibid., p. 259). Research conducted by the University of Nairobi found that 75 percent of radio listeners had accepted the concept of smaller families and many women indicated that the program "caused their husbands to allow them to come for family planning" (Ibid., p. 259).

One of the most dramatic examples of the success of soap operas as a persuasional mechanism toward family planning is the series *Humraahi* (Come Along with Me), which began airing on Indian television in 1992 and, by May, ranked as the top show on Indian television. It focused on the status of women, age of marriage, age of pregnancy, gender bias in childbearing and child rearing, equality of education, and spouse selection. At the end of each episode, information is presented and a post office box number in Bombay is displayed on the screen. The number of letters generated by this program, and a similar previous one, has been phenomenal. Population Communications International is concerned, however, about the coordination between the show and proper follow-up to viewers' needs. An effective response requires translators for twenty of India's major languages and personnel to provide health and social counseling.

Brazil's multimedia model has been very successful, and three dramas originating there have been dubbed into Spanish and other languages and disseminated to twenty-six countries. UNFPA credits Brazilian media campaigns with an 80 percent increase in the number of vasectomies performed monthly at Pro-Pater male health clinic and a 97 percent increase in the number of new clients (Sadik, 1991).

How Can Men Be Encouraged to Share the Responsibility of Birth Control?

Feminists complain that family planning discourse is sexist because it makes pregnancy prevention solely the woman's responsibility. Furthermore, in most cultures of the world, child care is a female activity; so not only are women blamed for having (or not having) a baby, they are also expected to do the necessary labor to ensure the child's survival for years afterwards and, increasingly, on their own. Despite the term "family planning," most programs focus on women. There are a few notable exceptions.

Traditional methods of preventing pregnancy—withdrawal or abstention—require male cooperation. In contrast, many of the more modern methods—the hormone pill, injections of Depo-Provera, the IUD, the Norplant implant, and the female condom—are exclusively female methods. They have the advantage of promising female autonomy, but they can pose serious health risks to users. In addition, they may serve to further shift responsibility away from men. Feminists accuse family planning clinics of pushing female methods at the expense of condoms and vasectomies. However, many health experts now recommend condoms because of their double protection against pregnancy and sexually transmitted diseases. Indeed, condoms are an increasingly acceptable method of contraception because of the worldwide AIDS crisis, and they are a method that requires male participation.

The Planned Parenthood Association of Ghana (PPAG) set up a "Daddies Club" in the western region of Ghana. Here, in workplace centers, men were encouraged to come after work to relax, hear lectures, and join in discussions about such matters as home management and family planning. Their football team jerseys featured a condom logo with a "wear me" message printed on the front. PPAG contends the "Daddies Clubs" are raising family planning acceptance rates in Ghana (Sadik, 1991).

In the Republic of Korea, family planners turned their attention to men in the 1970s, partly out of concern that the traditional preference for sons threatened efforts to curtail the birthrate. The Planned Parenthood Association of Korea (PPFK) and The Korean National Council of Women enlisted the cooperation of the military to integrate family planning and sex education into the annual training of the Homeland Reserve Forces, which touches the lives of most Korean men between ages twenty-five and thirty-five. Family planning indoctrination also became part of in-service training courses for civil servants (mostly male). The UNFPA reports that these efforts were successful and that the number of men who accepted family planning more than doubled within the two-year period of education and promotion (Sadik, 1991).

SUCCESSFUL PROGRAMS DESIGNED FOR AND BY WOMEN

Of the world's twenty poorest countries, only Bangladesh has registered a fertility decline. The government of Bangladesh committed to family planning when the country won independence in 1971; the population was eighty million, and they had hoped to stabilize it at 150 million. Although this figure was optimistic, the trends in fertility reduction have been laudable. Women in their childbearing years reduced their average number of children from seven in 1970, to under 4.5 in 1994. Contraceptive use for couples was only 6 percent in 1974 and had risen to 45 percent by 1994. Muslim fundamentalists who wish to curb family planning operations and keep women in a subordinate role clash with moderate Muslims in Bangladesh. Pressure from the conservative faction led then–Prime Minister Khaleda Zia to cancel her plans to go to the Cairo population conference. Nevertheless, family planning programs continue in Bangladesh, and women are both running them and participating in them (Burns, 1994).

The Bangladesh Women's Health Coalition presents a model of the change in focus discussed at the Cairo conference. This program began in 1980, by offering abortions, but it has expanded into a network of 3,000 local and regional clinics, some with the provision of basic health care services, literacy, legal aid, and employment skill training (Kalish, 1994).

In addition to providing clinics, Bangladesh is one of many countries that utilizes field workers. Most of the 50,000 outreach workers are women, and most come from the very villages they serve. A *New York Times* article uses the example of Anwara, a thirty-eight-year-old worker from the village of Pirojali, to illustrate the outreach approach. People in her village were originally suspicious of her efforts, but her patience and persistence finally won their acceptance. Workers try to talk to couples as much as possible, but most have found that once women are convinced that they want to control future births, they will take the lead in convincing their husbands and others of the necessity (Burns, 1994).

African countries pose the greatest challenge to reducing fertility, and although much remains to be done there, successful programs are operating. The governments of both Zimbabwe and Kenya have committed to family planning, with positive results. In Zimbabwe, opposition to family planning included the Catholic Church and many in the male-dominated parliament. Robert Mugabe, now President of Zimbabwe, once maintained that birth control was a racist plot—a form of genocide of the black population. After Mugabe assumed power, however, it became obvious that plans to improve the living standards could not be met unless the birthrate declined. Now there is official sanctioning of family planning projects. The government of Zimbabwe is one of the few to pay health care workers a monthly wage. Many of these community workers are women (see Chapter 5).

On bicycle, Maureen Dick carries a knapsack with blood pressure gauge, a logbook, a supply of pills and condoms, and a seven-inch wooden penis for demonstration purposes from hut to hut along the African countryside. (Zimbabwe has a budding export business selling these wooden penises to family planning programs in other countries.) At the last official study, 36 percent of Zimbabwean women were using contraceptives, compared to the average of 14 percent in sub-Saharan Africa. Most are using pills, injections of Depo-Provera, or condoms, which are encouraged to prevent the spread of AIDS.[21]

In Kenya, the U.S.-sponsored Centre for Development and Population Activities (CEDPA) outreach workers took advantage of an estimated 10,000 women's self-help groups already existing at the village level. Representatives from these groups received two weeks of management training in Nairobi. Afterward, they facilitated gatherings of women, in which needed services were identified and strategies to reach goals were discussed. One success story occurred in the village of Kamuthanga, Kenya, where an increasing number of young women were dropping out of school and becoming pregnant. The women's committee there planned a combination training and health center. They helped to fund this project by opening and running a bakery. The center has been in operation since 1982 and has become a focal point for other educational and economic ventures. The health center is one of the most active distribution points for contraceptives in the region (Kak and Signer, 1993).

SUMMARY

Historical and cross-cultural evidence suggests that women's freedom to be sexual or not to be sexual is closely connected to their well-being and prestige in society. Feminist pro-choice philosophy means that motherhood is a woman's decision. It is problematic to deny women access to reproductive control and equally problematic to insist that they limit the number of children they bear.

High fertility worldwide has created a population explosion. Demographers predict that the already present high population may double in the next thirty years, with 90 percent of this increase occurring in developing countries. The consequences of overpopulation are human misery (starvation, malnutrition, poverty) and destruction of the environment (resource depletion and pollution). The developed, more industrialized countries of the world pose the greatest threat to the environment. The overconsumption patterns of those citizens with a high standard of living means that even a small increase in their numbers will have an undesirable impact on the environment.

Women's status is integral to controlling the world's population. Although forward-looking thinkers such as Emma Goldman and Margaret Sanger long ago made the connection between women's equality and the birthrate, the theme had not received full international recognition until the 1994 World Conference on Population and Development. Recognition of the importance of women's status, both as an end in itself and as a means to limit world population growth, has been long overdue. The task now, however, is to fund and implement programs that empower women.

Men, especially in their relationship to women, are also crucial in the effort to lower reproduction. Some programs try to convince men that it is in their best interests to have small families. Surveys show that women often wish to have fewer children, and if they could obtain their husband's support, actual fertility would come closer to desired fertility. On a much deeper level, there is still a worldwide need to reveal to men (and women) the destructive forces of sex/gender inequality. Sex equality would mean that men and women could discuss and plan together, with mutual respect, their sexual behavior, choice of contraception, and the number of children they wish to have.

KEY WORDS
Agency for International Development (AID)
Antinatalist policy
Birthrate
Death rate
Demographic transition theory
Demography
Fecundity
Fertility
Global carrying capacity
Machismo
Marianisma
Migration rate
Natural fertility planning (NFP)
Population explosion
Population growth rate
Pronatalist policy

Chapter 4

Women and Work Worldwide

WOMEN'S WORK

Women make up 97 percent or more of:

- nurses in Japan, Bulgaria, and Poland,
- Kindergarten teachers in France and the United States,
- secretaries in Sweden,
- child care workers in China.

Several generalizations characterize women's work almost every-where: Women work longer hours than do men (United Nations, 1991a); much, but not all, of the work assigned to women is different in nature from the work assigned to men; women's work is vital to the political economy, but it tends to be devalued in most cultures and in the international accounting system. Some positive change has occurred, especially within the past thirty years, with some promis-ing developments for women in the workforce. However, before considering these issues, let us consider the situation typical of most women in the world today.

REAL WORK AND PERCEPTIONS OF WORK

Anthropologist Gail Lee Bernstein (1993) observed life for women in Bessho, a Japanese farming community. She reports on the daily activities of Haruko, who defines herself as "just a house-wife" and as having "free time." Bernstein realized that Haruko, similar to other women in Bessho, was the busiest member of her family. She discovered that women who labor side by side with men in the paddies, transplanting rice seedlings in late spring or early summer, weeding with other women during the summer, and again working with men to harvest in the fall, refer to such work as "helping my husband." Only activities performed for wages constituted "work."

The following description gives the reader some idea of Haruko's lifestyle:

> Haruko's daily round of chores began at six o'clock. Every morning she prepared a breakfast of misoshira, boiled rice, and green tea. After sending the children off to school at eight o'clock in a flurry of last-minute searches for clothing and books and hastily delivered instruction, Haruko ran a load of wash in the washing machine and hung it out to dry. As the woman of the house, Haruko also had several community obligations that were impossible to shirk.
>
> In addition to being a homemaker, Haruko was the family's chief farm worker. Haruko also worked with her mother-in-law and husband on a neighborhood team husking rice. One of Haruko's principal farm chores was feeding pigs. Twice a day, once in the morning and once at night, the couple fed the ninety pigs and cleaned the pigsty.
>
> By early November, Haruko usually looked for part-time wage-paying jobs. Haruko was taken on as a dokata, or construction worker (literally a "mud person"), and she worked on a team with two other women and three men. In most other wage-paying jobs women and men worked apart, at distinct kinds of work, but on the construction teams they worked side by side. The female dokata's work was physically demanding: women hauled heavy boulders, climbed down into trenches to lay irrigation pipes, constructed bridges over irrigation ditches and shoveled snow from steep mountain slopes. (Bernstein, 1993, pp. 226-229)

The description above is unique only as it reflects the specific work of a Japanese farm woman. The amount of work, the multiple roles fulfilled, and the devaluation of the effort put forth are typical of women's work throughout the world. Myths persist that work performed by women, usually within the family or in family enterprises, is not "real" work. This idea is so pervasive that it has obscured the official records of who works and who does not.

INCLUDING WOMEN IN INTERNATIONAL ECONOMIC ACTIVITY

"In 1990, out of the 828 million women officially estimated to be economically active, 56 percent lived in Asia, 29 percent in the developed world, 9 percent in Africa, and 5 percent in Latin America and the Caribbean" (United Nations, 1991a, p. 39). The notion of economically active, used by the International Labor Office (ILO) of the United Nations and by most national governments, fails to include much of the real work that women do. This inequity persists despite the ILO's broadened definition of the economically active population in 1982 to include "all work for pay or anticipation of profit" (Ibid.). The redefinition prompted statistical change in some areas but not in others. In India, initial estimates of 13 percent of women as economically active were revised to nearly 88 percent following the new guidelines (Ibid.). Even so, established categories exclude activities such as gathering fuel and water, keeping a kitchen garden, processing crops, and raising animals. Neither agricultural work in the developing world nor domestic work throughout the world is included in these statistics. The example of Arab women's work in rural regions provides an overview of the contrast between the real demands of women's work and the statistical invisibility of this work.

During the 1980s and 1990s, economic activity rates of Middle Eastern women ranged from a low of less than 7 percent in Jordan, Syria, Algeria, Iran, and Egypt to highs of 18 percent in Kuwait and 22 percent in Turkey (Moghadam, 1993). These figures fail to reflect adequately women's work in agricultural production, food processing, sewing, making handicrafts, tending livestock, and caring for family members. The United Nations Development Programme (UNDP) (1991) reports that Arab "women themselves may also hide their jobs, to keep up appearances in a culture which dictates that the man should be the sole supporter of the family" (p. 11).

The 1981 Population Census of Pakistan records only 3.2 percent of all women, aged ten and above, as working or looking for work (the figure was 14 percent in 1992). A sizable proportion is said to be "house-keeping" and therefore not working. The United Nations estimates that in Pakistan a rural woman spends sixty-three hours a week on domestic work (United Nations, 1991a). Many Pakistani women work on the farms of their fathers, husbands, and brothers, but the population census shows that only 176 women in the whole of Pakistan are agricultural and animal husbandry workers.

Women workers who escape official recognition include those working in family businesses; wool preparation and paper making; spinning, weaving, and dyeing; food and beverage processing; tailoring and dress making; shoe making and leather goods making; jewelry and precious metal making, etc. (Khan, 1989); and volunteer in community work (see Example 4.1).

The national economy of Pakistan, as with most developing countries, relies on the informal economic sector. This part of the labor force is officially overlooked, thus creating a distortion of national statistics upon which policies are based. The real harm comes from the lack of recognition given to the workers in this sector, causing them to exist outside a legal framework that could ensure a basic level of existence. Women who perform work not considered

EXAMPLE 4.1. Women and Volunteer Work

Both women and men perform voluntary, unpaid work for their community; however, the type of work, the scope of the work, and the social recognition for the work is likely to differ by gender. Women's volunteer activities, usually geared to assist and improve the quality of the lives of others, are often less prestigious and more life encompassing than the volunteer work performed by men. Women often volunteer to serve meals to the needy, stuff envelopes for campaigns, or staff busy hours in schools, while men tend to volunteer to chair boards, serve on governing committees, or to consult with organizations.

Sometimes volunteer work is women's only route to a public role. Often it leads to personal satisfaction and self-actualization. However, it is work; it requires talent and energy, and it is not calculated in national accounting systems. Marilyn Waring (1988) estimated that in 1980, 52.7 million women in the United States participated in voluntary work, valued at $18 billion.

Mary Prado argues that the term volunteer work carries a middle- to upper-class connotation. Her research of working-class Mexican-American women's unpaid community labor reveals that poorer women do even more work and do it because they "have to" for the safety and welfare of their families. All community work helps women develop skills and social networks (Prado, 1997). Feminists debate whether volunteer work enslaves or liberates women.

"work" are usually isolated from each other, and there is little chance of them joining a collective to improve overall standards.

Housework

Housework is most closely associated with women and the primary example of important but invisible work. No national governments in the world today include those activities loosely described as "housework" in their system of reckoning productive economic activity.

Marilyn Waring (1988) recounts the work days of Tendai, a young girl in the Lowveld, Zimbabwe, and Cathy, a middle-class North American homemaker. Tendai starts her day at 4 a.m., when she walks eleven kilometers to fetch water in a thirty-liter tin. Upon returning home, almost five hours later, Tendai eats a little food and then it is time to gather firewood. At midday, she cleans the eating utensils and prepares a lunch of sadza for her family. She is also in charge of clean-up duty after lunch and then must go out in the hot sun and gather wild vegetables for supper. Toward early evening, she again heads out on foot to procure water. At 9 p.m., after cooking supper and putting her younger siblings to sleep, she can rest.

Cathy is a North American, middle-class, "stay at home" mom. During a typical day, she buys, prepares, and serves meals to her family; she clears food and dishes from the table and cleans up after meals and snacks. Much time is consumed by child care: diapering, dressing, driving to school, watching them, teaching them, and playing with them. Cathy's other chores include dusting, doing laundry, making beds, caring for pets and plants, paying bills, sewing, putting away toys, talking to salespeople, answering the phone, vacuuming, sweeping, scrubbing floors, lawn and garden work, "cleaning the bathroom and kitchen and putting the children to bed" (Waring, 1988, p. 15).

Although the lifestyles of Tendai and Cathy vary because of the economic and technological level of their culture, they have something important in common: both are considered "economically inactive, unproductive and unoccupied" by economists (see Example 4.2).

Example 4.2. The International Wages for Housework Campaign
Women Count—Count Women's Work

IWFH is a network for women in third world and industrialized countries who have been organizing since 1972, for the recognition of, and compensation through governments, for the unwaged work that women do, to be paid by dismantling the military industrialized complex.

Within the IWFH campaign, black women/women of color, lesbian women, prostitute women, and women with visible and invisible disabilities organize independently—the best protection that our campaigning on any issue will express the needs and concerns of women from the bottom up. In particular, the IWFH campaign is petitioning every government to implement the following UN decision and to count the contribution to the economy of all women's work so that it is recognized and reflected in every gross national product.[1]

"The remunerated and, in particular, the unremunerated contributions of women to all aspects and sectors of development should be recognized, and appropriate efforts should be made to measure and reflect these contributions in national accounts and economic statistics and in the gross national product. Concrete steps should be taken to quantify the unremunerated contribution of women to agriculture, food production, reproduction, and household activities" (United Nations, 1985).

The United System of National Accounts (UNSNA) collects statistics on "productivity" from all nations, and these figures are then used to identify areas of the world needing economic assistance. If women's work was visible, more women in developing nations would be eligible to receive direct aid. Marilyn Waring (1988) believes that if housework and other unpaid work were officially counted, there would be corresponding social policy benefits for these workers. She also claims that reassigning economic value to the productive and reproductive work which mostly women perform will cause societies to question their current (misguided) priorities (e.g., excessive military expenditures).

Maid Work

In countries and areas of countries in which there is sufficient economic stratification, there is a demand for poor women to do domestic work in the private residences of wealthier families. An analysis of attitudes toward maid work involves the culmination of sexism, classism, and often racism. In this case, unlike the other forms of work we have discussed, women leave their homes to work for somebody else in a different setting. Women often migrate great distances to take these jobs.

Domestic work is an extension of work in the family relegated to women worldwide, and it is often one of the few employment options open to women at the bottom of the class system. The nature of maid work varies significantly with respect to wages, benefits, and job security. It is fair to say that the work is usually perceived as low in value and prestige. At its worst, domestic workers are virtually slaves to their employers, acquiescing to unreasonable and degrading demands because they need the work to survive. One such scenario may be found in South Africa where the legacy of apartheid produced conditions in which nearly all maids are black South African women working for white South African women.

The relationship between maids and madams in South Africa was explored by Jacklyn Cock through a series of interviews conducted in 1978 and 1979. The significance of her findings has not diminished with time. Apartheid has been dismantled, but the economic disparity between blacks and whites in that country persists, and racism, classism, and sexism keep this employment pattern in place. News reports claim that life continues to get harder for South African domestic workers (Wilkerson, 1994). Moreover, many aspects of Cock's analysis (1990) apply to the dynamics between domestic workers and their female employers throughout the world. The observations present a challenge to simplistic notions of sisterhood.

In South Africa, over one million black women are employed in domestic service. Their work is characterized by low pay, low status, long hours, hard work, no pension or benefits, and lack of job security. Continuation of employment is arbitrary, based on the wishes of the employer. Many black domestic workers in South Africa must leave their homes and their families to take employment in a white household. They take the jobs out of economic necessity and because they wish to support children and other family members.

The unequal race/class structure causes blacks to serve whites, and the unequal sex/gender structure, which defines housework and child care as women's province, causes black women to perform these duties for white women. This creates a form of liberation for white women, yet this liberation is not achieved through sex equality but rests instead on the backs of other women. Cock (1989) believes the maid system to be a microcosm of the social order in which it exists, and at the same time, it recreates this social order. White children are nurtured by black nannies—someone they must depend on—whom they often love, but these relationships also represent their first contact with the racial group ideologically considered to be inferior to themselves and from whom they must separate. Besides economic deprivation, black children in South Africa experience inequality by being denied a mother. Black children sometimes hardly know their mothers, and they resent the fact that their own mothers are spending more time caring for white children than for them.

Cock reports that the notions that madams have about their maids are usually distorted by paternalism and stereotypes. It was common to have madams say that they considered their maids to be "one of the family," yet this claim was not borne out in either observed behavior, further questioning, or in the responses of the maids. Cock found that only 10 percent of the employers in the in-depth sample knew their domestic workers' full names. Of the employers who knew that their servants had young children, 67 percent did not know who looked after the children while she was at work, and most did not know whether or not she had to pay anyone to look after her children (Cock, 1990).

Stereotypical notions about servants clouded perceptions and expectations. Many madams believed their maids to be childlike, stupid, incompetent, untrustworthy, lazy, and passive. These notions are particularly ironic given the importance of the tasks that maids perform, especially their child care function. The view of the passive and acquiescent domestic worker allows employers to exploit services without worry of retaliation. Interviews with maids revealed that external deference was a necessary facade, a behavior expected in this type of occupation. The vast majority reject the legitimacy of their situation and believe that change for the better will and should come. This account illustrates the gulf between women employers and the women whom they employ. However, both roles are products of the larger system, and an interactional analysis alone obscures the structural and patriarchal framework that fosters this type of unequal work situation.

Although the supply and demand of domestic work has long been mediated through the internal stratification of any given nation, Enloe (1989) observes that more recently it has become an international business with political implications. By quoting advertise-ments from cosmopolitan newspapers, she documents the trend of families from developed and/or wealthier nations actively searching for women to do child care and household work. Typically, the demand is generated because middle- and upper-class women in developed countries are in need of help at home to be able to earn money themselves and pursue careers. The supply is created by desperate economic conditions and lopsided international debt poli-tics, exacerbated by the prescriptions of the International Monetary Fund for debtor nations and played out in the lives of women who have to support children and other family members. Enloe points out that when a woman from Mexico, Jamaica, or the Philippines goes to the United States, Canada, or Kuwait to do domestic work and sends money home, she is doing her part to balance trade and pay off her government's debt (Enloe, 1989).

A hierarchy exists among domestic workers, and this stratifica-tion is especially noticeable among workers who cross international boundaries for employment. Professional nannies, sometimes gra-duating from nanny training schools, command a relatively high salary and do not usually do housework. An international associa-tion of nannies seeks to ensure a professional veneer and sets nan-nies aside from other household workers. Young women who are au pairs are usually in this position temporarily, using the opportunity to travel and learn another language. Frequently nannies and au pairs are white, and they are disproportionately European. Although both nannies and au pairs experience job stress, discrimination, and loneliness, they are better off than the scores of women across international boundaries who work as maids. The bottom rung of the hierarchy is composed of poor women who are economically dependent on their position with a particular family. They often enter a culture very different from the one they left, face a language barrier, and experience racial/ethnic discrimination, as well as sexual harassment. Because of their legal and economic status, they are particularly vulnerable, as they fear deportation:

In Britain, France, Saudi Arabia, Japan, and the United States, immigrant domestic workers' relationships with each other and with their employers are shaped in large part by political debates over immigration. These debates, so indicative of a society's own national identity and what it thinks of its place in the international system, are usually riddled with assumptions about male and female citizenship. (Enloe, 1989, p. 190)

Another type of women's work related to class and national boundaries obscures connections between women. It is the type of maid service and related activities performed in public buildings, particularly in hotels and motels and on cruise ships and airplanes worldwide, and its growth is closely associated with the development of tourism as a global economic industry. Enloe (1989) reminds us that tourism is labor intensive. Tourists of both sexes need and expect to be waited on, and in most countries, women make up a disproportionate share of those who prepare and serve food, clean rooms, make beds, and do laundry. Women, imaged as sex objects, entice male tourists to travel on a certain airline or to a certain exotic location. Sex tourism, tours for elite men (usually from the developed world) for the sole purpose of sexual activity with female prostitutes (usually sex workers are poor and from disadvantaged economies), is an aspect of gendered tourism. (See Chapter 6 for further discussion on the violence of prostitution.)

Sex Work

One of the most controversial issues in international women's studies is the debate over whether prostitution and other forms of sex work (e.g., nude dancing, modeling for pornographic magazines, working peep shows) always constitute forms of violence or may be considered freely chosen work.[2] Providing sexual services for money, goods, or survival is almost always specific to women. Sex workers (those who are in a position to have their voices heard) point out the common economic similarity between prostitution and marriage. Many prostitutes maintain that they identify with feminist values of female solidarity, economic independence, and financial autonomy. The growing number of international prostitute rights organizations (mostly in northern countries, e.g., the United States, Great Britain, the Netherlands, Canada, and Germany) challenges the myopic view that all sex workers have been enslaved or coerced and provides an opportunity to evaluate the meaning of this work for those women who perform it (Ward, 1996).

Home-Based Production

Work that women perform at home for cash is one of the fastest growing industries throughout the world. Reliable statistics are difficult to come by on both the national and international levels, but we do know that this type of work, sometimes known as cottage industry, is prevalent in developed countries, where it may involve office work and microelectronic assembly. Cottage industry is massive in many developing nations, especially in Asia, where there is a broader range of types of work. Home-based workers are frequently self-employed; however, increasing numbers are engaged in piecerate work for companies or subcontractors.

There are many benefits for the person or corporation employing women workers in this fashion. For example, there are no overhead costs, little investment in equipment, no unions to contend with, and little or no legislation regulating employee wages or benefits (see Example 4.3). Unfortunately, the same features that are advantageous to employers are liabilities to the employee. She usually works for very low wages and has no contact with others doing the

---

EXAMPLE 4.3. The Zoë Baird Case

Zoë Baird was nominated by newly elected President Bill Clinton to be the first ever woman Attorney General of the United States. Forty years old at that time, Baird was about to cap a career that had been "meteoric." However, twenty-nine days later she was forced to withdraw her nomination. Sources revealed that she had employed illegal immigrants in her household—a Peruvian couple, the wife as a nanny to her child and the husband as a chauffeur. She had paid the couple "off the books" and had neglected to pay their Social Security taxes. There was a tremendous public outcry over the issue and much adverse press coverage. The American media portrayed Baird as a wealthy lawyer who did not play by the rules.

Beyond the question of propriety or even whether this transgression should have cost Baird the nomination, this case illuminates societal focus on women's domestic/child care responsibility, the mediation of social class in this realm, and the international trends that have arisen to accommodate wealthy career women by employing poor women often from economically disadvantaged countries. It is no surprise that the first woman Attorney General-designate was sabotaged by the thing that sabotages women day after day: the struggle for good, surrogate care for kids is hard to find even if you are well-to-do and near impossible if you are not.

same work or with union representatives; the hours she puts in are considerable and often fragmented to allow her to complete other household demands; and her income depends on the flow of incoming work, which may be inconsistent or nonexistent (Singh and Kelles-Viitanen, 1987). There are reasons why, despite all these detractions, women engage in home-based work. Sometimes it is the only way they can make money, and sometimes they find it a viable alternative to going out to work. The belief that "a woman's place is in the home" is still alive and well in most cultures. The structural aspects of raising children and doing household labor remain female tasks almost everywhere. When a woman does paid work at home, she is fulfilling her traditional obligations, and she is also making some money, which often will be put back into raising the standard of living for her family.

In India, home-based industry has included beedi making, food processing, lacemaking, and various aspects of garment production. Rukmini Rao and Sahba Husain (1987) interviewed women working at home for the garment export industry in Delhi. They found that, for the majority, home-based work was crucial economically and was the best type of work for these women, as they could incorporate it into their daily routine, allowing them to do all their housework and receive wages for the piecework they did. The women interviewed reported that male family members either did not make enough money to support the family or they were absent from the home:

> Women gave several reasons for accepting home-based work. Many of them resorted to home production as a last means of earning a livelihood. . . . As one woman reported, "My husband's work is very irregular. Whatever little I earn also sustains the family." In some families, even when the men earned, the money was not available to the household. "My husband drinks a lot. He does not give me any money. I have taken up this work for the children's sake."
>
> Another woman complained, "My husband has gone away and does not send me any money. There is no one to look after my small children. So I have taken up this work."

Women also mentioned the lack of employment opportunities, whereas put-out work was available in practically every lane of their locality. Some younger women, who would have preferred to work in a factory and earn a better wage, were prevented from doing so on the plea that they had to safeguard their "family honour." One young woman said that her husband did not like her to go out at all. (Rao and Husain, 1987, pp. 56-57)

Rao and Husain observe several negative outcomes of home-based production for the women with whom they spoke. In this locality, as in others similar to it, there was a surplus of women willing to do this work, some desperate enough to undercut each other's wages. The subcontractors maximized this competition. Despite living in close proximity, these workers were isolated from each other as well as from the hierarchy of production. Their contacts were almost solely with their subcontractor, usually someone belonging to the same ethnic group as the worker. The resulting interaction might range from one of trust to one of dependency. It is usually true that the women workers involved have little control over most aspects of their work or their future working lives. In fact, no job security and threats of termination reinforce the powerlessness of these workers. With growing international competition, there is likely to be increased use of women working in home-based production.

THE GLOBAL ASSEMBLY LINE

Perhaps no type of international work is more closely associated with both female and third world exploitation than that work provided by multinational corporations. Multinationals, also called transnational corporations (TNCs), are corporate enterprises that, although headquartered in one country, conduct operations through subsidiaries they own or control around the world.

These worldwide webs of economic activity have already achieved a degree of global integration never before achieved by any world empire or nation-state. The driving force behind each of them can be traced in large measure to the same few hundred corporate giants with headquarters in the United

States, Japan, Germany, France, Switzerland, the Netherlands, and the United Kingdom. The combined assets of the top 300 firms now make up roughly a quarter of the productive assets in the world. (Barnet and Cavanaugh, 1994, p. 15)

Many analysts charge that multinationals represent a disturbing trend in world economic and political power, creating a situation properly called "neocolonialism." Their influence in less developed nations includes the level of wages, the type of crops grown, and how national resources are allocated. They are run by a tiny elite of managers and directors, whose major goal is profit, and are not under the control of any one country.

The availability of a cheap labor force is the main reason that corporations based in core or developed countries establish work sites in developing countries. International competition has encouraged a growing number of companies to use this strategy. The initial expansion began in the 1960s when operations were established in Hong Kong, Taiwan, South Korea, Mexico, Singapore, and Malaysia. "From 1960 to 1969, investment in offshore manufacturing by U.S. firms mushroomed from $11.1 billion to $29.5 billion. In the mid-1970s, Thailand and the Philippines became corporate favorites" (Fuentes and Ehrenreich, 1984, p. 8). These sites were chosen deliberately to keep wages low and sidestep trade union demands, pollution regulations, and occupational safety controls prevalent in more developed countries. The trend for TNCs to look for opportune locations coincided with the increased popularity of an export-led industrialization strategy favored by many third world nations and recommended by the United Nations Industrial Development Organization (UNIDO), the World Bank, and the International Monetary Fund (IMF). Free trade zones or export processing zones (EPZs) emerged as primary features to attract foreign industry and investment, jobs, technology, and monetary resources to purchase desired imports. Within these zones, companies can import raw materials, components, and equipment without paying a customs tax. The companies are usually given significant local tax incentives. National companies are often kept out of the EPZs unless they invest jointly with a foreign venture. The main attraction of all these "come-ons" is cheap labor. Some zones "resemble a huge labor camp where trade unions, strikes, and freedom of movement are severely limited, if not forbidden. A special police force is on hand to search people and vehicles entering or leaving the zones" (Fuentes and Ehrenreich, 1984, pp. 10-11).

Women account for 80 to 90 percent of workers in lightweight assembly. Primarily, they are hired in the garment or textile industries, electronics industries, chemical plants, food processing, aspects of agribusiness, and many other product assembly industries. Multinationals prefer to hire women workers. Local and worldwide traditional conventions regarding female subordination allow companies to pay women lower wages and dismiss them more easily. There is the belief that women workers are infinitely pliable, obedient, docile, and patient. Women are also thought to be more skilled at detailed work than men because of their greater manual dexterity.

Many corporations deliberately hire young, unmarried women workers. An advertisement from a Mexican newspaper asks for female applicants between ages seventeen and thirty, single, and without children. Hiring such workers offers several benefits to the company. These workers are more likely to have health and vitality and may be expected to leave to get married after several years, thus avoiding extra pay for seniority. Companies also try not to have to pay maternity benefits, and some factories insist on regular pregnancy screening exams. "In the Philippines' Bataan Export Processing Zone the Mattel toy company offers prizes to workers who undergo sterilization" (Fuentes and Ehrenreich, 1984, p. 13). Not all companies use young women. Another exploitive use of female labor is to hire homemakers for part-time shifts. This option "seems" beneficial to many women because, in theory anyway, it gives them time to meet their family obligations. Studies show that part-time workers give maximum productivity during working hours, and because the work is not full time, benefits and job security are sacrificed.

Considerable debate has arisen, some of which emanates from empirical studies, as to whether female work in multinationals is oppressive, tantamount to slavery, or a form of liberation. Linda Lim (1991) has observed that women who work for multinational corporations make better wages and have better working conditions than women who work in the informal sector or in local factories. She asserts that this work can help women acquire experience and possessions and free themselves from the patriarchal control of their families. Other researchers conclude that this type of employment utilizes local patriarchal norms to the advantage of the corporation and that the opportunities for upward mobility within TNCs are very limited (Fernandez-Kelly, 1983). To make any sweeping generalization as to whether women's work in TNCs is exploitative or liberating is misleading.[3]

The situation for women who work in multinational corporations varies from location to location. The case of Mexican women working under the maquila program provides an example of some processes discussed thus far and shows how women's lives are influenced by their work. The Border Industrialization Program (BIP), commonly known as the maquiladora or maquila system, began in 1965, after the termination of the bracero (guest workers) program. The U.S.-Mexican agreement called for industries to establish plants in both the United States and along the Mexican border under the guise of mutual benefit. The U.S.-based corporations received tax advantages and low-cost labor, while Mexico expected to benefit from employment, skills acquisition, and technology. The program has been in existence for almost thirty years, with approximately 2,000 border factories operating to the almost exclusive advantage of the corporations involved. The Mexican side of the border suffers from poverty and pollution, without adequate housing or public services, and is subject to the demand of these corporations, which are backed by the U.S. government. Many observers fear that the North American Free Trade Agreement (NAFTA) between the United States, Canada, and Mexico will further exploit the people of Mexico and that U.S. workers will lose jobs as more companies relocate south of the border.

The wage rate for Mexican workers in multinationals remains one of the lowest in the world. More than 80 percent of the maquiladora workforce is female (Tiano, 1994). The majority are between sixteen and twenty-five years of age. These women average forty-eight hours a week on the job and earn less than $1.00 per hour. The largest category for female employment is the electronics industry, followed by the garment industry, the chemical industry, and agribusiness.

Tiano (1994) claims that many electronics assembly plants are large, modern operations and "give the illusion" of a safe, pleasant work environment. Garment maquilas are more diverse, ranging from modern facilities to poorly ventilated sweatshops. The expectation of a healthy work environment is usually not met in the maquiladora system. Many female workers are exposed to toxic chemicals daily, but employers defend this practice by saying that they do not work there long enough to produce any serious damage. This is not true, and some occupational health problems that have been documented include chronic back pain, asthma, conjunctivitis, bronchitis, and brown-lung disease (Fuentes and Ehrenreich, 1984).

In the 1960s and 1970s, many women who work for the Mallory Corporation making television capacitors were exposed to chemicals that caused them to give birth to babies having defects ranging from mental retardation to webbed feet and hands. These children, now teenagers, and their families initiated a lawsuit against the company; however, a successful outcome is doubtful since the ownership of the corporation has changed hands several times since. In 1992, up to thirty cases of babies born without brains were documented in Brownsville, Texas, most within a 2.4 mile radius of the border. In Matamoros, Mexico, just across the border, forty-two cases were identified in the same period:

A joint study was conducted by the federal Centers for Disease Control (CDD) and the Texas Department of Health (TDH). The study was highly criticized for its narrow focus and for failing to include significant environmental factors. The study used a standard, twenty-year-old questionnaire when interviewing mothers who had anencephalic children and failed to survey the families in Matamoros afflicted with the birth defect, thereby excluding half of the study population. The CDC/TDH never contacted the National Toxic Campaign whose test, analyzed in the EPA-approved lab, revealed that during the period in which the anencephalic babies were conceived, Stephan Chemical was discharging highly toxic xylene into an open canal behind their facility at levels 53,000 times the U.S. permissible level. Studies have linked xylene with the types of birth defects found in the area" (Meeker-Lowry, 1993, pp. 3-5).

New economic arrangements worldwide such as NAFTA, affecting Canada, the United States, and Mexico, and GATT (a worldwide General Agreement on Tariffs and Trade) will likely affect women workers. Apprehension has been strongest surrounding the negative consequences of NAFTA on female workers. Critics fear that women from the United States and Canada will suffer from unemployment, while NAFTA will exacerbate the problems of low wages, occupational health risks, and human rights violations for women in Mexico (*Connexions*, 1994).

WOMEN'S OFFICIAL LABOR FORCE PARTICIPATION

Two features characterize the labor force participation of women in virtually every country of the world: (1) fewer women than men are employed in the mainstream, officially counted labor force, and (2) a universal and pervasive disparity exists between the wages of women and those of men.

With respect to the number of women who work for pay outside the home, wide variation and fluctuation occurs by country. The female proportion of the labor force ranges from under one-fifth in traditional societies (e.g., Pakistan and Algeria) to approximately one-third in many developing countries (e.g., Ireland, Mexico, and Venezuela) and comprises close to half in many other countries (United Kingdom, Australia, Finland, and Zimbabwe). Table 4.1 uses selected countries to show how common it is for a woman to be employed (first figure) and the size of the female labor force as a proportion of the total labor force (second figure).

Several variables influence the likelihood that women will be employed outside the home in any given society. If a shortage of available male workers occurs, as often happens during wartime, the demand for workers necessitates women's inclusion in the workforce. The ideology and attitudes of the culture regarding women's proper role play a large part in determining official policies that either encourage or discourage employment for women. A country's overall level of development influences the number and type of jobs available as well as the education of women.

Table 4.1. Women's Share of the "Official" Labor Force by Region and Selected Countries

Sub-Saharan Africa		South and Central America/Caribbean	
Burundi	47%	Jamaica	46%
Mozambique	47%	Haiti	41%
Niger	46%	Brazil	36%
Central African Republic	45%	Cuba	33%
Uganda	40%	Uruguay	32%
Kenya	39%	Argentina	29%
Ethiopia	37%	Panama	28%
Zimbabwe	34%	Nicaragua	26%
Sudan	23%	Colombia	22%
Chad	21%	Ecuador	19%
Mali	16%	Guatemala	17%
North Africa and Middle East		**Europe, North America, and Oceana**	
Israel	42%	Slovenia	50%
Egypt	23%	Moldova	48%
Iraq	22%	Russia	48%
Morocco	21%	Sweden	48%
Iran	19%	Finland	47%
Kuwait	16%	Poland	46%
Yemen	14%	United States	46%
Jordan	11%	Canada	45%
Algeria	10%	Denmark	45%
Libya	10%	United Kingdom	44%
Afghanistan	9%	Australia	42%
United Arab Emirates	9%	France	42%
Saudi Arabia	8%	Norway	41%
		Germany	40%
Asia		New Zealand	36%
Vietnam	47%	Italy	32%
North Korea	46%	Ireland	30%
Thailand	44%	Spain	25%
China	43%		
Japan	40%		
South Korea	40%		
Philippines	31%		
India	25%		

Adapted from Neft, N. and A. Levine. *Where Women Stand,* 1997, pp. 52-55.

The number of women who are working outside the home has risen in most industrialized countries throughout the last twenty years and continues to rise in many developing countries. The trend toward more women workers has, to some extent, been the outcome of the worldwide movement for gender equality. However, economic need is the largest single factor in the overall increase. More married women with small children have to share the economic support of their families with their husband or partner, and an increasing number of women are the sole support of their families.

The "wage gap" refers to the fact that the average take-home pay for women in the labor force is lower than for men, and this disparity is universal. In the Republic of Korea, women receive only 50 percent the pay of men; and in Japan, 52 percent. Both Iceland and Sweden have decreased their gender pay gap to 10 percent, but the international average continues to reflect that women make between 30 and 40 percent less than men do (United Nations, 1991b). There are multiple explanations for the pervasive lower pay accorded to women. No doubt misogynous attitudes have resulted in both outright discrimination and more subtle practices that amount to discrimination but somehow avoid this accusation.

Some main factors involved in explaining the wage gap are: (1) women's greater commitment to family; (2) differences in education and training by gender; (3) gender segregation of the labor force; and (4) prejudice, stereotypes, and resulting covert discrimination. These variables are not mutually exclusive, often operating in combination with each other. The components are mediated through cultural norms and social/economic history of various countries and become part of the rate of change in ideology and industrialization within societies.

BALANCING WORK AND FAMILY

This chapter has already devoted considerable space to documenting the invisible, behind-the-scenes work that women do. Examples previously given attest to the large role family responsibilities play in determining women's overall work. Almost everywhere, women's work outside the home is considered subordinate to their roles within the home, particularly child care. Various practices and structures have developed in response to the greater domestic involvement of women. Many of these have the net effect of keeping women in jobs that pay less and have no or low job mobility.

As discussed, the rise in home-based production is one adaptation to accomplishing both domestic work and paid work. In many developing countries, (for instance, throughout Latin America), women are employed in the informal sector where they can make and sell crafts and other products while they care for children. Women in

many traditional African communities perform the greatest proportion of farming, food production, fetching water, cooking, and caring
for their children, simultaneously. As children grow they become an
economic asset by looking after each other, running messages, taking
care of small livestock, and washing dishes. The Luo women of
Kenya combine farming with small trade and depend upon children
to share many daily duties (Guyer, 1995).

Cross-cultural studies consistently show that, although women are
moving into occupations outside the home, men are much less likely to
increase their share of the domestic workload. In some nations, such as
the former Soviet Union, public policy called for women's full inclusion in public life, but there were no actions taken to free women from
domestic labor. Zoy Khotkina (1994) claims that this situation continues in Russia today. Women who are stressed from their double life are
not equipped to compete for better jobs and higher wages.

In many countries, women are far more likely than men to be
employed part time and to have work patterns with long interrup-
tions. Table 4.2 illustrates the widespread feminization of part-time
work. Several studies show that women with small children, who
work part time, have less stress and are more satisfied than either
women who work exclusively in the home or women who work full
time.[4] The trend toward part-time work for women, however, does
little to promise equality in the workplace. Most part-time jobs are
so poorly paid that they are only suitable as an income supplement.
It is also true that part-time workers tend to lack job security and
fringe benefits, such as paid vacation, sick leave, health insurance,
workers compensation, a retirement plan, etc. (Stoper, 1988).

TABLE 4.2. Percent of Women's Share of Part-Time Employment in Selected
Countries (1995)

United Kingdom	82.3
France	82.0
Sweden	80.1
Iceland	78.6
Australia	74.4
Netherlands	73.6
United States	68.0

Adapted from United Nations, Report on the World Social Situation, 1997, p. 143.

EDUCATIONAL AND TRAINING INEQUITIES

The United Nations (1991a) reports that 33.6 percent of the world's females are illiterate. This contrasts with 19.4 percent of the male population. Illiterate women are invariably caught in a cycle of poverty and powerlessness. They also lack the basic skills required for employment in technological, higher paid jobs.

Liberal feminists believe that education and training of girls and women are the keys to equality. Strides toward closing the gap on literacy and education were made during the prosperous years of the 1970s and early 1980s, but with the worldwide economic crises and increased military expenditures in many countries came massive cuts in education.

In Africa and southern and western Asia, over 40 percent of young women are still illiterate. Although illiteracy rates for young women fell between 1970 and 1990, they are still much higher than those for young men (see Table 4.3).

The United Nations reports remind us that the decline has affected females more than males. The cultural norms of male dominance mean that families, supported by their communities, choose sons to attend schools and to train for future employment. Daughters, on the other hand, may be taken out of school to help with domestic and agricultural work or may be married early to reduce their financial burden on the family or to gain profit from a bride-price. Unequal schooling is accentuated by the implementation of school fees in many areas. In Zambia in 1985, for example, parents had to allocate over one-fifth of their per capita income per child for school supplies. When parents are faced with educating six or seven children and must select one or two, gender is often a leading determinant (United Nations, 1991a).

Today, especially in affluent countries, it is ever more likely that girls will learn to read and write, attend primary and secondary school, and even go to college. It is encouraging that in some countries, such as Quatar, Lesotho, Bulgaria, and Portugal, more women are enrolled in institutions of higher education than their male counterparts (Ibid.). Despite gains, however, U.S.- and European-based studies reveal that sexism interferes with the actual type of learning offered to girls as compared to boys.

Table 4.3. Decline in Female Illiteracy 1970 to 1990

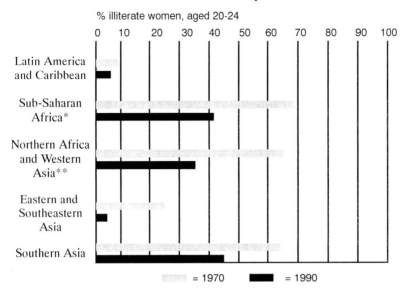

% illiterate women, aged 20-24

*Includes Sudan; excludes South Africa
**Includes Somalia and Mauritania; excludes Cyprus, Israel, and Turkey

Source: United Nations. *World's Women 1970-1990*, p. 46.

Girls tend to attain better results in primary school and, to some extent, in secondary school than do boys. Data from France, Ireland, Greece, and Sweden support this claim (Wilson, 1991). Most observers believe that girls are high achievers in school because their behavior more closely conforms to the model of the "good pupil" and that this outcome is the result of diverse gender socialization and gender expectations of teachers. According to this premise, it is not surprising that the self-image and aspirations of girls begin to falter when they approach adolescence. Reporting on interviews with secondary teachers in Spain in 1987, "teachers, like parents, anticipate the problems that girls are going to face in the labour market. They discourage girls from following certain careers, knowing that they will experience discrimination, and often abdicate responsibility to parents by claiming it is the job of the family to advise the child" (Alberdi and Alberdi, 1991, p. 166).

The comprehensive 1992 AAUW (American Association of University Women) report, *How Schools Shortchange Girls,* found covert discrimination in classrooms across the United States in places where educators believed that there was no differential treatment. Some findings of this study include: (1) girls receive less attention from teachers than do boys, with African-American girls receiving less than European-American girls, although they try to attain it more; (2) sexual harassment of girls by their male peers is increasing; (3) textbooks and examples used still marginalize the experiences of girls and women; (4) there is an "evaded curriculum," meaning that real-life issues of sexism and sexuality are seldom considered relevant subjects for study and discussion; and (5) girls are directed away from math and the hard sciences. The researchers concluded that the state of inequality in American education systemically discourages girls from taking courses that would benefit their economic well-being, thereby contributing to the feminization of poverty (AAUW Report, 1992).

HIGHER EDUCATION

The good news is that today, more than ever before, an increasing proportion of women all over the world receive a college or university education. This is a revolutionary feat considering that in the early years of the twentieth century it was very unusual for women to go on to college. Indeed, women were systematically denied entrance into institutions of higher learning. Opponents to women's entrance into higher education have argued that women's brains are not sufficiently developed to profit from advanced learning, women's proper sphere is the home—they do not need college work to perform their duties at home—and women in college classes will interfere with the ability of men to study.

These arguments still surface. For instance, Islamic fundamentalists in Egypt and Algeria have been battling with Islamic moderates to require female students to wear the hijab, or Islamic head scarf. They also have pushed for female students to move out of dormitories and live at home. At Cairo University, Islamists have succeeded in instituting a ruling that male and female students must ride in separate buses on university trips. In Saudi Arabia, men are not allowed to instruct female students in person, and therefore, women students must watch lectures on closed-circuit television (Bollag, 1994). In traditional cultures, advocates of women's education have found that they achieve greater success by emphasizing how higher education for women will enhance their family roles, making them more interesting and ·useful to their husbands and better able to educate their children. A majority of women in the teaching profession in most countries has been a further impetus to educate women.

The experience of women students in universities in much of the developed world, for example, throughout Europe and the United States, has been remarkably similar. Their numbers are increasing, and commonly one-half or more of undergraduates are women. However, there is considerable sex segregation by curriculum. In France in 1988, 82.8 percent of candidates for the Baccalaureate in Literature and Philosophy were women but only 3.3 percent of candidates for the Mathematics and Technology option were female (Charles, 1991). In Greece, educational reform resulted in a dramatic rise in female university enrollment, but women students are concentrated in the humanities and social sciences. Kontogiannopoulou-Polydorides (1991) reports that women's limited participation in science and engineering is somewhat based on self-selection. She also notes that women students' achievement level is comparable to that of men students. Female undergraduates outnumber male undergraduates in Sweden but again are underrepresented in the areas of science and technology and overrepresented in teaching, social studies, and nursing (Wernersson, 1991). The segregated curriculum in institutions of higher learning is the educational culmination of gendered socialization, and it leads to gender-segregated employment patterns. The challenge for women is twofold: on the one hand, all areas of study and work must be made accessible to both sexes, and on the other hand, women's specialties must be valued, respected, and rewarded.

ROLE MODELS IN EDUCATION

Teachers themselves provide role models for students, and the teaching profession has offered advancement to women in developed countries since the nineteenth century. Teaching was seen as an occupation suited to women because it combined employment with child care. Female teachers, who are also role models, predominate in the lower grades. For example, in the mid-1980s, the proportion of female teachers at the preschool levels was above 90 percent in England, France, Ireland, Greece, and Sweden and above 70 percent for primary levels in these countries. Although women constitute the majority of teachers of young children, the majority of administrators in primary schools are men, and as the grade level of education increases, the number of women teachers decreases (Wilson, 1991).

The number of women faculty at the university level rarely exceeds 25 percent; women faculty are often clustered into traditionally female subject areas (e.g., languages, humanities, and nursing) and tend to be at the bottom of the academic hierarchy. The number of full professors in most universities in North America and Europe during the 1980s and 1990s was and remains under 10 percent. The educational structure sends an overwhelming message of the limits of female power. This message is internalized to students of both sexes and contributes to a reinforcement of male dominance in the world of work and other public institutions.

GENDER SEGREGATION OF THE LABOR FORCE

The extensive practice of channeling women into female-dominated jobs and professions is correlated with wage disparity, low mobility, low job security, and the lack of fringe benefits. A cross-cultural similarity exists in the types of occupations filled by female workers, with notable exceptions. An extensive study of twelve industrialized countries found that women predominate in clerical, service, low prestige sales, and select professional areas. They are less likely to be managers or administrators (Roos, 1985). In Sweden, 95 percent of practical nurses, 100 percent of domestic helpers, and 98 percent of counter clerks and cashiers are women, and in Finland, 94 percent of clerical workers are women (Stockard and Johnson, 1992). In Hungary, 100 percent of the typists and wage clerks are women. The Organization for Economic Cooperation and Development reported that between 1975 and 1985, women filled 50 to 80 percent of all service jobs in twenty-four nations (United Nations, 1991a).

Medicine is often regarded as an appropriate form of work for women since it is an extension of the nurturing role. But, within this profession, women often assume subordinate or lower echelon positions. In the United States, 96 percent of nurses are women, while only about 16 percent of physicians are women. Female physicians, pharmacists, and dentists are more common in European countries than in the United States. In Poland, 82.1 percent of dentists and 86.8 percent of pharmacists were women in 1985-1986 (Szydlowski and Dudziak, 1991). Approximately three-quarters of all doctors are women in the former Soviet Union, and this fact has long been used to signify sex equality. However, the control and prestige of doctors in Russia and the former Soviet Union is considerably lower than it is in the United States (Stockard and Johnson, 1992).

Employment in the media industry, particularly television, is extremely important because, similar to teaching, the decisional nature and the visibility of the roles affect perceptions of viewers regarding women's capability and authority. Wilson reports that 60 percent of the women employed in European television in 1986 were in clerical positions, while women constituted only 4 percent of technicians, 26 percent of middle-level management, and 7 percent of boards of directors. Women were depicted on screen in a narrow range of roles, and women newscasters were younger than their male counterparts and chosen for a favorable appearance as determined by cultural standards (Wilson, 1991).

Gender segregation in the workforce is, by itself, an inadequate explanation for women's lower pay. The ideology of male superiority and the corresponding mythology about appropriate gender roles causes most societies to devalue female-dominated jobs. Any extensive remedy will not only train and hire more females for nontraditional occupations, but will also work to enhance the image and value of female-dominated areas.

PREJUDICE, STEREOTYPES, AND DISCRIMINATION

Women in the workplace all too often find that they are treated as women first and as workers second. Men, and even women with one another, make assumptions about the capabilities of women based on social learning experiences and gender as it is defined within the total cultural context. Although there is some cultural variation regarding which traits are masculine and which are feminine, managerial roles and other work roles associated with power and authority are heavily identified with characteristics considered masculine—aggression, dominance, risk taking, and being firm and just. Many societies expect men to be naturally better suited for powerful roles, and if a particular woman excels or shows leadership potential, she is often deemed "masculine." Feminine characteristics (e.g., nurturance, sexuality, helplessness, emotionality) are applied to most women in the workplace and serve to undermine the respect they receive and the power they can attain. U.S. studies of gender and managerial style show there are few work behavior differences between women and men, but behavior is viewed through the lens of gender. Women are caught in a no-win situation: if they are too tough, they are not feminine; if they are too feminine, they are not tough enough (Franklin and Sweeney, 1988).

The effects of stereotyping can be seen in every country, but Russia, with the collapse of the Soviet Union and economic crisis, provides an account of changing female stereotypes and shows that the ideology of the new Russian "democracy" is not necessarily liberating for women. The Soviet Union had officially enshrined sex equality, and their propaganda boasted of women as workers and comrades. Khotkina (1994) reports that this image was never accurate, and further, women's labor force participation was engineered by the government depending on need. Much of the work assigned to women was heavy, boring, and monotonous. However, she notes that current work conditions for women in Russia are worse. Today, unemployment is a women's issue, with 70 to 80 percent of the registered unemployed being female.

The stereotype of the unfeminine woman comrade worker is being replaced with familiar Western models of sexy and subordinate images. There is a negative connotation associated with feminism. Sexual harassment in the workplace is rampant in today's Russia, with job advertisements specifying youth, sex appeal, and "no inhibitions" as criteria for employment (Khotkina, 1994). According to a 1994 *New York Times* article, most Russian men dismiss the issue of harassment as a Western hang-up, and most Russian women shrug it off as an "unpleasant fact of life" (Stanley, 1994, p. 8).

ENCOURAGING TRENDS

Women's Enterprises

Women, especially in the developing world, make up a significant number of self-employed "microvendors." In the past, these women have been unable to obtain credit to expand their businesses because many are illiterate and/or lack necessary collateral. In 1976, a rural banking project designed to help microventures in Bangladesh became so successful that it has spread to developing and developed countries alike.

The Grameen Bank, as it came to be called, has extended credit to women from Zambia to Appalachia and, in the process, has extended its banking concept to other lending institutions. For example, Women's World Banking (WWB) was formed in 1979 to lend global support for women's business efforts and exigency matters such as workshops on health care and balancing work and family. Women in solidarity groups, with five- to eight-member vendors, are good candidates for credit. Lenders have greater confidence in the group mechanism and believe that members offer each other motivation and assistance. The repayment rate has been excellent.

In Latin America, successful ventures by women have taken place in Ecuador, Bolivia, Columbia, and the Dominican Republic (Berger and Buvinic, 1989). An illustration of a particularly successful program has been the H-P Women's Development Company in Zambia. Besides providing women opportunities for credit, investment, training, and employment, H-P also provides legal services, child care, and housing (McDonnell, Himunyanga-Phiri, and Tembo, 1993). The collective experience with women's enterprises has been extremely positive and establishes the foundation for women's greater empowerment and independence.

Changing the Workplace—Policies and Legislation

Declaring equality in the workplace through ratification of United Nations' conventions (e.g., the 1960 Convention Concerning Discrimination in respect to Employment and Occupation) or governmental antidiscrimination legislation provides no guarantee that sexist practices will be eliminated. Legal measures are only effective if they are strictly enforced and they will be strictly enforced only if there is societal commitment to the principles of sex equality. Japan has implemented successive legal reforms toward sex equality in the Japanese labor force. Presently, Japanese women are well educated and usually become employed as young adults, although not often for career positions. They frequently interrupt their employment for marriage and motherhood and return when children are older. The result of this pattern and discriminatory practices is that the wage gap in Japan is one of the greatest worldwide. A 1985 Equal Employment Act was called a step in the right direction but did little to remedy the situation as there were no consequences for violators of the law (Brinton, 1994). In contrast, an Equal Pay Act passed in Great Britain in 1970 threatened employers with negative penalties for violation. The result was a 19 percent increase in women's wages (Zabalza and Tzannatoes, 1994).

Sweden has legislated work policies considered by many to represent a model of what is needed to bridge the wage gap. The evolution of their system clearly illustrates how change in the workplace may be influenced by the entry of women workers. The present policies were the result of intensive debate during the 1960s, in which many policymakers believed the gender structure was detrimental to men as well as women and that work and personal life had to be considered simultaneously.

Powerful trade union influences and relative economic property are two factors closing the wage gap in Sweden. Women earn roughly 90 percent of what men make. There are many concessions made to parents of both sexes. Those with children under eight may reduce their work hours to six instead of eight; parental leave (usually taken by the mother) following the birth of a baby may extend to nine months at 90 percent of earnings and job protection; Swedish fathers are permitted up to a ten-day allowance after a birth to share home responsibilities; and either parent may take up to sixty days leave per year for caregiving. Many men do not take advantage of these leave opportunities, and studies show that career concerns may be a big factor (Sidel, 1987). The Swedish system has not revolutionized gender roles, but it has made it much easier for women to balance work and family. This example and similar workplace changes for corporate and government employees in much of the developed world raises questions about which accommodations are best for women workers and whether these options will result in real equality.

FUTURE CHALLENGES

A top priority to improve women's status and self-esteem as global workers is to expand the definition of "economically active" to include all the productive paid and unpaid work that women do. Communities must begin brainstorming ways to reduce the drudgery of the day-to-day work largely performed by women. This can only be done through a focused effort beginning with the realities of work and dedicated to equal sharing among all people. Its foundation rests on the premise of equal distribution of goods and services and therefore will always be hampered in a competitive market economy.

Women's continued strides in education are vital for improving their work circumstances as well as boosting their leadership potential. In this regard, efforts should be made to close the literacy gap; girls should be enrolled in all levels of education along with boys, and hidden sex discrimination should be eliminated. Within the educational structure, textbooks should convey messages of strong, capable females, and women in the teaching profession should be promoted to administrative positions. Higher education presents an opportunity for the tenure of competent women professors. Positive female role models and mentors are a key to future workplace equality.

Legislation to guarantee fair hiring, promotional opportunities, pay equity, parental leave, and child care is important to an equitable and humane work environment. This legislation needs the support of society. As the formal workplace embraces women employees in all positions, unfavorable stereotypes will be replaced with favorable ones. Financial security for women will improve women's global status and provide a better quality of life to women and their families.

SUMMARY

Women's work holds up more than half the sky, but much of it is unpaid, underpaid, and devalued. Often women's work as "helpers," homemakers, and volunteers is not even defined as work. Within the official labor force in every country, a persistent wage gap exists. Reasons include blatant discrimination, family obligations, less or different education, and segregated work. Stereotypes influence the type of jobs and careers assigned to women. More privileged women may get ahead or keep afloat by hiring other women to clean their houses or care for their children. Multinational corporations make profits by utilizing women's cheaper labor. This process rests both on gender and global economic hierarchy. Reports indicate that women are often successful as entrepreneurs; microlending strategies work because women are industrious and repay their loans. Employment advances for women rest on eradicating illiteracy, opening up all academic levels and specialities to girls and women, and providing legal tools for fair employment.

KEY WORDS

Cottage industry

Economically active

Export processing zones (EPZs)

Feminization of poverty

Global Assembly Line

Gross National Product (GNP)

Home-based production

International Labor Office (ILO)

International monetary fund (IMF)

International Wages for Housework Campaign (IWFH)

Multinational or transnational corporations (TNCs)

North American Free Trade Agreement (NAFTA)

Sex-segregated work

United System of National Accounts (UNSNA)

Wage gap

The World Bank

Chapter 5

Women and Health Care

INTRODUCTION

Women's health concerns and available health care are critical and substantiated global concerns.[1] Historically, the symptoms of illness and disease among women have been delegitimized as a serious consideration or as a source for critical exploration in research. This lack of response to the health needs of women is widely documented.[2] The impact that poverty and malnutrition have on women's worldwide morbidity and mortality across the life course is staggering (Jacobson, 1993). These factors create the conditions for disease development and increase the prevalence of death due to disease.

Women across the globe face health concerns that affect their quality of life. Although no women are free from the risk of disease development, the incidence of specific illnesses varies throughout the world. Within developing regions, disease and premature mortality are frequently related to inadequate nutrition, inadequate health care resources, and inadequate economic and environmental structures.[3]

Empirical researchers have addressed the impact of inadequate nutrition and environmental resources on the health of women in developing areas. Evidence ties health problems to poor nutrition in many developing areas. Inadequate diet, observed in most developing regions, leads to stunted growth (WHO, 1992). This lack of optimal size influences the development of obstructed labor and maternal mortality. Stunted growth is a result of childhood protein-energy malnutrition. Researchers estimate that 450 million adult women are stunted in growth from protein-energy malnutrition during childhood (The World Bank, 1994). The highest levels of malnutrition are among women in South Asia; however, women in Africa and other developing areas fare little better.

In South Asia, 60 percent of the women of reproductive age are both underweight and suffer from anemia (WHO, 1992). Within developing areas, 55 percent of pregnant women and 44 percent of all women suffer from nutritional anemia, while only 17 percent of pregnant women and 12 percent of all women in developed regions face anemia (Ibid.).

Why is malnutrition so pervasive in many developing regions? The malnutrition that many women face throughout developing areas is a result of a number of related factors. Developing areas are characterized by an inadequate food supply. Regardless of the actual food available to families, communities' "male preference" frequently disadvantages women, making them the last to eat or not a priority in the allocation of food. Developing areas frequently lack effective ways to store food for long periods of time; therefore, food is more likely to become unfit for human consumption. Women in many developing areas have restricted accessibility to education,[4] thus knowledge of nutritious foods is limited.

Finally, many cultures within developing areas maintain taboos against nutritious foods, effectively curtailing access to such foods. Poor nutrition and anemia not only contribute to complications during childbirth, but also reduce women's productivity within their communities, decrease their resistance to infectious agents, and increase their susceptibility to numerous debilitating conditions.[5] These issues also impact economically disadvantaged women in developed areas where lack of income makes appropriate nutrition and health care less likely.

Women and Smoking

Morbidity patterns among women worldwide are also a consequence of environmental hazards, substance abuse, and life choices.[6] Smoking patterns in developed regions offer a dramatic example. Cigarette smoking is currently identified as the major single cause of disease and premature mortality in developing regions (Graham, 1994). Estimates indicate that 20 percent of all deaths in developed countries are attributable to smoking.[7] In addition to its links with coronary heart disease, chronic obstructive pulmonary diseases, cancer of the mouth, esophagus, pharynx and larynx, smoking has been implicated as a primary cause of lung cancer in developed and developing regions (Peto et al., 1994).

The British Secretary of Health indicates that 80 percent of the lung cancer deaths in Britain are the result of smoking (Graham, 1994). Although smoking behavior and lung cancer rates are declining among males in many developed regions, they continue to increase among females. Over the last twenty years, death rates of women from lung cancer have more than doubled in Japan, Norway, Poland, Sweden, and the United Kingdom. Dramatic increases of 200 percent have been noted among women in Australia, Denmark, and New Zealand. In the United States and Canada, women have experienced a phenomenal increase of 300 percent mortality due to lung cancer in this same time period (Smyke, 1991).

Although smoking is increasing among women in developed countries, women in disadvantaged categories within capitalistic hierarchies are revealing even greater levels of smoking behavior (Graham, 1994). Smoking also affects the reproductive health of women. Women who smoke are at higher risk for miscarriage, low birth weight babies, and early onset menopause. Few feminists offer an analysis of the increasing rate of smoking among women in developed areas. Traditional patterns still maintain smoking as a male activity in many developing regions. Issues of equal access to smoking has complicated the development of a clear argument concerning smoking behavior. Thus, by applauding women's rights to smoke (if they wish to), feminists expose women to the risk of developing lung cancer and other related disorders.

Women and Cancer

Worldwide breast cancer continues to be a major health concern for women.[8] Lung cancer is replacing breast cancer as the leading cause of death for women in many developed areas. However, breast cancer continues to take a staggering toll on many women. Among women within developed regions (particularly those aged forty-five to sixty-four years), breast cancer continues to be a leading cause of death. The issue of breast cancer has benefited from a great deal of feminist discussion and debate. Included in these discussions is a recognition that it causes both physical trauma and emotional distress.[9] The emotional trauma is sometimes particularly intense because the breast is closely connected to both breast-feeding and sexual allure. Thus the loss or disfigurement of a breast signals deficiency in certain culturally defined attributes of woman-hood, as well as the reminder that a greater risk, death by breast cancer, is a possibility.[10] For women who have not had children (including lesbian women without children) and women who have postponed childbirth until their late thirties or beyond, the risk of breast cancer is doubled (Travis, 1989).

Cancer continues to be a serious health concern in both developed and developing areas; however, the greater likelihood of maternal mortality and death by infectious disease in developing areas makes it less likely for those women to die of cancer. Breast and lung cancer take a great toll on women in developed areas, but women in developing areas are more likely to contract cervical cancer (WHO, 1992). Developing areas commonly do not have appropriate diagnosis and treatment procedures for cervical cancer. In many cases, cervical cancer is diagnosed in the latest stages or upon death. The morbidity and mortality patterns worldwide are related to a host of factors specific to the regions under investigation.

Reproductive Health

Worldwide, forty to sixty million women resort to having an abortion to end an unwanted pregnancy. Estimates suggest that 125,000 to 200,000 female deaths occur annually as a direct result of unsafe abortions (Dixon-Mueller, 1993b). Abortion-related mortality is highest in countries that do not legally sanction abortion or limit access to safe abortion services. Henshaw and Van Hort (1992) report that worldwide accessibility to abortion services ranges from no restrictions to a total prohibition. This report reveals that 40 percent of all countries have no restrictions on abortions, 23 percent permit abortions for social or medical reasons, 12 percent permit abortion when the life or health of the mother or fetus is at risk, and 25 percent only to save the life of the mother or child, or it is not permitted. Developing areas of the world tend to be characterized by fewer restrictions, but new battles are fought each year to maintain lower levels of restrictions. The fact that 500,000 women die worldwide each year in childbirth underscores the importance of these issues, and 99 percent of these women are in developing countries (Koblinsky, Campbell, and Harlow, 1993). In Africa, 1 in 21 women have a lifetime chance of dying from pregnancy-related causes; in Asia, 1 in 54; and in Latin America, 1 in 73; while in Northern Europe, the lifetime chances are 1 in 10,000 (Jacobson, 1991).

Reproductive tract infections (RTIs) create serious consequences for women. These infections fall into three general categories: (1) sexually transmitted diseases (STDs) (HIV/AIDS, syphilis, gonorrhea, etc.), (2) bacterial vaginosis caused by overpopulation of vaginal organisms, and (3) infections that are caused by the introduction of bacterial or other organisms into the reproductive tract through unhygienic practices. The consequences of RTIs include death (as caused by HIV/AIDS or untreated syphilis), infertility, chronic pain, pelvic inflammatory disease, or complications during pregnancy and delivery. These infections are seen worldwide but are common in all developing countries. Younis and Zuray (1993) report that 50 percent of a community sample of Egyptian women had one or more kinds of reproductive tract disease. Many women throughout the world are further disadvantaged due to the lack of recognized symptoms associated with some STDs. Thus, women may not know they are infected and therefore do not seek medical attention.

CASE STUDIES

Three case studies are presented here describing the health care concerns of three diverse groups of women that are attempting to grapple with how to obtain and sustain adequate and appropriate health care for themselves and their families. These women are recipients, participants, and also providers of health care. Health care advocates within the spheres described here are individuals and countries who are struggling with the demands of life-threatening concerns, as they make progress toward meeting the health care needs as defined by women, communities, and their families (Pitts, McMaster, and Wilson, 1991).

The death of a mother, particularly in countries that are largely rural, jeopardizes the health of the whole family. Women do much more than domestic work; they are the health promotors, health providers, and health educators of their entire families. Women also hold a central place in the economic production of many communities. The loss of this key figure in the life of the family leaves not only an emotional and familial void, but also a loss of a central producer and the family health coordinator and implementer. In addition to women providing care on an informal basis, the majority of formal health care providers worldwide are also women, although they are disproportionately located in lower status positions with less financial remuneration (Koblinsky, Timyan, and Gay, 1993).

This chapter, through the use of case studies, explores key aspects of health care in three vastly different areas of the world. The first case study addresses the formal and informal health care systems in rural Zimbabwe, the second case study explores the health care available for women in Norway, and the third examines health care and the use of the Family Doctor Program within Cuba. Finally, the importance of health promotion and education in all countries is discussed.

The contrasts between these areas provide a context to understand the diverse needs of women worldwide, as they try to gain needed health care for themselves and their families. The common thread in these examples is the search for needed health resources. The dissimilarity is evidenced by the societal distinctions and varied structures women encounter when seeking needed services. Thus the customs, health beliefs, and the political climates modulate much of the experiences of these women.

HEALTH CARE FOR ZIMBABWEAN WOMEN

The health care needs of the Zimbabwean population were seen as an immediate priority by the newly independent nation in 1980. As the development of the present health care system was sought, the new government attempted to make the most out of the lengthy legacy of colonial discrimination. (See Table 5.1 for facts concerning Zimbabwe.) The definition of the needed changes within the health care system consists of: (1) a reallocation of health care services in order to serve the needs of all the population; (2) a need to address the unique demands of the urban and the rural majority population; (3) the necessity for additional health care providers and facilities at all levels; and (4) the decision to use traditional and indigenous health care workers who had historically provided health care to the indigenous population of Zimbabwe.[11]

TABLE 5.1. Facts Concerning Zimbabwe

Population:	11,423,175
Birthrate:	31.7 births per 1,000 population per year
Death rate:	19.0 deaths per 1,000 population per year
Fertility rate:	3.9 children per woman
Ethnic divisions:	98% African
	Shona 71%
	Nbebele 16%
	other 11%
	1% white
	1% other
Official languages:	English, Shona, Sindebele
Government:	parliamentary democracy
Independence:	from United Kingdom, April 18, 1980

Source: *World Fact Book*. Washington, DC: Superintendent of Documents, U.S. Government Printing Office, 1997.

The health care needs of Zimbabwean women and their children were a critical focus in the expansion and development of an effective health care system. In 1980, the mortality due to problems associated with pregnancy was 170 per 100,000 women (Mhloyi, 1992). This rate, which is far from the highest (2,000 per 100,000 in Ethiopia) was nonetheless a staggering loss (Turshen, 1991b). This astounding rate was a consequence of several related factors. Women were plagued with the "four too's."[12] The lives of these women were and continue to be frequently characterized by "too" many births, "too" closely spaced, and either "too" early or "too" late in life (Mhloyi, 1992). In addition, when these women prepared for birth, they were frequently attended and assisted in delivery by a traditional village midwife. These women possessed a great deal of skill and knowledge concerning normal births but attended these births utilizing traditional practices that were potentially life threatening for both the mother and the new child.

Many Zimbabwean women, similar to many of their sisters in other developing countries, engaged in hard labor in the field from sunup to sundown with little control over the fruits of this labor.

Women were, and continue to be, the primary producers of Zimbabwean agricultural products (Lowenson, 1991). The contribution made by these women is estimated at 80 percent of the farming in rural Zimbabwe. Life in the rural areas for these women consists of intense agricultural labor, serial births, and surviving the day-to-day burdens of subsistence living. This combination places women at risk for a host of diseases during the life span, as well as for complications during pregnancy and childbirth.

In the seventeen years since the success of the revolution and the establishment of a health care system that hoped to address the needs of Zimbabwean women and families, several significant changes have occurred in both formal and informal health sectors, thus affecting the health standing of the Zimbabwean population.

The Formal System

The formal health care system had critical shortcomings and unequal distribution of health care facilities among provinces at the beginning of independence.[13] The old system was inappropriate to address the needs and concerns of the country because it had developed unequally in a number of ways that required immediate attention. Most of the health facilities were located in areas that were not accessible to the majority of the population. Particularly, they were not accessible for the majority population within the countryside, but they were also not equally accessible for individuals in all communities within urban areas. The previous segregated health care arena had created a system in which the majority of the population had poor or no health facilities available. As housing developed in high density areas, appropriate health care facilities were constructed to provide the necessary services to this portion of the population.

To meet the heavy needs of all the population, a three-tier level of formal health care was established. Central, provincial, and district level facilities were established to address these needs. In some cases, already existing health units were renovated and used at the various levels, and in other situations, particularly for rural areas, new rural health centers or clinics were built. The primary focus was to cover the population's health care needs with appropriate health structures located throughout the country.

Hand in hand with the establishment of facilities was the rapid need to train persons to work within health care services. The education of these practitioners was an additional focus. In achieving this goal, Zimbabwe rapidly trained health providers and reached out to other countries for assistance: in particular, Zimbabwe sought training assistance for health professionals in the United Kingdom, the United States, and Scandinavian countries. Many health providers trained abroad; others trained within Zimbabwe, and foreign practitioners came to Zimbabwe to provide services.

Health Promotion and Education

Health care administrators quickly recognized that health needs for women were much more than having access to health care practitioners. As Turshen (1991c) states "health care is one of the first social services offered by every independent government, whether to prove that it can carry on the services provided by the former regime or to distinguish itself by democratizing the health system" (p. 206). Health care, particularly for rural women, is much more involved than merely providing formal health care services. Health can only be achieved and maintained by developing a process to ensure healthful food, clean water, a sufficiently sanitary environment, and protection from disease carriers within the environment. This difficult aspect of health care requires health education and health promotion.

The promotion of health and the education concerning these issues permeates the formal health care system. This plan can most clearly be seen in two aspects. On the district level, clinic nurses and other health practitioners hold sessions to educate the community on health-related manners. Much of this education focuses on maternal and child health, as well as on appropriate sanitation. Both formal and informal sessions are held to teach appropriate sanitation practices, cooking skills, warning signs of problems during pregnancy, signs indicating childhood illnesses, the importance of immunizations, etc. In this way, the formal health sector provides women the opportunity, with guidance, to explore healthier habits and healthful practices.

District level prevention became the focus for preventative medicine and allied health work. In order to achieve this level of prevention, clinics developed a "supermarket" philosophy. Families are able to come to a clinic en masse without an appointment. During a visit, each member of the family chooses services they need from the clinic. In this way, families can make one trip to the clinic and obtain multiple services. Therefore, a mother can have a prenatal visit, while children get immunizations, a father obtains a prostate check, and an elder has his vision screened. In this manner, the health care system respects the integrity of the family, provides maximum coverage to all members, and only necessitates one trip to the clinic, which may be far from the home village. As one woman awaiting treatment in a clinic in Matabeland South stated:

> We walked all morning to get to Natisha clinic. My baby needs to be looked at because her eyes are red and my boy's ankle has been hurting and he needs shots. . . . I'm going to get an exam, too . . .[14]

Although they will spend most of the day awaiting various services, they will obtain multiple levels of preventative and acute care.

The second aspect of health promotion has been the establishment of allied community health workers. Assisting in preventative care are health care workers who perform health promotion and education on a village-to-village basis. These village community workers are all female. When asked why the village community workers (VCWs) are all women, one district nurse echoed a repeated theme.[15] She stated:

> The message is better received in the community from a woman; people don't want men coming into their houses and villages talking about health and personal matters.[16]

These village community workers are paid a small fee to provide direct services within their communities, to develop practical projects (putting in toilets, wells, testing water, etc.), and to engage in health promotion activities for families (checking on immunizations, teaching first aid, encouraging healthier habits, discussing contraceptive possibilities, etc.). In all aspects, these female allied health workers provide ongoing and intense health education among their communities. Village community workers work long hours for little pay. They work within their own villages approximately five to eight hours a day but are typically on call twenty-four hours a day. These women are salaried governmental employees and are paid seventy Zimbabwean dollars a month.[17] The common complaints expressed by these women were that they worked such long hours with so little pay and that they felt unheard when they expressed their concerns to their supervisors.

The supervisors of these women are the ward community coordinators. These positions are always held by men. Mr. M., a forty-five-year-old ward community coordinator described why village community workers were paid only seventy dollars a month: "It was always to be a part-time job. They are not required to be available all the time."[18]

However, regardless of the assertion that these women were part-time employees, the reality was quite different. The community perceived these women to be accessible and full time. As representatives who were nominated and voted for by their village peers as appropriate to be VCWs, these women feel obliged to perform twenty-four hours a day.[19]

Central to health promotion for women in Zimbabwe has been a focus on contraceptive use. Zimbabwean women, as in many interfamily decisions, have little power in deciding if they will use contraceptives.[20] Both the need to have many workers in agricultural areas and the male domination of female sexuality and reproduction have created a climate where serial births are common (Lowenson, 1991; Mhloyi, 1990). Thus, birth control promotion is woven within a set of contradictory and pervasive traditional beliefs.

The Zimbabwean government supports a cadre of workers to promote contraception within communities as a means of spacing children and as a means of enhancing both the life of the mother and the children within the family system. The contraception device promoted throughout the country is the oral contraceptive (birth control pills). The Ministry of Health reports that 90 percent of the population has information concerning contraception, but it is not known what percentage actually uses contraceptive devices either effectively or ineffectively.

Although contraception information can be obtained at all levels of the formal health care system, the community-based distributor (CBD) provides direct contraception information to women in the community. These positions (CBDs) are considered full-time allied health positions. CBDs move back and forth between villages discussing and dispensing oral contraceptives. These women travel across large distances to work ten hours a day for a monthly salary of $500 (Z). The CBDs carry sample pills, use screening mechanisms to ascertain whether women are likely candidates for oral contraceptives, and dispense pills.

Women receiving oral contraceptives through the CBDs are referred to the local district clinic and are encouraged to develop a relationship with that clinic. These CBDs are the frontline persons in dispensing contraception, especially in rural Zimbabwe. The CBDs also have condoms and are trained to discuss their use with men and women as both birth control and safe-sex devices. On interviewing several CBDs, one stated, "I am prepared to talk to men, but only a few want to talk about condom use." Thus, as throughout the world, birth control is a woman's issue that is seldom discussed by men within the family system.

Informal Health Care

The informal health care system has a rich history that far precedes the existence of the formal system. This system historically was the only health care vehicle available for indigenous Zimbabwean women. As with many other countries, these informal structures coexist today with formal health care.[21]

Two major practitioners within the informal health care system are traditional midwives and traditional healers. In the early years, postindependence, the Health Ministry decided it must employ all possible sectors in providing adequate health care to its population. Thus, traditional practitioners were explored as adjunct providers within the system. The interaction and use of midwives is a success story; however, the use of traditional healers has been much less successful.

Midwives

Efforts have been made to provide training to the women operating as traditional midwives in Zimbabwe. This encourages the country to recognize and appreciate the contributions of these women to the communities they work in but also allows the formal health system to provide traditional midwives with information that would create the climate for a healthy birth atmosphere for both mothers and children.[22] Beginning around 1982 and continuing, albeit slowly, today and funded by governmental monies and international sources, traditional midwives have been provided with training and information. These one-week training sessions, provided by district nurses, are centered around: (1) traditional practices that were not healthful; (2) the development of sanitary practices for both the midwife and the mother she is attending; (3) the ability to screen problematic births before getting to the delivery stage; (4) the ability to recognize problems that would require a transport to the clinic; (5) the development of skills to care for a newborn and the ability to access afterbirth difficulties for mothers and children; (6) a focus on basic nutrition; (7) a knowledge of normal birth processes and how to enhance the process (management of first-, second-, and third-stage labor); (8) handling minor problems during pregnancy and delivery (e.g., vomiting, headaches); (9) umbilical cord care; (10) family planning; (11) recognition of STDs and AIDS; and (12) record keeping and use of the midwifery kit.

After training, traditional midwives (TMs) received from the government a birth pouch (midwifery kit) that contained midwifery supplies when monies were available. Since this training began, deaths due to pregnancy complications have decreased 50 percent (Mhloyi, 1992). Traditional midwives interviewed reported no deaths since their training but spoke solemnly of the women who died or had serious complications earlier in their practice.

Midwives who have received training operate as an informal resource center for TMs not yet trained, providing further coverage of the information imparted by the formal health care sector. In describing how this resource center works, one fifty-nine-year-old midwife stated, "Everyone in the village knows when you've had your training and the TMs come to us. They want to know what we know. Especially when a mother is having problems, then they come to me and say: 'What would you do?' and 'What did that nurse tell me to do when she's bleeding this much?'" In this way, the knowledge that is acquired by one midwife is shared with others, allowing the village to further benefit from the upgraded training of any individual midwife.

Comparing Traditional Midwives and Trained Traditional Midwives

In the fall of 1992, sixty-one traditional midwives were interviewed in a southern province of Zimbabwe concerning the nature of traditional midwifery today and how those who have been trained have altered their practices. Table 5.2 indicates a summary of the traditional practices described by these midwives, and Table 5.3 provides a summary of practices after training.

Traditional midwifery, as described by these women, seldom provides care before the onset of labor contractions. Midwives indicate they often knew women in their village were pregnant, but they had no conversations or interactions with them before the woman in labor needed someone to assist her birth. As one sixty-year-old midwife who had been practicing for twenty years stated, "I see women and I know they are pregnant and I pay attention that they will be giving birth soon, but I wait to be called at the birth." When

TABLE 5.2. Traditional Birth Process

1.	A call comes to a traditional midwife (TM) that a woman is in labor and a midwife is needed. Frequently, the TM has never checked this woman before but is generally aware that she is a pregnant woman within her village.
2.	On arrival, the TM prepares a birthing spot in a private place, usually the kitchen, by:
	a. spreading an old sack on the floor and
	b. spreading cow dung or mud on top of the sack.
3.	She assists the birthing mother in squatting (sometimes with the help of a stick) over the prepared area.
4.	After the birth of the child, the TM cuts the cord with a sharp object and then puts ashes or cow dung on the umbilical stump.
5.	She buries the placenta by tradition of the village, usually in the corner of the birthing room or behind the door of the same room.
6.	The TM announces the birth of the baby to the men and the rest of the family.
7.	She attends to the needs of mother and child until mother feels strong (which includes household chores, other children, cooking, etc.).

asked if there are exceptions, they stated that they talk more frequently with family members, especially their daughters, and provide prenatal care and consultation for relatives and close friends. These sessions centered around questions and concerns that were plaguing the pregnant women.

Midwives, traditionally, are called to the birth by a member of the family—the mother of the woman giving birth, an older child, or a neighbor. When the TM arrives at the home, she prepares the birthing spot. The location of the birth is often the kitchen or food area and is always an area considered private. Typically the TM and the birthing mother are alone, but on occasion, the birthing woman's mother or another woman may be present. If others are present, they generally are merely observers and take no real part in what is going on during the birth.

Birthing customs varied somewhat within rural villages within Zimbabwe, but all prepared the birthing spot by laying something on the area, a piece of cloth or a sack was frequently named. Customarily, cow dung or mud was spread on top of the birthing area. When one midwife was asked why this was done, she stated that "We used to believe that it was necessary to absorb the liquid from the woman, but now since training, we've been taught that that's not the best way."

After preparing the area, women are assisted by the TM to either sit or squat over the prepared area to birth the baby. Sometimes, a stick is used to assist the mother in supporting herself while squatting. Traditionally, after the baby is born onto this area, the cord is cut with a sharp object and either ashes or cow dung are placed on the stump to dry the cord.

Following the birth the baby is wrapped in a cloth and given to the mother; then the TM buries the placenta in an area within the home. Midwives report the placenta is often buried behind the door of the room in which the birth occurred, although this ritual varies between villages and communities.

The TM announces the arrival of the child after the birth. The midwives' rituals for announcing the new birth vary tremendously. One TM stated, "I go to where the father and family are and say the child and mother are well, then return to tend to them." Another midwife spoke of going to the hut where the men were after a birth.

She then kneeled down and began to chant louder and louder until someone came and looked at her. That was the sign that they knew all was well and she, without saying a word, returned to care for the mother. Another midwife described that usually a female member of the family would come and wait outside of the hut as the birth neared and upon hearing the baby's cry would come in and see that all was well, and she and the midwife would together announce the arrival of the infant to the family. The midwife's specific role varies in the announcement of the birth, but in all cases, she has a central role. After the family is aware of the birth, the TM spends hours, days, and sometimes weeks caring for and assisting the new mother. The amount of time depends on the needs of the new mother and the assistance she has within her family network.

The description of the birth process after training is a reflection of a blend of traditional beliefs and conventional medical practices. Midwives begin visiting the pregnant women early within their pregnancies (as early as possible). During these visits, midwives discuss with women the screening process and the focus on healthful habits, nutrition, and cleanliness.

The Zimbabwean Ministry of Health estimates that 50 to 60 percent of traditional midwives in Zimbabwe have received this additional training. These women are advised to send women who are birthing their first child (primigravida) to the clinic for delivery, as well as those who have had five or more children. These women are at the greatest risks for complications. These higher-risk births are only handled by trained midwives in emergencies.

In preparation for the birth, once called, trained midwives prepare a clean spot in a private place. They first typically lay down a sack and after washing their hands thoroughly (and wearing rubber gloves when available), they assist the mother in the traditional squatting position.

When the baby arrives, they cut and tie the cord, check the vital signs of the baby, and give the child to the mother. They discard the placenta following the traditions of the mother and her family. Again, the traditional midwife announces the birth given the traditions of the village. After the birth, the TM stays with the new mother to attend to her postdelivery needs. Typically the next day, the midwife goes with the mother and new child to the clinic to register the birth and obtain any advice the mother needs from the district nurses. The TM attends to the needs of the new mother and child as long as she is needed.

These informal female health providers receive a variety of forms of payment for their work as midwives. Within rural communities, money is seldom the form of payment. When money is exchanged, $1(Z) or $2(Z) is paid to the TM for her services. Most typically, other tokens of appreciation are given. Common payments include a piece of soap, an old maternity dress, or some food or drink.[23] TMs are considered to hold high status in village communities. The trained midwife has been successful in integrating the new knowledge, while maintaining the integrity of the traditional customs concerning birth that were not harmful to the life of the mother or the child (Conway-Turner, 1997).

Traditional Healers

Within both rural and urban areas within Zimbabwe, an alternative to the formal health care system is the traditional healer. These men and women heal by tapping into the collective wisdom of ancestors who hold healing powers and skills. Although a few formal clinics have traditional healers that work within their facilities, most do not. The opposing orientation between the formal health care system and the traditional healer makes it an uncommon alliance. Many Zimbabweans utilize both the formal and informal spheres when facing a health crisis.

The traditional healer describes him/herself as a channel for the traditional information and flow of health care information.[24] Through the use of meditation, prayer, or chanting, these healers engage ancestral spirits to guide them in curing illnesses. Traditional healers are sometimes directed to give herbs to a patient, provide advice on exercise or nutrition, or manipulate the body by massage, stroking, or elongation. Central to the practice of traditional healing is that the cure comes not from the healer but from the ancestors. Both the traditional healer and the formal health care provider view each other with a mixture of curiosity and suspicion.

Women, particularly in the countryside, visit traditional healers. Women in need of care commonly combine and use the advice of both systems. Thus, the Zimbabwean health care system includes a well-developed formal system that continues to make strides and an informal system that at times works in concert with the formal system, but most frequently at odds with it.

Lack of sufficient resources continues to inhibit how well the health care systems can respond to the needs of women and their families. However, Zimbabwe's health care model attempts to use all resources available to them. The formal and informal systems are partners (although not equal partners) in meeting the health care needs of the citizens of Zimbabwe.

HEALTH CARE IN NORWAY

Health care policy within Norway is grounded in the country's overwhelming support for public policies. This support reflects society's norms and values concerning achieving policies that favor the whole population. According to Siem (1986), Norwegian health administration policy tends to be public in nature, uniform in their application, and liberal in their orientation. This philosophy is held in place by a complex and hierarchial bureaucracy that governs and ensures the working of the health administration. (See Table 5.3 for facts concerning Norway.)

TABLE 5.3. Facts Concerning Norway

Population:	4,399,993
Birthrate:	13.3 births per 1,000 population per year
Death rate:	10.2 deaths per 1,000 population per year
Fertility rate:	1.8 children per woman
Ethnic divisions:	Germanic (Nordic, Alpine, and Baltic) Lapps (Sami), 20,000
Official languages:	Norwegian
Government:	constitutional monarchy
Independence:	from Sweden, October 26, 1905

Source: *World Fact Book*. Washington, DC: Superintendent of Documents, U.S. Government Printing Office, 1997.

Coupled with a policy that mandates uniform health coverage is the Norwegian National Insurance that guarantees it:

> The basis of Norwegian National Insurance is that it is a right, not a privilege granted at someone's discretion, to receive support from society when one's welfare is impaired by disease, pregnancy, old age, unemployment or the like. (Siem, 1986)

Coverage of National Health Insurance

The national health insurance is quite broad, covering virtually all persons living within Norway. In addition, it covers employed individuals who live in Norway but hold legal residency elsewhere, as well as citizens of Norway who are temporarily outside of their home country.

Excluded from the national health insurance are individuals and their family members who are residing in Norway but are paid employees of foreign countries or international organizations. For all practical purposes, all Norwegian families are covered by this policy.

Coverage for Families

The coverage provides a blanket of protection for individuals needing medical care. The range of care covered includes physician care of all types, midwifery care, dental treatment, psychological services, and prostheses. Central to the inclusive list is the undergirding philosophy of complete coverage for all members of the family.

Such issues as sick leave and maternity are carefully detailed within the Norwegian plan. Employees are entitled to 100 percent of their gross earned income for sick leave. The first two weeks' payments are paid by the employers, and additional days needed are paid by the national insurance, thus providing comprehensive insurance (Siem, 1986).

Women are entitled to a six-week paid maternity leave postdelivery, regardless of past work history. However, if she was employed six of the last ten months before delivery, she is guaranteed ninety days. Fathers may opt to take paternity leave instead of the mother; however, the maximum period of leave for fathers is sixty days.

Most health care for women, men, and children throughout Norway is provided by a system of "local health stations" located throughout the country. Care is provided in the local health station by a team consisting of a health nurse, a midwife, and a physician. These individuals refer any specialist care that is needed to "area" physiotherapists, psychologists, dentists, pediatricians, or other needed specialists.[25] The major focus of local health stations is on early detection of diseases and prevention. In addition to direct health provision, these providers consult with families and provide training that will enhance prevention (see Table 5.4).

TABLE 5.4. Functions of Norwegian Local Health Stations

1. Monitor growth and development of individuals and families
2. Physical examination by a physician or nurse
3. Immunizations
4. Parental counseling on:
• breast-feeding
• nutrition and eating habits
• general questions concerning child development (e.g., sleep problems, sibling jealousy, etc.)
• lifestyle issues (e.g., smoking, stress)
• health promotion in general
5. Wellness
6. Home visits
7. Individual consultation
8. Group consultation
9. Classes on health-related topics (breast cancer, sexually transmitted diseases, contraception, etc.)
10. Referrals to specialists or allied agents

The focus of the health care services within Norway is not only on prevention, but also on equal access to all individuals. The policies governing such provision allow equal benefits to individuals regardless of gender. For example, the rights provided for parents with sick children apply to both mothers and fathers. These rights include:

- Up to ten days paid leave from work per year to take care of sick children. These ten days are shared between the parents, if they live together.
- If a child is hospitalized, one or two parents may stay the entire hospital stay.
- If a child has a disease that is life threatening, parents may take leave from work with full salary for up to one year.

Although obstacles to access have been eliminated for Norwegian women, some women have greater health care needs because of the class they represent. Norwegian women from lower economic classes have greater health care needs, as they do throughout the world.[26] Reducing access issues is a major step, but tackling issues that contribute to unequal development of disease and biased treatment by the formal system must also be addressed.

Addressing Women's Unmet Needs

Addressing the needs of women within the health care system is a complex process. Central to this process is understanding how women's health concerns are understood and treated by health providers in Norway. Feminists argue that greater numbers of women practitioners in medical care would ensure sensitive physicians to address women's health needs. Although the vast majority of physicians in Norway are male, over two-thirds of the general practice consultation force is female (Malterud, 1992a). Women come into a medical hierarchy that is characterized by overtly expressed male domination. Buxrud (1993) concluded in a recent study that, although the numbers of female physicians are increasing in Norway, these female physicians experience more stress and feel constrained by a male-centered medical model. This is clearly reflected in female physicians' reports of more stress, more work-related health problems, and a higher risk of suicide.

Women as recipients of health care face gender-specific concerns. One concern is the tendency of the medical community to view female distinctiveness as abnormal. The medical management of menopause reflects this tendency. Menopause, a natural course within the life cycle of women, is translated into a hormone deficiency disease.[27] This medicalization of a normal part of women's reproductive life cycle exists throughout Western medicine.

Additionally, the current Norwegian medical model is not sensitive to the medical complaints of most women. Practitioners argue that women's complaints are vague and do not fit valid medical models (Malterud, 1992b). Consequently, women's voices are often ignored as they articulate their health concerns, and these same women are often labeled as hypochondriacs. Incongruence between women's health complaints and connections with established medical criteria are labeled as not authentic and unworthy of medical intervention.

Malterud (1992b) argues that, in order to obtain information to understand what underlying disease is creating the illness symptoms perceived by women, a new questioning approach must be established that is sensitive to gender.

Malterud challenges other women practitioners to use the following strategic guidelines:

- Speak out about women's experiences and observations.
- Speak out loudly as female practitioners about medical ignorance regarding women's health problems.
- Investigate clinical approaches for empowering the voices of female patients.
- Obtain and refine the extensive knowledge about women's illness experienced by female doctors.
- Create research methods capable of obtaining observations of women's medical concerns, and build supportive networks including practitioners and patients.
- Construct a female epistemology that can be communicated convincingly to the medical culture (1992b).

Central to women's health in Norway is understanding social class differences in disease development and empowering women as health care recipients and providers.

WOMEN AND HEALTH CARE IN CUBA

Major changes have taken place within the political, economic, and social fabric of Cuba since the revolution in 1959. The area of health and education has gone through dramatic changes that have been instrumental in improving the access and quality of health care for women in Cuba. The focus on health maintains its energy as both the country and the women of Cuba continue to see health care development and delivery as a priority. (See Table 5.5 for some other facts concerning Cuba.)

Formal Health Care After the Revolution (1960)

The formal health care system in Cuba in 1960 was inadequate in both the quality and quantity of health care facilities available. In 1959, there was only one rural hospital and few polyclinics within the entire country (Catasus, 1988). Thus, the focus on building appropriate health care facilities was absolutely necessary. According to the Cuban Ministry of Public Health, 50 percent of Cuba's 6,000 doctors fled the new socialist country in 1960, creating an inability to deliver sufficient health care services to the Cuban population.

TABLE 5.5. Facts Concerning Cuba

Population:	10,999,041
Birthrate:	13.2 births per 1,000 population per year
Death rate:	7.4 deaths per 1,000 population per year
Fertility rate:	1.5 children per woman
Ethnic divisions:	51% mixed 37% white 11% African descent 1% Chinese
Official language:	Spanish
Government:	Communist
Independence:	1959 Triumph of Communist Revolution

Source: *World Fact Book*. Washington, DC: Superintendent of Documents, U.S. Government Printing Office, 1997.

To fill this health care need, Cuba, spearheaded by the commitment of Fidel Castro, has engaged in an intensive thirty-two-year program to develop a policy that addresses the unmet needs in health care. The advancements within the area of health care are a consequence of a federal policy that has made health care access and quality care issues a priority within Cuba. Unfortunately, the present economic conditions in Cuba have crippled many of these advances.

Cuban health care policy has focused on acquiring doctors and developing health care facilities. The focus on physicians incorporates both quantitative and qualitative changes. In the early 1960s, the Ministry of Health set an ambitious goal to have one physician for every 253 persons. In order to achieve this goal, massive promotional activities began to encourage and demonstrate the importance of physicians for the enhanced quality of life of the Cuban population. As of January 1992, there were 42,000 doctors in Cuba, a substantial gain toward meeting the goal set in the 1960s. Approximately 4,000 doctors graduate from Cuban medical schools each year. These programs are six-year postsecondary educational programs, with approximately equal numbers of males and females within the present classes.

Since 1959, both the development of appropriate health facilities and the training of large numbers of health providers have been crucial components in improving the quality of health care. The increased quality can be demonstrated by exploring health indicators for women and children. In 1958, infant mortality was 60 per 1,000 live births, and the maternal mortality was 100 per 100,000, a result of insufficient preventative care due to inaccessibility of health care and the economic disarray of capitalist Cuba. In order to tackle this specific need for preventative health care, the health of women and children was established as a priority, which led to the development of a policy to address the health needs of the population.

Family Doctor Program

The family doctor program integrates medical care within the community in order to provide continual preventative care.[28] Each family doctor unit consists of one physician and one nurse. This team shares work and living space with each other and their families. The family doctor and nurse serve the community of which they are members, such that neighbors are both a part of the family doctor's community and the client catchment area served by the team. The number of clients each unit is responsible for varies, but the goal is to reach 200 to 300 persons. The typical client load in 1992 was 600 to 800 persons.

As one family doctor stated:

> I have 192 families that we take care of, we know them all. I know who is pregnant and who will need immunizations soon and how many old people are sick and who is out of work because of illness.[29]

Consistent with the spirit of the family doctor program, this family doctor is describing preventative care across the life course of the family. In addition to a family doctor, each area is served by a polyclinic consisting of multiple clinics available for the needs of the community. The polyclinic operates as a community hospital that can address most nonspecialized procedures. Highly specialized procedures are funneled to the specialty general hospitals.

The significance of this focus on the lives of women can be seen in the decrease of deaths due to pregnancy-related causes, dropping from 100 per 100,000 in 1958, to 26.7 per 100,000 in 1973, and then to 14.6 per 100,000 in 1990. The infant mortality rate is the lowest of all developing countries and is nearly comparable to the industrialized market economy countries. The infant mortality rate of 10.1 per 1,000 reflects a drastic drop from the 60 per 1,000 rate before 1960 (*Informe Annual*, 1990).

Physicians were only a part of the overall increase in needed medical personnel. All aspects were encouraged—nursing, technicians, researchers, therapists, etc. Dr. Alba Abela, Chair of the Committee on Public Health, described the importance of women in the struggle for appropriate health care:

> They are both the majority health workers and the ones who have historically been abused by the health care practices that preceded the triumph of the revolution.[30]

Thus, great strides have been made in the area of health care services and access for Cuban women, but this was fundamentally in response to an old order that had created deplorable conditions for women and families.

Community Involvement in Health Care

Supportive mechanisms exist for reinforcing appropriate healthy practices among Cuban women. The removal of cost as a barrier to appropriate health care has multiple effects for women. This is significantly reflected in both prenatal care and contraceptive use. Prenatal care is virtually universal, and contraceptive information is widely available and utilized. Doctors are used to seek out information, discuss health-related behaviors, and gain and discuss medical procedures. Cubans view doctors as readily available resources who are involved in the daily needs and concerns of the Cuban population.

The Grandparents Circle

The Grandparents Circle is a group of community elders who serve as support within the areas they reside. This support is often directed toward children, pregnant women, young mothers, and ill individuals within their communities. They informally encourage healthy habits and reinforce appropriate community health standards.

The Federation of Women

The Federation of Women is a national organization that engages in health and health promotion activities through its committees and its direct work with women in Cuba. These women support health promotion among women and are advocates for women's health within federal arenas.

Cuban health care explores the possibilities of health within the standard advances of medicine but recently interest in nontraditional health practices has surfaced. Acupuncture, acupressure, herbal treatments, and holistic measures are now being considered as the economic crisis makes Western medical practices financially prohibitive. The philosophy that doctors should be accessible and available seems to permeate all aspects of health care, and doctors are now exploring alternative practices.

New Crises in Cuban Health Care

Recent events outside Cuba have had major consequences for the health care of the Cuban population. For years, Cuba has led developing countries in health care, and it now finds itself grasping for ways to respond to the needs of its citizens. The thirty-four-year U.S. embargo continues to create difficulty for a country that produces a small fraction of its population's needs (Kuntz, 1993), but the additional loss of its major trading partner in 1989 has been a devastating blow to Cuba. The collapse of the Soviet Union ended the flow of billions of dollars in aid, fuel, food, and medicine to Cuba.

The United States continues to tighten the embargo and, fueled by anti-Castro forces, has intensified punitive measures. The strain on the Cuban system is obvious throughout the country. The inability to trade has created nutritional deficits that are beginning to affect the health of pregnant women, children, and elders.[31]

Inability to obtain gasoline has made health care facilities less accessible and people have difficulty finding public transportation as well. Hospitals have insufficient medical supplies to combat illness. In an article in *The New York Times,* Golden (1994) reports a situation in which scarcity of medicines and medical-related supplies is profoundly affecting the delivery of health care. Cubans are unable to obtain diagnostics tests due to a lack of diagnostic chemicals and equipment, are unable to transport patients by ambulance due to shortages in gasoline supplies, and frequently find themselves without the basic necessities for comfort while in the hospitals (clean sheets, disposable supplies, and air-conditioned rooms). This lack of adequate resources negatively impacts health care provisions, making critical medicines and medical supplies nonexistent.

Optic and peripheral neuropathy have become widespread in Cuba, as well as corrosive esophagitis.[32,33] Optic neuropathy causes blurry and progressive loss of vision. Peripheral neuropathy is characterized by loss of coordination in the limbs as well as pain, fatigue, weakness, and tingling sensations. Although the major suspected causes are viral agents or toxic substances, physicians believe that the lack of adequate nutrition has been a contributing factor. Over 45,000 Cubans have been diagnosed with neuropathic illness since 1991, when both forms first appeared (American Health Association, 1993).

This, in addition to the expected long-term negative results of poor nutrition and inadequate health supplies, creates serious health consequences for women and children. The incidence of babies born with low birth weights and the incidence of anemia among expectant mothers is on the rise, although it has not yet created a comparable increase in maternal or infant mortality.[34]

Health care providers and those who wish to aid in the maintenance of health in Cuba have organized to provide medical assistance. This aid is welcomed by Cubans although it reaches only a small portion of the population (see Example 5.1). The health condition of Cuban women and their families does not appear bright, and accounts indicate that the situation worsens with each day. The supplies get shorter, the need becomes greater, and a crippling health crisis is apparent. How the Cuban government will respond as the health care crisis escalates is the question of the hour. Certainly the international community watches, waits, and sometimes attempts to influence local governments' relationships with Cuba, as a means to increase medical exchange.

EXAMPLE 5.1. Pediatricians and Parents for Peace

PPP was organized in 1992 to provide medical aid to the people of Cuba. The group consists of physicians, professionals, parents, and other supporters who feel it is inhuman to deny medical supplies to the people of Cuba. Focusing on the needs of children and their mothers, this international group collects and delivers medical supplies to Cuba in defiance of the U.S. embargo. The U.S.-based group is often joined by Canadian, Mexican, and other supporters in their efforts.

RESPONDING TO WOMEN'S HEALTH NEEDS

In the three countries discussed in this chapter, all responses to health needs address issues of health promotion. These countries, similar to most, see health promotion as central to preventative health care for their populations.

Health promotion and education activities are particularly important when addressing the health care needs of women. Women's health needs are in many ways strikingly different from those of their male counterparts (Begum et al., 1987). Whereas men have high mortality levels overall, women in most countries have higher levels of morbidity (Haavio-Mannila, 1986). These findings typically have generated great interest in understanding the physiological, genetic, or environmental factors attributing to the higher mortality rates in men. However, this type of research, backed by financial resources, has not explored the issue of women's higher morbidity. Thus, education and exploration concerning health issues faced by women are extremely important.

Health Promotion and AIDS

Today the need is imperative for women worldwide to understand the HIV virus and the potential ramifications for themselves and their families. More than three million women are infected with HIV (Bruyn, 1992). It is estimated that during the 1990s three million women and children will die of AIDS (Chin, 1990). Like no other disease before it, the HIV virus will kill women in record numbers. HIV/AIDS is spreading in Africa at an alarming rate. WHO estimates that by the year 2000, over 6 million women will be infected.

Women are susceptible to contracting AIDS because: (1) the disease is shrouded in stereotypes; (2) they have inadequate information concerning AIDS; (3) they are predisposed due to biological and health-related factors; (4) they are at risk with certain sexual practices; and (5) they are vulnerable because the male partner often decides he will not wear a condom.

Throughout many countries of the world, the stereotype persists that AIDS is a disease of homosexual males.[35] This belief encourages women not to take the epidemic seriously and makes them view themselves as immune to the HIV virus, thus placing women at risk throughout the world. Coupled with this notion is the belief that the only way a woman could acquire AIDS is if she is either promiscuous or a prostitute. Both views give the typical woman an illusion of invulnerability that is not grounded in fact (Pitts, Humphrey, and Wilson, 1991).

Women residing in developing areas have less accessibility to information. Cultural environments often prevent women's exposure to information by isolating them from news. Illiteracy rates are higher among women, particularly in developing countries, limiting women's ability to gain information by reading. Both rural environments and poverty preclude access to television and radios for many women.[36]

Health-related practices can put women at risk for HIV infection. Women in many parts of Africa, Asia, and Latin America are assisted during childbirth by traditional midwives. These women often use unsafe practices and, particularly, do not follow sanitation standards that would prevent the passage of HIV from woman to woman or from laboring mother to birthing attendant (Bruyn, 1992). In this case, the passage of the virus through birthing practices can be accelerated. There is a documented relationship between STDs and AIDS. Women suffering from STDs, who have ulcers or sores, can more easily be infected with the HIV virus. These women, particularly in poor communities and developing countries, may go for long periods of time with untreated infections that increase their risk of contracting AIDS.

Several types of sexual behavior can predispose women worldwide to the HIV virus. Polygynous relationships and multiple partners provide more opportunities for infection and passing HIV/AIDS along to other partners. The common practice of men working outside their communities can create a similar situation. These men frequently have sexual relationships away from home and, if infected, will bring the virus back to the home family. Unprotected sex with multiple partners is common worldwide; this increases the risk of exposure to a wide variety of sexually transmitted diseases, including AIDS. Anal intercourse is commonly seen as a homosexual act; however, heterosexual men and women interviewed in several countries report that anal intercourse is practiced, although it is generally not as common as vaginal intercourse.[37] This type of intercourse is commonly unprotected; this is dangerous because frequent tears that are a consequence of this sexual behavior create a channel to the bloodstream, which increases risk of infection.

The need to provide HIV/AIDS information to educate women worldwide is imperative. This requires policies that recognize the importance of health education and promotion (Eshleman, 1997). In the case of AIDS, education is the best hope to slow the ravages of this disease on women worldwide, within both developing and developed countries.

SUMMARY

Developing an appropriate and accessible health care system for women is a worldwide concern. The three cases described in this chapter have addressed the needs of women within the health care system. Each country has a different history, legacy, and set of resources to address the critical issues affecting health care. In each case, significant movements were made toward providing needed health services. The economic systems of these countries vary immensely, which leads us to believe that despite such political differences as capitalism and socialism, health care can be made a priority.

The major indicators of health care in all countries discussed here revealed remarkable improvements when the financial barriers to health care access were removed or significantly reduced. In these case studies, financial obstacles to access have been reduced (for now), yet issues still exist. In Zimbabwe, the struggle continues to provide adequate health care to all women. Remote areas and insufficient personnel continue to plague this country. The impact of a long-lasting drought makes resources scarce. Norway, which has structural and financial advantages, still must face the inequity of delivery based on gender. This issue is only underscored by the paternal nature of Norwegian health care and its lack of responsiveness to female illness. Finally, in Cuba, progress has been reversed as economic devastation takes its toll. With the continued embargo by Cuba's natural trade partner, the United States, and the loss of eastern European countries as trading partners, Cuba's health care system cannot maintain its previous standard. Thus, as we approach the year 2000, the struggles continue in all countries, illustrating the problems within the health care arena for women worldwide.

The dilemmas addressed by each case study are quantitatively different. The history and resources of a developed country such as Norway with equal access to health care is vastly different from the continuous problems and tenuous advances of Cuba and Zimbabwe. For many developed countries, the issue resides in ensuring equal health care. However, in developing countries, the existence of adequate care is not guaranteed, and providing basic health care is an ongoing challenge.

KEY WORDS
Acute care
Birthrate
Formal health sector
Informal health sector
Midwife
Morbidity
Mortality
Preventive medicine
Traditional healer
Traditional midwife (TM)

Chapter 6

Women and Violence

> Peace includes not only the absence of war, violence and hostilities at the national and international levels but also the enjoyment of economic and social justice, equality and the entire range of human rights and fundamental freedoms within society.[1]

Created at the culmination of the U.N. decade for women and reasserted at the Fourth World Women's Conference in Beijing, this comprehensive and positive definition of peace stands in stark contrast to the violence which directly or indirectly affects the lives of women throughout the world. The quest of women to stop the violence which threatens their safety, restricts their freedom, and endangers the survival of humanity is an issue that has the potential to connect women around the world. Large-scale violence, often organized and legitimized by governments or in resistance to governments, is a gendered phenomenon. Women and men play separate roles in this activity.

Although it is true women may support and/or participate in wars and revolutions, the most common consequence of military force, for women, is victimization. Women are also victimized by systematic structural violence and by interpersonal violence. This chapter presents cross-cultural examples that examine the scope of violence and its impact on women's lives.[2] Omnipresent violence exacerbates the global oppression of women, and this oppression escalates into additional violence. Ridding the world of the horror of violence is intrinsically connected to the elimination of gendered power structures and sexist ideologies.

WHAT IS THE RELATIONSHIP BETWEEN IDEOLOGY, GENDER, AND VIOLENCE?

Jean Lipman-Blumen (1984) observed that in all societies gender roles (socially constructed expectations for masculine and feminine behavior) are intertwined with biological sex. She theorized that the power dimension of the sex/gender system provides "the blueprint for all other power relationships" (p. 5). Many believe that gender ideology is an integral part of all types of violence, from war and revolution to interpersonal attack. Patriarchy ("rule of the fathers") asserts the superiority of males and the inferiority of females. "It also provides the rationale for sexual terrorism. The taproot of patriarchy is the masculine/warrior ideal" (Sheffield, 1997, p. 112). Men are offered confirmation of their manhood and a sense of superiority over women from their participation in the military (Thompson, 1991).

In many societies, characteristics regarded as masculine contribute to men's proclivity to engage in violent behavior. The qualities that are valued by patriarchal society include aggression, force, strength, power, toughness, dominance, and competitiveness. The intent of these common cultural notions of masculinity is to win, to conquer, and to be in control. Myths and propaganda facilitate the cultural acceptance of these values and, hence, promote acts of violence. Feminine weakness, dependence, or virtue may be invoked as a justification for men to engage in armed conflict. Women are asked to trust that men have their best interests at heart. The roles of "protector" and "protected" further subordinate women (Stiehm, 1982).

Gender ideology is also useful in explaining many types of family and community violence. Structural violence against women (e.g., genital mutilation) may be justified by saying it is necessary to preserve virginity or to ensure matrimony. Rape and sexual harassment are often defended by invoking the notion that the woman was "asking for it." Both men and women in vastly different cultures are likely to believe in these rationales. One of the tasks confronting international movements to eliminate violence against women is to reveal the interconnections between gendered values and surrounding rhetoric and the violence in women's lives. We begin by examining women's participation and victimization in large-scale conflict.

International military conflict, civil wars, and wars of resistance take up a disproportionate amount of space in history books and constitute much of the worldwide daily news. These activities are overwhelmingly male dominated, from leadership to foot soldier to negotiators in the peace process. The perception that women have not been involved in these conflicts, however, is false. The diverse roles that women assume in conflict situations have, until recently, been both unrecognized and undervalued.

DO THE ROLES WOMEN ASSUME DURING WAR LEAD TO LIBERATION?

Women's participation in wars and revolutions varies depending on the particular historical, social, and economic circumstances and women's relationship to these circumstances. When conditions arise within a society where much of the population endorses armed conflict, propaganda directed at women may urge them to participate; many women may want to participate. Overall, women have been supportive, willingly made sacrifices, and been enthusiastic supporters of conflicts, even encouraging men to fight (Thompson, 1991). One reason for this cooperation is the implicit expectation or actual promise that women who work for the defense of the country or the cause will reap benefits in improved status and lasting respect. The evidence suggests that more often the gain is likely to be short in duration and does not result in a permanent change in status nor ongoing movement toward equality.

Women have served in clandestine resistance networks, in battle preparations, and in combat. They have been especially prominent as freedom fighters against colonialism. The roles of women revolutionaries are documented in struggles fought against repressive governments in Zimbabwe, Mozambique, Namibia, and South Africa. The illustration of women's role in the liberation of Algeria from France, between 1954 and 1963, provides a familiar example of how women's status is subject to change before, during, and after an armed struggle.

Algeria suffered tremendously under French colonialism, where Algerians were deprived of land ownership, citizenship, and the use of their native language and were forced to live under French laws. The National Liberation Front (FLN), which eventually won independence for Algeria, was a coalition of leftists and Muslims. Islamic values became intertwined with nationalist ideology, and the effort to win independence incorporated protection of Muslim identity. Algerian women participated fully in the struggle for independence. They served as an inconspicuous means of transport for FLN ammunition.

Some of the norms of Muslim tradition were suspended to meet the imperatives of war. Algerian women communicated freely with men to plot strategy. When on a mission disguised as Europeans, they traveled without the traditional Muslim garments, the haik and the veil. The French considered Algerian women dangerous and targeted them with peace propaganda. After the war, the National Liberation Front made an official statement of women's equality, which was codified in Algeria's 1963 constitution (Benallegue, 1983).

For a period, there were attempts to appease both the new progressive socialist government and the Islamic faction. The fervor over women's status, however, was not easily resolved. Laws began to reflect fundamentalist Muslim practices, starting with the 1966 Algerian Penal Code, which provides a sentence of one year for male adulterers and two years for females guilty of the same offense. Marriage outside the Muslim faith is prohibited to Algerian women. Divorce by repudiation is the husband's right; a wife must petition the courts for a divorce. The 1970 Family Code reaffirmed the customs of polygyny and arranged marriage (Marshall and Stokes, 1981). In Algeria today, most women either desire, or have submitted to, living by Islamic codes. Many are afraid of murder or attack if they don't conform. Amnesty International (1995) describes the case of sixteen-year-old Katia Bengana, who was murdered for her public refusal to wear Islamic dress. Others want to protect their family status and to avoid the leers, stares, and offensive public treatment of Westernized women by males. Strides toward public equality during and immediately after the revolution for independence were reversed, and goals for women were redefined.

South Africa is another and more recent example in which both women and men have struggled against injustice. Until 1992, a small white minority forcefully imposed a policy of racial segregation on a large nonwhite majority. The apartheid system contained over three hundred racial laws that required blacks, Asians, and people of mixed-race ancestry to use separate facilities in such public institutions as hospitals, schools, and colleges. In addition to the laws of apartheid, there were further restrictions for African women. For example, married women were considered legal minors who could not engage in contracts or even open credit accounts without their husband's permission. Local customs, such as the "lobola," or bride-price, further undermined the rights of African women. Despite this context, many South African women fought for freedom. They carried on every conceivable activity in the antiapartheid movement and experienced arrest, imprisonment, sexual harassment, exile, and severe mistreatment during detention. Women died beside men in the struggle. Diana Russell (1989) interviewed Mavivi Manzini (full-time worker for the women's section of the African National Congress and former member of the South African student movement) along with sixty other female freedom fighters. Example 6.1 describes another view of how women react to military struggle.

Manzini states that, time and time again, it was the women who led demonstrations, often facing guns and bullets. They mistakenly thought the police would hesitate before shooting women. She and others interviewed believe that women's emancipation cannot be separated from the struggle for national liberation (Russell, 1989). Although there are many examples of women's support and participation in armed struggles, both currently and historically, women are far more likely to be victims in the entire process of war. The rationale of protecting "women and children" is ironic in light of evidence that they are the very class of people who suffer the most.[3] The following sections explore indirect and direct female victimization caused by war.

EXAMPLE 6.1. Women in Nicaragua's Sandinista Revolution

The Sandinista National Liberation Front (FSLN) arose in the 1960s to combat poverty and injustice, which was largely a result of U.S. imperialism and the authoritarian power of dictator Samoa. Women's lives were characterized by illiteracy and an endless cycle of pregnancies, child care, and domestic labor.

The entrance of women into the revolutionary movement had a profound effect on their status. They participated in protests and hunger strikes, and in covert operations, they acted as spies, hid weapons, and smuggled radio equipment. As political prisoners, they were raped, tortured, and killed.

With victory in 1979, women had enormous expectations of how the new people's government would change their lives. By 1990, with the defeat of the Sandinista party, women in Nicaragua were disappointed and battle weary. Feminist survivors of years of struggle question past assumptions as they organize in an independent, internationally connected movement in which they hope women and men will really be equal partners (Randall, 1998).

HOW DO THE ECONOMICS OF WAR AFFECT WOMEN?

Modern warfare involves the development of "sophisticated" weapons—chemical agents, a vast assortment of high-tech bombs, missiles and delivery systems—more expensive and more deadly than ever before in human history. The international military establishment employs over 100 million people, and world military expenditures in 1986, the "international year of peace," were a record $900 billion (Robertson, 1987). The use of all types of assault weapons increases the likelihood that conflict will be settled through force; at the same time, it increases the number of civilian casualties. It is not true that warriors alone die so that the civilian population, notably women and children, can be safe. In 1987, there was a new high in regional military conflict. There were twenty-four wars and four-fifths of the casualties were civilians (United Nations, 1991a).

Global military costs consume an immense and growing proportion of human financial, material, and personal resources. Ruth Sivard (1996) reports that "of 160 countries, half the countries spend more on military programs than on health care. All except the Russian Federation are developing countries; 15 of them spend more on military than on health and education" (p. 35).

The success of the worldwide movement for women's equality depends on channeling substantial monetary resources into human services by governments and other agencies in the international community. Attention needs to be directed to the following areas. National health care budgets must be increased to provide primary health care; existing health facilities must be improved and maintained; clean water and sanitation facilities require improvement. Also needed are subsidized medications; funds for reproductive counseling; increased funding to reduce the education gap between males and females, including development of adult literacy programs, and development of services to reduce time spent in child care and domestic workload (United Nations, 1991a).

Table 6.1 illustrates an economic equation of human services that could *be purchased by reducing the level of military spending* (Sivard, 1991).

The continuous deflection of resources for armed conflict prevents women from improving their status. Countries suffering from eco-

TABLE 6.1. Choices

It is time to redefine national protection. A commitment to social welfare and gender equity requires prioritizing government spending away from military programs and toward programs to alleviate hunger, disease, and illiteracy in low-income countries. The figures below weigh the cost of acquiring selected military weapons against selected social spending alternatives.		
Costs of Protection		
Weapons	Dollars	Other Options
Seawolf nuclear-powered submarine	$2,500,000,000	Immunization program with vaccines and micronutrients for the world's children
Intercontinental nuclear and conventional Stealth bombers	$2,200,000,000	Supplying family planning services to 120 million women in developing countries
Aegis guided missile destroyer	$969,000,000	One year of primary schooling for 11,400,000 girls in impoverished countries
Multiple launcher rocket system loaded with ballistic rockets	$29,000,000	One year's rural water and sanitation service for 2,000,000 people in developing nations
Tomahawk cruise missile	$1,730,000	1,200 wells with hand pumps, for families lacking local water resources

Adapted from Sivard, *World Military and Social Expenditures*, 1996, p. 39.

nomic crises, often exacerbated by militarism, cause reduced expenditure for social programs. Military expenses around the world, within the past quarter-century, have increased by over 40 percent in developed regions and by almost 130 percent in developing regions. At least twenty-seven nations spend more on defense than health and education combined (United Nations, 1991a).

WOMEN'S LIVES DESTROYED BY WAR

Wartime violence differs from peacetime violence in the sheer magnitude of devastation. Women as well as men lose homes and property, families and loved ones, but war will affect women's lives in several different ways. Women are more likely than men to be displaced from their homes. It is often women, with dependent children, who must go on alone, and whether in combat zones or in refugee camps, women become targets of rape and brutality. Later, women, as life givers, must "pick up the pieces" and repopulate society (Peterson and Runyan, 1993).

WHAT CONDITIONS FACE WOMEN REFUGEES?

Repressive governments, military regimes, and civil wars in Latin America, the Middle East, Asia, Africa, and Eastern Europe result in personal loss, community devastation, and population decrease. In 1991, the known number of refugees was 17 million and growing. The real number of refugees is likely to be much higher because those who flee to non–United Nations locations are not counted. The United Nations estimates that 80 percent of the population affected are women (often widowed) and dependent children (United Nations, 1991a). At the present time, the U.N. High Commissioner for Refugees (UNHCR) has adopted a policy statement to better protect refugee women and an international NGO Working Group on refugee women continues to focus attention on the problem. Martin (1992) charges that, despite recent efforts, programming and policy development do not take into full consideration that the refugee population is disproportionately female. Women who are refugees, or displaced within their own country, often find that months stretch into years and the prospects of returning home are increasingly bleak.

The physical conditions of most refugee camps are dismal. Housing consists of makeshift barracks. The quarters are crowded, and there is a lack of property, goods, and services. Many camps are devoid of men; others have a more balanced sex ratio. In either case, gender hierarchy becomes exaggerated. Sexual violence and harassment is a pervasive problem, and reports of women who bribe guards with sex to obtain basic necessities, such as water or firewood, are common. Boredom, melancholia, and crying indicate psychological distress. Considering the reality of refugee conditions, Lindsey (1994) and others commend the perseverance of women who manage to keep their families together through multiple hardships.

During the 1980s, over two million people were displaced in Central America, as peasants were driven from their land (Manz, 1988). The plight of female refugees from the largely Indian population of Guatemala illustrates some of the atrocities facing all women refugees. The unprecedented exodus of tens of thousands of Guatemalan Indians in the 1980s was the result of government violence, which had escalated by 1979 to the point of 100 to 200 deaths per month. Amnesty International accused the government of mass murder:

> The victims were peasants, leaders of cooperatives, students, rural organizers, labor leaders, political reformers, and church activists among others. At times, the victims were snatched off the street and never reappeared: in other cases mutilated bodies were dropped by the roadside; in some instances people were shot down in front of friends, family, or coworkers. (Ibid., pp. 14-15)

Even prior to militarization of the countryside, peasant life was one of poverty, economic and social discrimination, and low political power. Many able-bodied men migrated considerable distances, often staying away six to eight months, to earn needed income. The flight from Guatemala to other countries, primarily Mexico, that took place in the 1980s varied by ethnic background, class, and region. Although some Ladinos (identified with the dominant Western culture) were persecuted as individuals, it was mostly the Indians in the highlands and the northern lowlands who abandoned communities, depopulating entire regions.

Refugee camps, ranging from fifty to five thousand inhabitants, were funded by the Mexican government, the United Nations, and volunteer organizations. Daily deaths occurred during the early stages of encampment. The military violence that preceded flight included both premeditated and indiscriminate rape of women, both in detention and in the community. Rigoberta Menchu, the Guatemalan activist, writer, and 1992 Nobel Prize recipient, did much to publicize the atrocities committed on the Indian population of Guatemala, especially to poor Indian women, companeras, in small rural communities. She explains her decision to leave her own village and work in other, more devastated villages: "I couldn't bear so many women—hundreds of women, young girls, widows—being pregnant because the soldiers had used them sexually. I was ashamed to stay safely in my village and not think about the others" (Menchu, 1992).

According to the testimony of residents of Quiche province, most girls between ages eleven and fifteen had been sexually abused by the army. Witnesses also claimed that women were targeted for sexual torture, including forced nudity and electrodes attached to the nipples and vagina. That refugee women were forced to witness the rapes, murder, and torture of others, often friends and family, was perhaps as devastating as their own torture (Aron et al., 1991).

An ongoing consequence of the horrors suffered by Guatemalan Indian women and other refugee women is post-traumatic stress disorder (PTSD). Some manifestations of PTSD include sleeplessness, depression, anxiety, flashbacks, and the inability to trust (Aron et al., 1991). Refugee status has impeded recovery, as these women find themselves in unfamiliar circumstances, often without emotional support systems. They may have lost family members to torture and death, and may have had to leave loved ones behind, sometimes children. These women fear both an uncertain future and revictimization.

WHY DO MEN RAPE DURING WARTIME?

Men have raped and terrorized women throughout history, across many (but not all) cultures, in times of peace and of war. Because rape is already a familiar part of the social fabric, war provides a rationale to vent existing contempt for women. Susan Brownmiller (1975) notes that the act of rape signifies virility for the aggressors but impotence on the part of the losers—the ultimate masculine humiliation. Systematic rape by victors demonstrates that the prime motivation of rape is the drive for power, not sex.

In war, rape is another type of defilement of property. Husbands, fathers, and sometimes whole families may reject a raped woman. She represents "spoiled goods," or she reminds them they were powerless to save her. Until the 1990s, with widespread reports of rape in the Balkans and in Rwanda, rape stories were underreported. Nevertheless, the rape of Jewish women in Nazi Germany (1930s and 1940s), of Vietnamese women by American troops during the Vietnam war (1968), of Bengali women by Pakistani soldiers during the invasion of Bangladesh (1971), and of Muslim women in the former Yugoslavia (1990s) illustrates that similar patterns of behavior occur despite cultural differences or historical periods.

News of mass rapes in Bosnia-Herzegovina (formerly Yugoslavia) in the 1990s shocked the world and outraged human rights groups. Complex political, ethnic, and religious animosities erupted in violent attacks, often between former neighbors. Both sides in this conflict used rape as a weapon, but it is the Serbians who are accused of the most vicious crimes against women. The atrocities include rape camps and forced impregnation. Modern video technology confirmed the reported rapes of Muslim and Croatian women. In one film clip, " . . . a woman near age thirty-five, with short, dark hair, was thrown on the ground, her hands spread and tied to a tree, her legs tied to her hands. Many men watched her raped in person; thousands more watched her raped on television" (MacKinnon, 1993, p. 28).

Vesna Nikolic-Ristanovic (1996) interviewed sixty-nine women refugees, temporarily settled in Serbia. She wanted to record their knowledge and experience with wartime violence and to use interview data coupled with statistical data to learn more about domestic violence during wartime. Although she spoke to mostly Serbian women in a situation where more Muslim women were violated, she found them quite willing to speak for Muslim and Croat women, as well as to tell their own stories. One repeated form of psychological torture was the forced witness of the torture, rape, and murder of women of all ages. This happened in private homes to mothers, wives, and young girls and in prisons or makeshift bordellos.

One interviewee described the brutal gang rape of a seventy-six-year-old Serbian woman by Moslem soldiers. She later died from the attack. Nikolic-Ristanovic analyzes the practice of forced impregnation: "Women are seen as objects, as dishes which passively accept men's seed . . . the identity of the child depends only on men; consequently women impregnated by their enemies give birth to children who belong to the enemies' ethnic group" (1996, p. 202). She goes on to describe the agony of women in this position: "Feeling the child of the rapist in her womb and being convinced that everybody will know that it's the child of the enemy, but knowing at the same time it is also her child, is the most cruel form of torture. . . . the husbands of raped women and other men detest and reject these women because they were raped and bore children to the enemy" (pp. 202-203).

In her related study, Nikolic-Ristanovic (1996) documents the increase in domestic violence as fighting escalated in the Balkans. The war propaganda (especially media coverage), real war experiences, and the availability of weapons led ordinary men to relieve anxiety, fear, and frustration by battering their wives. The cruelty of men toward their wives was exaggerated when spouses belonged to two different ethnic groups. One Muslim woman, married to a Serb, found herself the scapegoat for all Moslem crimes. He beat her every night after drinking with his friends, and when she tried to flee with her child, he stopped her, insisting that the child is Serbian and stays with him.

The violence women experienced in Rwanda was similar to Bosnia in that it was an ethnic clash in which tens of thousands of Tutsi women were raped and impregnated by Hutu fighters and neighbors. Officials at a maternity ward caring for many of these women say over half of them were also mutilated with machetes, scissors, or acid. Rwanda is a highly conservative Roman Catholic society where abortion is illegal and raped women are viewed as traitors. Mothers in such a desperate dilemma frequently abandoned their children to poorly staffed orphanages. Those who keep the children are coping with extremely mixed feelings. As one Rwandan mother, whose husband and other children were killed by her young son's father, said, "I am obliged to love him" (Sullivan, 1996, p. 51).

Rape and sexual violence were given a new priority at two 1997 war crimes tribunals: ICTFY, International Criminal Tribunal for the Former Yugoslavia, and ITC, International Tribunal for Rwanda. Previously, sex crimes against men were acknowledged, but those against women were not. Despite an official step forward in this regard, relatively few suspected rapists were indicted; there is no documentation of rape as genocide, and women judges are under-represented ("Will War Crimes . . .", 1996).

HOW DOES PROSTITUTION CONTRIBUTE TO GENDER VIOLENCE DURING WARTIME?

Both the Korean Council for the Women Drafted for Military Sexual Slavery and recommendations to the U.N. Human Rights Commission direct Japan to formally apologize for war crimes against approximately 200,000 Asian women forced into prostitution during World War II. Demands made by, and on behalf of, surviving former "comfort women" also include monetary compensation, a memorial to the victims, and the correction of Japanese history books, to teach the truth about this atrocity (Soh, 1996). By all accounts, Japan started building "comfort stations" in the 1930s, and between one and two hundred thousand women were brought as captives or lured to work as prostitutes in these shanties. Most were children or teenagers from Korea, a Japanese colony from 1910 to 1945. A Japanese schoolteacher, working in Korea, recalled how she was ordered to select physically well-developed girls for the war effort, unaware of how they would be used. Women and girls were confined to military-run quarters and were forced to have sex with soldiers, who were often rotated through the "comfort stations" day and night at fifteen-minute intervals. Venereal disease was rampant. Thousands of women died, including many who were apparently killed by the soldiers (Sanger, 1992).

When the survivors of these brothels returned to Korea, they were often shunned by their families and society. Virginity is a prerequisite for marriage in Korea; therefore, most of these women were considered ineligible for marriage. Their lives were destroyed both socially and psychologically. Until 1992, the Japanese government denied that this outrageous practice had been sponsored by the government. Japan maintained that the practice had been engineered by private industry until Mr. Yoshiaki Yoshimi, a history professor, discovered documents proving these were *military* brothels and that "recruitment" of women was a military function. The apparent rationale behind the comfort women initiative was to provide supervised sexual outlet, control the spread of sexually transmitted diseases, and reduce the likelihood that Japanese soldiers would commit sexual crimes against women in occupied territories, as they had done in Nanjing, China in 1937 (Son, 1996).

The U.S. military in Vietnam recommended local women's bodies as reward and release at a time when wives and girlfriends were unavailable. Although Vietnam had a history of prostitution before the American presence, economic conditions had deteriorated so badly by the mid-1960s that prostitution was the only viable option for many Vietnamese women. The custom had become so extensive that, in 1966, a Committee for the Defense of the Vietnamese Woman's

Human Dignity and Rights was organized in Saigon (Brownmiller, 1975). Except for the Marine Corps, which tried to enforce a strict moral code, other branches of the U.S. military promoted the use of prostitutes to "pacify" the troops. In military-controlled and -regulated brothels, women were tested for venereal disease and "tagged" if they were disease free. Officially sanctioned prostitution contributed to a climate in which women, especially Vietnamese women, were treated as merchandise.

An exaggerated masculine-feminine dynamic was established by the difference in phenotype of the large, strong American man and the small, fragile Vietnamese woman. This dynamic contributed to an atmosphere that permitted gang rapes to occur. Official statistics relating to rape and subsequent convictions are highly questionable. Many believe that they appear low because of the power differential between victims and perpetrators, the partisan nature of official bureaucratic sources, and the fact that rapes are, in general, underreported. There were many documented rapes by American soldiers in Vietnam, and the recounting of just one such case is enough to illustrate how racism, sexism, and the "pressure to be masculine," result in unspeakable acts.

In November 1966, a squad of five men on reconnaissance entered the tiny hamlet of Cat Tuong. The members of the squad collectively decided to bring along a young girl from the village for sexual purposes while they scouted for Viet Cong. They knew that at the end of their five-day tour they would have to kill her and dispose of her body. Mao was chosen because they fancied her gold tooth. The other women in the village cried and cowered, and Mao's mother ran after her with her scarf, knowing that she was powerless to stop the kidnapping. Later, it was revealed that acts of excessive cruelty, as well as rape, had been performed on Mao prior to her murder, in what appeared to be a contest of masculine dominance. One of the five men in the patrol, Private First Class Sven Eriksson, did not participate and reported the crime to his superiors, who initially took no action but instead transferred Eriksson for his own protection. The case was examined when a sympathetic chaplain alerted the Criminal Investigation Division and Mao's body was discovered. During the separate court martials of the four other men involved, Eriksson's manhood was called into question over and over. Although the four defendants were found guilty, the most severe sentence (life imprisonment) was commuted to eight years (Brownmiller, 1975).

In addition to Vietnam, prostitution is openly acknowledged around other American bases. The widespread incidence of "hospitality women" surrounding American bases in the Philippines has created the most attention. Prostitution became the center of Filipino controversy over the American presence there. By 1985, the U.S. military had become the second largest employer in the Philippines. There were between six and nine thousand licensed "entertainment" workers and as many as twenty thousand unlicensed workers in Olongapo City, adjacent to Subic Bay Naval Base. Thousands of poor women viewed prostitution as a means of survival. They served both military and civilian clientele and were required to have compulsory VD and AIDS testing twice a month (Enloe, 1989).

In 1987, twenty-five HIV-positive cases were identified. These women became a rallying point for the members of "Gabriela," the umbrella feminist organization active in the antibase movement. Gabriela demanded that women be given counseling and medical care. They further objected to blame being placed on the women and began the campaign to make the government of the Philippines insist that the U.S. military not allow service personnel showing any signs of AIDS on Philippine soil. They accomplished this objective in 1988, when such a policy was enacted.

An additional consequence of the extensive sexual exploitation of Filipino women has been the high number of illegitimate children born and abandoned. Many of these street children are lured or sold into prostitution to serve American pedophiles. According to Cynthia Enloe, there is a price differential based on the racial heritage of these children: Caucasian-looking children could be sold for $50-200; children appearing black brought $25-30. As mentioned, eradication of military-sponsored prostitution in the Philippines has been the target of several organized opposition groups. One organization, cofounded by Filipino feminists at the end of the women's decade conference in Nairobi, Kenya, in 1985, is called the Campaign Against Military Prostitution (CAMP). Their effort is international, extending to all parts of the world in which military installations support prostitution (Enloe, 1989).

FEMALE SEXUAL SLAVERY:
PROSTITUTION AND SEX TOURISM

The process of labeling and defining women sexually has been a primary source of social control over them. Although the specific criteria by which women are judged "good" and "bad" may differ from culture to culture, women's sexual lives are generally (despite occasional notable exceptions) the primary criteria used to judge them. Once a woman is driven or coerced into a sexually active role outside of marriage, her value to society diminishes, and the roles she can assume are restricted. The social reactions toward a woman who exchanges sex for money range from pity to contempt. Kathleen Barry (1979) uses the concept of "female sexual slavery" to designate situations in which women find themselves trapped in a lifestyle that subjects them to sexual exploitation and violence. Barry believes there are similarities between the rape victim and the prostitute because neither considers the act sex. Although other feminists view prostitution as dangerous to physical and mental health, there is controversy as to whether sex work differs substantially in violence and danger from other women's work.[4]

International sexual exploitation of women continues to be a serious problem, a problem fostered by both sexist notions about women and the spread of capitalism throughout the world. Pornography, sex tourism, and trafficking in women reduce women's bodies to commodities. These practices reinforce the ethos that sex can be readily disassociated from personal feelings. They link male eroticism with extreme brutality and with the forceful domination of women. These particular crimes against women are circular in nature. That is, they are both causes and consequences of violence and discrimination against women.

HOW HAS GLOBAL ECONOMIC INEQUALITY
CONTRIBUTED TO SEX TOURISM
AND TRAFFICKING IN WOMEN?

"Sex tourism" relies on a worldwide stratification system in which the power and the choices of the women involved are extremely limited. Although the practice exists elsewhere, it is well documented in South Korea, the Philippines, Indonesia, Sri Lanka, and Thailand.

Local governments seeking foreign capital are anxious to have wealthy businessmen and businesses spend money in sexualized travel. Male clientele often come from the developed countries (e.g., North America, Western Europe, Japan, and Australia) or from elite strata within developing nations (e.g., the Middle East) to destinations in the developing world. Cynthia Enloe (1989) describes sex tourism in the Pat Bong section of Bangkok, Thailand. Loopholes surrounding the entertainment industry circumvent the ban on prostitution to bring in revenue from male tourists, who outnumber female tourists there three to one. "In 1986, Thailand earned more foreign currency from tourism—$1.5 billion—than it did from any other economic activity including its traditional export leader, rice" (p. 37). Potential clients are encouraged to take Thai tours, with promises of "girls" who are beautiful, exotic, and subservient.

The women who work in the approximately 119 massage parlors, 119 barbershop-*cum*-massage parlors and teahouses, 97 nightclubs, 248 disguised brothels, and 394 disco-restaurants come from a variety of backgrounds, including rural settings that cannot support high populations. Although they remain at the bottom of the economic system that employs them, they earn, on the average, five times more than they could in a nonentertainment-type job. The work is inherently exploitative and there is no job security, as the women work as long as there is a steady flow of male tourists.

Indeed, Enloe reports that, in 1987, Thai officials became concerned about a sharp decrease in male tourists. The number of years that a woman can work as a prostitute or in sex entertainment is limited by age and appearance, and they are always at risk of customer brutality, venereal disease, and AIDS. Two Thai women's organizations, "Empower" and "Friends of Women," were formed in the 1980s to educate the women about protecting themselves from AIDS and to give them English lessons, designed to somewhat equalize the interaction between themselves and their English-speaking clients. Representatives from these organizations also investigate the commerce that has developed around exporting women from Thailand and other third world nations to industrialized countries for marriage, entertainment, and prostitution (Enloe, 1989). Sex tourism relies on a combination of social, economic, political, and historical conditions that interact to place women in an especially vulnerable position.

As global poverty worsens, some women from almost all countries are finding "sex work" their only means of survival. Increasingly, girls and women are kidnaped or lured into forced prostitution through international groups that profit from "trafficking in women." Simons (1993) presents the case of three Hungarian women who thought they were traveling to Belgium to work as waitresses. On arrival, according to one woman, her work papers were confiscated and she was literally "jailed" in a brothel for three months, until the police raided the establishment and liberated her by arrest.

Since the end of the cold war, thousands of women from Russia, Bulgaria, Poland, and other Eastern European countries have been brought to Germany, the Netherlands, France, Switzerland, Italy and Greece. Some know that they will be prostitutes, but many are duped and/or forced. The red-light district of Antwerp advertises girls of every race and nationality and promises that there will be new girls every week (Simons, 1993). In New York City, Asian Organized Crime has been charged in a smuggling ring in which Asian women were lured into prostitution. One Thai woman said they had promised to let her go after she had slept with 300 men. Customers reportedly paid $130 for an hour with a prostitute, and the only money the prostitute got to keep was the tips. Although there is an international outcry against this type of exploitation, the ongoing combination of economic inequality and sexism impedes lasting remedies.

STRUCTURAL VIOLENCE AGAINST WOMEN

The structural violence discussed in this section refers to the pain, suffering, and in some cases, death inflicted upon women within given cultures by acts that are, or have been, condoned as necessary or even beneficial within that culture. These acts of violence are patterned and deliberate rather than random. They apply to women within certain circumstances, who fall within a certain social location, defined by age, social class, and/or marital status. These forms of violence are deeply embedded in the culture and are widely accepted because cultural justifications that are passed down as "common knowledge" make the violence seem reasonable. Structural violence against women also differs from other versions of violence because it is often women who directly victimize girls or other women.

Chinese Footbinding

Chinese footbinding is an historical example of structural violence and was a routine practice in China from the thirteenth until the twentieth century. The purpose of binding was to make the feet small. The ideal of small (albeit deformed) feet as objects of beauty and sexuality became institutionalized in Chinese society. Consequently, women of all classes were subject to the procedure, although the feet of girls in the lower strata of society were not usually bound as tightly because they needed to walk in order to work.

Andrea Dworkin (1983) describes the process, usually performed by her mother when a girl was between five and seven years of age. A bandage, about two inches wide and ten feet long, was wrapped from inside the instep, over the small toes. The large toe was left out of the binding. The other toes were bent under, bringing the heel and toes as close together as possible. The method was then repeated until the entire bandage was used. The foot of the young child was thereafter submitted to unrelenting pressure. Bound feet often became infected, bled, oozed pus, and sometimes one or more toes dropped off, toenails grew into the skin, and circulation was extremely poor.

From the moment binding occurred, the pain was excruciating, and the woman was effectively crippled. Upper-class "ladies," whose feet were most severely bound, were incapacitated. These women served as "ornaments," enhancing the prestige of men who could afford to keep a woman in idleness. Myths about the advantages of bound feet were widely accepted despite lack of supporting evidence. It was believed that footbinding changed the contour of the vagina so that sexual pleasure would be more intense for the man. The size of a woman's feet became a criterion for marriage, an important family matter in Chinese society where the custom of arranged marriage traditionally prevailed. The parents of the groom-to-be would inspect the feet of the prospective bride as the most important standard of evaluation. Although the bound feet of women in ancient China were admired and considered sexually attractive, they increased a woman's vulnerability, since a woman with bound feet could not run away and would experience intense pain if her feet were assaulted (Dworkin, 1983).

Although footbinding is now obsolete, it serves as a prototype of structural violence against women. In retrospect, it is easy to unmask the absurd rationale for binding Chinese women's feet and to see that the real intention of this brutal practice was to limit women to a particular social role.

Female Genital Mutilation (FGM)

Structural violence in the form of what is known euphemistically as "female circumcision" remains a contemporary challenge. This practice is not confined to a single country: United Nation's estimates indicate that eighty million women in Africa alone and millions more in the Middle East, as well as African and Middle Eastern populations residing in Europe and the Americas, are victims of genital mutilation (United Nations, 1991a).

There are three primary varieties of this practice and many local variations: (1) sunna "circumcision," or removal of the prepuce and/or tip of the clitoris; (2) clitoridectomy, or the excision of the entire clitoris (both prepuce and glans), plus the adjacent parts of the labia minora; and (3) infibulation, or removal of the entire clitoris, the labia minora, and the labia majora, plus the joining of the scraped sides of the vulva across the vagina, where they are secured with thorns or sewn with catgut or thread. A small opening is preserved by inserting a sliver of wood (commonly a match stick) into the wound during the healing process, thus allowing passage of urine and menstrual blood.

An infibulated woman must be cut open to permit intercourse, and cut further to permit childbirth. Often she is closed up again after delivery and thus may be subject to such procedures repeatedly in her reproductive life (Morgan and Steinem, 1980). Therefore. female circumcision is very different in nature from male circumcision. The practice destroys the woman's capacity for sexual pleasure and has severe health consequences including immediate death from hemorrhage, shock, or septicemia, as well as chronic conditions such as incontinence, scarring and keloid formation, recto-vaginal fistulas, vulval cysts and abscesses, urinary retention, delayed menarche, and infection. There is no genital satisfaction during sexual intercourse and sometimes excruciating pain. Sterility is a possible consequence of the cysts and swelling of the vaginal wall. If pregnancy occurs, there are numerous risks to a healthy and uncomplicated birth, such as the increased likelihood of infection and head injury during delivery. Psychological reactions range from temporary trauma to frigidity and psychosis.

Up to 90 percent of Somali and Sudanese women are circumcised. With increased patterns of immigration, doctors, social workers, and legislators in developed countries are dealing with this issue: Mary Ann French (1992) describes a chilling example of culture clash, when a fifteen-year-old Somali girl entered Washington, DC, General Hospital in advanced labor. Doctors looked between her legs and gasped; they quickly moved her to an operating theater, where the attending physician cut away at "thick, unyielding keloid" scar tissue to allow the baby's head entrance. Repeated injections of painkillers could not stop her screams during the next hour and a half, as they sewed up the jagged wound. The "equivalent of Stone Age surgery" was performed when this girl was seven years old. A dozen strong hands held her down as a sharp object severed her clitoris and cut loose the inner lips of her vagina, scraping away surrounding flesh. Eventually, the outer lips were sewn together with catgut and acacia thorns. This process of infibulation left an aperture barely wide enough to pass urine and menstrual blood. "Not allowed to cry, she was told to bite on a stick of wood to bear the pain. For weeks, her legs were tied together, held motionless, while her would healed" (French, 1992, p. F1).

Explanations for this type of structural violence include tradition, family honor, marriageability, cleanliness, initiation into womanhood, prevention of promiscuity, and the belief that it heightens male sexual satisfaction, that it increases fertility, and that it serves as a contraceptive. Myths deconstructed from the Mossi of Upper Volta and the Dogon and Bambaras of Mali seem to suggest the practice was associated with a fear of masculine traits in women and of women's sexuality in general (Morgan and Steinem, 1980). The practice also existed in the West. Doctors in both England and the

United States in the nineteenth century recommended clitorectomies for nymphomania, masturbation, insomnia, sterility, and unhappy marriage (Ibid.).

Several African countries have outlawed FGM and Muslim opponents to the practice observe there is nothing in the Koran to justify this procedure, but local social pressure to have daughters circumcised is enormous. Efforts to eradicate FGM met with retort that once again Westerners are interfering in affairs that do not concern them. The drive to retain indigenous customs becomes a primary stimulus in women's compliance with the procedure.[6]

In recent years, however, there has been condemnation of the practice from numerous sources. In February 1979, the World Health Organization initiated a meeting of physicians, midwives, and health officials from ten African and Arab nations to discuss traditional practices and health. Among their recommendations were that governments should adapt clear national policies against "female circumcision" and intensify education about its dangers (Davies, 1983). In the 1990s, several women's groups in Africa are implementing strategies for change. Two of these are Maendeleo Ya Wanawake in Kenya and the Association for the Progress and Defense of Women's Rights (APDF) in Mali (Mekuria, 1995).

African women often prefer Western feminists to concentrate on priorities such as starvation, general health, and agricultural and industrial development. Ellen Gruenbaum (1993), after exploring clitoridectomy and infibulation in Sudan, states that it is a mistake to insist that international organizations take firm stands against this practice because this heavy-handedness will produce a backlash. She believes that, to be effective, the impetus must come from national movements and from women themselves. Nevertheless, we take the position that the practice of genital mutilation constitutes a crime against women and should be eradicated.

Suttee and Dowry Murders

Women in India face harassment, abuse, and murder in disputes surrounding marital status and/or marriage arrangements. The custom of suttee (widow burning) has a thousand-year history, and reports, starting in 1981, indicated a revival of this practice. Beliefs surrounding immolation of widows on their husbands' funeral pyres involve both the notion that her death will help the deceased atone for his sins and will "spare" widows temptation when alone. Mary Daly (1983) describes the intolerable situation in which a widow found herself, and how death was the only real "choice" she could make. Religion forbade remarriage and there were no viable methods of self-support, except prostitution, in which case she would be shunned by her entire family. Underlying this custom, and the tolerance of other abusive patterns in India, is the high value placed on family honor.

In the ancient custom of suttee, widows were often blamed for the deaths of their husbands. In many cases, they were child brides of elderly men, possibly in their sixties, at the time of marriage. There is little to suggest that young women wanted to die in this way, and yet, the cultural definition of what occurred during suttee was that the widow "willingly" cremated herself. She was ritually bathed, attired, and drugged in preparation for her fate, and if necessary, she would be pushed into the fire. The practice of suttee was officially banned in 1829; widows were permitted to remarry in 1856, yet custom remained so strong that it was necessary to outlaw it again in 1956 (Daly, 1983). The reports that it has resurfaced in the latter part of the twentieth century indicate that outlawing entrenched traditional customs is no guarantee such practices will disappear.

In India, more recently, the crime of dowry burnings remains a serious source of concern. The harassment and violence of women by husbands and in-laws because of insufficient dowries must be examined within the context of several other cultural practices. The custom of arranged marriage (a legal convention, provided that the couple consent) is widely practiced in India. Arranged marriage takes the marital union out of the realm of individual romantic choice and places it within the context of families joining socially and economically with other families, presumably for mutual benefit. The dowry payment in Indian custom (in the form of cash, clothes, furniture, or appliances) is made by the bride's family to the groom's family. This payment was outlawed in 1961, punishable by heavy fines and jail sentences for those found guilty of demanding gifts from a bride's family. But, once again, the law is neither obeyed nor well enforced.

In 1975, the Indian Commission on the Status of Women reported that the dowry issue was one of the gravest problems affecting women in almost every Indian state (Morgan, 1984). The United Nations (1991a) reports that approximately five women a day are burned in dowry-related disputes, and activists claim the figure is actually much higher. Traditional residence patterns, following marriage in India, are patrilocal, meaning the bride is frequently isolated or removed from the protection of her own family and surrounded by her in-laws. In the case of a dowry being considered inadequate, the new wife may be exposed to harassment, battering, or burning or murdered in another way. In August 1982, thirty women's groups in Delhi demonstrated to call attention to dowry crimes and to demand that police handle these matters more effectively. Subsequently, a special unit was organized to investigate suspicious deaths of women who have been married six months or less. These deaths are often ruled suicides, although the authorities are cognizant that family ridicule may have driven the victim to self-destruction (Kelkar, 1985).

Expectations for dowry payment account for other forms of systemic violence against women in India—female infanticide and greater neglect of female children with resulting lopsided sex ratios in many parts of the country. But is it fair to blame dowry for the violence against these females? These injustices could not occur without the preexisting ideology of female subordination and devaluation.[7] Although the particular societal customs discussed here represent the more sensational effects of global misogyny, almost all societies are plagued with violence against women. The problem of domestic violence, of child and wife abuse, seems to be endemic throughout most of the modern world.

BATTERED WOMEN: CAN SAFETY BEGIN AT HOME?

Domestic violence is prevalent in all patriarchal cultures and in both developed and developing nations. Family members, especially women and children, are physically, psychologically, and sexually abused within the privacy of the home. The International Women's Movement, as well as women's movements in most countries, condemns domestic violence, wants to dispel myths that reinforce the behavior, and aims to enact policies to assist women who are battered. Despite educational awareness and some improvement in the handling of domestic violence cases, this form of abuse remains staggering in proportions and extremely resistant to remedies. In many countries, the battering of women is not officially recognized. Social custom frequently condones domestic violence and considers it a normal part of marriage—a private matter rather than a crime.

Worldwide statistics on wife abuse are unavailable, but the following figures suggest that the phenomenon is widespread: (1) In the United States, a woman is beaten every eighteen minutes; between three and four million are battered each year; however, estimates conclude that only one in one hundred cases is reported; (2) in parts of New Guinea, 67 percent of all women are victims of family violence; (3) in Bangladesh, half of the 170 female murder victims between 1983 and 1985 were victims of domestic violence; (4) in Colombia, approximately one-fifth of patients in a Bogota hospital were battered women; and (5) in Austria, almost 60 percent of divorce cases cited domestic violence as the cause (United Nations, 1991a). The widespread incidence of wife abuse is part of a legacy of patriarchal family relations which assumes that the husband has the right to physically punish or control his wife with physical force.

Throughout the seventeenth, eighteenth, and nineteenth centuries, legal codes in much of Europe and the United States permitted a husband to beat his wife. Some statutes were designed to ameliorate the degree of violence while still allowing it to occur. For instance, eighteenth-century French law restricted violence against wives to blows, thumps, kicks, or punches on the back, if they leave no traces, and forbade the use of sharp-edged or crushing instruments. The expression "rule of thumb" originated from English common law, which permitted a man to beat his wife with a stick, provided it was smaller than his thumb.

In 1910, in the United States, the Supreme Court ruled that a woman could not press charges against her husband because it would open the door for a public display of private accusations (Sheffield, 1997). In the United States, during the 1970s, the problem was redefined from a private one to a public one and placed into the category of a condition requiring community action. Personal testimony served to garner support, to further explore the concomitants of the abusive situation, and to attempt solutions. Dobash and Dobash (1997, pp. 267-268) provide familiar testimony from numerous countries:

> He once used a stick, he hit me once with a big fiberglass fishing pole, six foot long. And he just went woosh, he gave me such a wallop with that. I had a mark . . . right down my back. I thought my back had broke.
>
> —Scottish woman

> He used to bang my head against the wall or the floor. I finally left him when I thought he was trying to kill me.
>
> —English woman

> I hid what was happening to me from everyone. I made excuses for my bruises and marks. I thought I should put up with it . . . accept my lot as being part of marriage . . . I wanted to keep it hidden.
>
> —Irish woman

Cultural mores sanctioning wife beating still exist. Men often believe they must assume and ensure their dominance through the show of physical force. Threats, real or perceived, to male supremacy may exacerbate violence. In this context, any one of a number of stressors triggers physical abuse. Precipitating factors include pregnancy, childbirth, sexual problems, jealousy, money, arguments over gender role expectations, or any combination of these. Alcohol is closely associated with violence against women, as its consumption is usually considered a male "privilege." Alcohol lowers inhibitions and provides an "excuse" for the behavior. Women are often blamed for their own victimization. A frequent question concerning wife beating is, "Why doesn't she leave?" Further, many may believe that she deserves it, especially if she is suspected of infidelity. This latter belief is often codified into law:

> According to a recent comparative study on the legislation of several Mediterranean and Arab countries (i.e., Egypt, France,

Iraq, Jordan, Kuwait, Lebanon, the Libyan Arab Jamahiriyas, Portugal, Spain, the Syrian Arab Republic, Tunisia, and Turkey), crimes of honour continue to absolve husbands and other male relatives, partially or fully, from charges of homicide or severe bodily injury to this day. (United Nations, 1991a, p. 70)

Tacit sanctioning, the lackluster response of authorities, and the emotional toll (e.g., poor self-esteem, "learned helplessness," and fear) all serve to make domestic violence one of the least reported crimes in the world. Many countries deny that violence against women in the family is a problem; others, such as India and Japan, report a suspiciously low incidence of this type of abuse. There are various interpretations of worldwide underreporting. Underreporting may be a consequence of cultural or official government definitions (in which case, women's grassroots efforts might yield quite different data), or as hypothesized by Gelles and Cornell (1983), it may be that in societies where male dominance is firmly entrenched violence is less necessary to ensure obedience.

Sometimes there are highly contradictory messages about women and domestic violence within a given culture. Peru offers an example of this disparity. In Peru, customs of chivalry and practices of machismo become intertwined with inequities of race, class, and gender. The expression "not even with a rose petal" (should a man strike a woman) exemplifies the ideal of protectionism toward women of European descent. Yet Peruvian machismo is apparent in the following statistic: between 70 and 80 percent of the crimes reported daily to the Peruvian police are cases of women who have been beaten by their husbands (Portugal, 1984). There are other Peruvian adages that attempt to justify the actual frequency of domestic violence, such as the Sierra folk saying, "The more you hit me, the more I love you" (Ibid., p. 552). The existence of both ideologies makes it even more difficult to combat wife battering. The rejoinder to assertions regarding abuse may be, on the one hand, that there is no problem because we do not approve of abuse, or on the other hand, there is no problem because the abuse is indicative of love!

David Levinson (1989) reports that wife beating exists in seventy-five out of ninety cultures studied in a comparative analysis of ethnographic data. He concludes that four factors are strong predictors of wife abuse: (1) economic inequality between men and women, (2) the normative acceptance of violence to settle conflicts, (3) patriarchal decision making in the home, and (4) the wife's inability to obtain a divorce. Societies with low abuse rates generally use nonviolent strategies to settle disputes, have basic respect for all members of the family, and share household labor. These societies allow couples to divorce when they do not get along.

Whereas it is difficult to completely change cultures, noteworthy efforts have been made to ameliorate worldwide domestic violence. The United Nations has requested that its member states adopt short- and long-term strategies to protect victims and punish perpetrators of this type of abuse. Some countries have complied with the request and have instituted programs. Examples of these programs include: (1) Australia has reclassified domestic violence as assault, and initiated a national educational and retraining campaign, establishing shelters in which 43,000 women and children sought refuge between 1986-1987; (2) Costa Rica has made the abuse of women illegal; and (3) in Zimbabwe, the Musasa Project (1988) provides counseling for women who have been raped or beaten by their husbands or lovers and informs them of their legal rights (United Nations, 1991a). Much more needs to be done. The 1993 United Nations World Conference on Human Rights and the 1995 World Women's Conference addressed wife battering, defining it as a violation of human rights requiring immediate action.

SEXUAL HARASSMENT: CAN WOMEN BE COMFORTABLE IN THE PUBLIC WORLD?

Sexual harassment on the street and in the workplace affects millions of women around the world. There is a broad range of behavior under this rubric. The behavior in question involves repeated unwanted and unwelcome sexual advances.

In public areas, unwanted behaviors include anything from catcalls and whistles to offensive and threatening touching. In the workplace, sexual harassment is sometimes associated with ultimatums regarding continued employment, for example, "If you don't sleep with me, you're fired." However, there are other less blatant forms of harassment that may be perpetrated by a superior, a peer, or even a subordinate. All of these behaviors have the effect of controlling women by making them feel uncomfortable and impairing their effectiveness on the job. Attitudes that condone this behavior require women to be constantly on guard. They are at risk of being blamed for their own harassment; they may lose their jobs if they report the harassment, or they may be ostracized by workers who prefer to maintain the status quo. Most nations of the world have no sex harassment policy. In Islamic nations, many women who cover their heads and/or faces explain self-protection is part of their rationale. It conveys a message to men that they are uninterested in any sexual involvement—that they are moral and religious.

In September 1980, the Equal Employment Opportunity Commission (EEOC), under the federal government of the United States, issued guidelines on sexual harassment that apply to both government and private employers. Sexual harassment was considered a form of sex discrimination and as such was prohibited under Title VII of the 1964 Civil Rights Act. In 1986, the U.S. Supreme Court finally ruled on a sexual harassment case, reinforcing its connection to the discrimination legislation (Martin, 1989). The employer is responsible for apprising employees of the sex harassment policy. Therefore, most large companies and organizations in the United States attempt to educate all employees of the EEOC guidelines, as well as drawing up their own policies to help clarify unacceptable conduct. Despite the concept of protecting employees from harassment gaining acceptance, the United States is still a long way from solving workplace sexual harassment and has yet to address, in any serious way, the problem of peer harassment or "routine" street harassment.

Although men occasionally report sexual harassment, the incidence of this for women is staggering. Women who are harassed at their workplace suffer both economically and psychologically, and even with a system for redress, it is difficult to know which course of action will be the most effective. Similar to rape victims, sexually harassed women feel humiliated, angry, and frightened, and often blame themselves. Their emotional response may cause them to leave their positions, miss time, and/or be inattentive at work. The experience may cause the victim to suffer psychologically for years after, even when the harassment has been apparently forgotten.

Europe has recently made advances in confronting sexual harassment. In July 1991, the European Community adopted a new code of Practice of the Protection of the Dignity of Women and Men at Work, which encourages employers to develop a policy statement that bans sexual harassment and to appoint trained personnel to handle complaints. In Spain and France, sexual harassment is a criminal offense, although their laws are described as vague and difficult for women to follow through in litigation (United Nations, 1991a). In much of the rest of the world, there are no policies regarding sex harassment and informal reports indicate that abuses are pandemic.

Female domestic workers are particularly vulnerable to this type of victimization. In El Salvador, unofficial statistics suggest that women working as servants and/or for multinational factories commonly face sexual assault from male employers (Morgan, 1984). The situation of foreign women working as maids in Kuwait made international headlines. There are approximately 100,000 domestic servants in Kuwait from Asian countries, including India, Sri Lanka, and the Philippines. These women are required to pay fees (about $500) before coming to Kuwait, with the promise of the return of their fees in less than a month. Some come so they can send substantial sums back to their families and children. They do not make the salaries promised (most earn approximately $165 a month), and they encounter abuse as a corollary of their work. Embassies receive between fifteen and twenty new runaways daily, who report they have been denied pay, locked up, given no time off or have been beaten, sexually harassed, and even raped by their Kuwaiti employers.

Women workers in this situation have little recourse. The Kuwaiti government has not volunteered to intervene on behalf of foreign female labor. In some situations, they are told they cannot have their passports returned until they repay the recruitment fee paid by their employers ($1,500) to be released from their contracts (Hedges, 1993b).

Street harassment is rampant throughout the world. This type of harassment involves offensive touching, sexual gestures, and personal remarks. The consequence for women is a hostile, uncomfortable environment. In India, sexual harassment, "insulting the modesty of a woman by word, gesture, or act," is a punishable offense that carries a penalty of heavy fines and imprisonment (Morgan, 1984, p. 300). This law was instituted in the 1970s in an effort to reclaim family honor through protection of the family's women. Despite the existence of the law, however, the custom of "Eve-teasing" has continued, and women demonstrated, beginning in the 1980s, for more "women-only" buses to protect themselves from harassment (Morgan, 1984).

RAPE

Rape occurs when a person uses force or threat of force to obtain some form of sexual penetration (vaginal, oral, or anal) with another person. Rape is yet another underreported crime. When Robin Morgan edited *Sisterhood Is Global* in 1984 and updated it in 1996, she surveyed the laws and practices of sixty-four and seventy countries, respectively. Morgan found rape to be illegal in the vast majority of them, but there were usually qualifications as to what constituted rape and who could be raped. Although there were laws that officially forbade rape in over half the countries surveyed, there was no data on incidence. Where there were statistics, they were suspiciously low. Scholars continue to debate the significance of these low reports. Rape, as with wife abuse and sexual harassment, appears to be less common in societies where seclusion and repression of women is most complete. Those who assume these crimes really are less frequent believe that force is used by the dominant group only when they feel their superior position is being threatened. Others believe that rape is just as prevalent in these countries, but women are afraid to report it, and government propaganda suppresses the reports that do occur. Worldwide sexism promotes norms, myths, and laws that excuse many forms of rape and creates a situation in which women are kept in fear and men are encouraged to assume that raping a woman is their right or the fault of the victim.

On July 10, 1991, seventy-one teenage girls were raped and nineteen were killed by their classmates at St. Kizito's boarding school in Meru, Kenya. The boys were retaliating against the girls for failing to join them in a strike against the school's headmaster. The *Kenya Times* reported that rape was a common occurrence and the deputy principal stated that, "The boys didn't mean to harm the girls, they just wanted to rape" (Heise, 1991, p. C1). This attitude is not unusual. The crime is often not taken seriously unless the woman who is raped "belongs" to another man. The Latin root of the word rape means "theft," and cultural responses to this violence often emphasize reclaiming the woman's lost value.

In many cases, rape is viewed not as a violation of a woman's body, but as an act that has dishonored a father, a husband, or a family. In these cases, the rapist must pay, sometimes at the expense of the victim. Middle Eastern and North African countries are particularly likely to mention family honor as part of their penal code outlawing rape. Morocco, for example, states that rape is a "crime and offense against family order and public morality" (Morgan, 1984, p. 446). The normal penalty is between five and ten years imprisonment. However, if the victim was a virgin, the penalty is between ten and twenty years (Morgan, 1984). The focus of attention is what to do with the woman who has been raped. If she is unmarried, the rape, with its consequent loss of virginity, may make it impossible for her to marry. If she is a married woman, her dishonored husband will likely repudiate their marriage. A 1981 study conducted by Gideon Kressel of Jerusalem's Hebrew University reported that, of seventy-two honor murders of Arab Israelis, five were against women who had been raped (Heise, 1991). Many more rape victims are cast out and become beggars or prostitutes.

This ubiquitous double standard creates a challenge for feminists to shift the burden of proof from the woman to the man. Mexican feminists rallied around Claudia Rodriguez Ferrando, who spent one year in jail and was facing a possible ten more years for shooting and killing a man who tried to sexually assault her. When he originally heard the case, Judge Gustavo Aquiles Gasca weighed the evidence in light of prevailing cultural norms. Mr. Cruz, Ms. Rodriguez's husband, had willingly stayed home with their five children to allow his wife to go out to a party. He had given her his pistol for safety. This seemed an odd type of marriage in Texcoco, Mexico. It did not seem unusual that Mr. Carbrera, the dead man, also married, was out with another woman. The fact that forensic tests confirmed that Mr. Carbrera's blood was saturated with alcohol further convinced the judge that the man was not responsible for his own actions. He concluded that Ms. Rodriguez "provoked him to attack her." Once women knew about the Rodriguez case, it became a symbol in their crusade for fair treatment. More than 500 women, including soap opera stars, legislators, and novelists signed a petition for her release (Preston, 1997).

A United Nations study (1991a) concluded that sexual violence and rape are often a part of wife abuse (discussed earlier in this chapter). For example, approximately one in seven wives in the United Kingdom has been raped by her spouse. Rape and sexual abuse within marriage or in intimate relationships is highly traumatic, as it constitutes a betrayal of trust and is the antithesis of what sexual relations are ideally supposed to mean. The absence of marital rape laws throughout the world underscores the concept that marriage essentially authorizes the husband to have sex with his wife, whenever he desires and regardless of her wishes. Only a few countries have incorporated marital rape into their penal codes; some of those that have are Canada, Denmark, Poland, Scotland, and Sweden (United Nations, 1991a).

Peggy Reeves Sanday (1997) has spent years collecting data and studying the cross-cultural variation in rape. Sanday's findings led her to compile profiles of "rape-prone" societies and "rape-free" societies. Rape-prone societies either allow or overlook sexual assault. Sexual conquest confers status on men, men are posed as a social group against women, and rituals may include rape. The Gusü culture of southwestern Kenya is a rape-prone society in which a "real man" makes his bride cry on her wedding night. Rape-free societies are characterized by sexual equality and the notion that both women and men are indispensable. Interpersonal violence is rare in rape-free societies. Sanday concludes that values which uphold female characteristics and the sacredness of life deter the likelihood of rape.

CAN VIOLENCE AGAINST WOMEN BE ELIMINATED?

The task of reducing violence against women is complex. It involves combating sexism, misogyny, and assumptions about male dominance and male supremacy; learning to settle disputes on all levels nonviolently; systematic governmental and international support of issues of importance to women; restructuring legal systems in ways that recognize women's inherent humanity; adjusting economic systems so that women are neither exploited economically nor forced into degrading work; regulating objectifying and pornographic media images of women; and developing ways in which men and women can relate without either dependency or dominance.

The violence that women throughout the world experience is fostered by ongoing and escalating regional, national, and international military conflicts. The challenge of reversing world military expenditures, and altering underlying world economic inequality that creates much of the conflict, seems formidable. It will take both women and men of many nations, acting in the best interests of humanity, to learn nonviolent methods of conflict resolution. Women have been absent from political roles that would involve them in decisions regarding military action, and they are likewise absent in peace negotiations. Many women have, however, been involved in voluntary organizations working toward peace and disarmament. One of the earliest efforts of this type was The Women's International League for Peace and Freedom (WILPF), founded on April 28, 1915. In that year, an international congress of women gathered at The Hague in Holland to formulate a plan to stop World War I and to promote a permanent peace that would rest on a foundation of equal rights, justice within and between nations, and national independence and freedom (Bussey and Tims, 1980).

In the 1980s, at least thirty all-women peace encampments protested the deployment of first-strike nuclear technology on three continents (Lederman, 1989). Also in that year, Feminists International for Peace and Food (FIPF) was formed by women from nearly twenty countries in South America, North America, the Middle East, and Europe. A specific goal of this organization has been to make people see the connection between the "way women are treated and the existence of war" (Wiser, 1989, p. 288). Some believe that an equal number of women to men in governmental decision-making posts will facilitate an end to global conflict. Whether or not this is the case, there is no question that women need to be represented in all delegations negotiating war and peace issues and international policy.

Koss, Heise, and Russo (1997) address the psychological, somatic, sociocultural, and economic consequences of interpersonal violence, especially rape, on a global basis. They believe that assembling a cross-national database to obtain reliable statistics is a priority, as recognition of the high incidence of violence against women will validate women's real experience and document the need for change. Countless local women's organizations throughout the world are dedicated to combating violence against women. Some of the best strategies include support services and shelters for raped and battered women, where psychological counseling, medical care, and legal advice can assist women to regain self-respect, weigh their options, and decide on a course of action.

To both prevent abuse and help women to recover from abuse, there must be concerted action on all fronts to eliminate sexual discrimination. A comprehensive agenda of health care, reproductive counseling, education, employment training, and opportunities for advancement can do much to raise the status of women and make them more likely to resist interpersonal aggression. Media campaigns of two different types can be beneficial in curtailing violence against women. The first type strives to eliminate violent pornography and violence in the mainstream media. The second type disseminates educational messages advising nonviolent solutions to conflict and spreads information about legal rights and support services.

Feminists and human rights activists have become increasingly active in efforts to reduce the worldwide violence against women. The United Nations 1979 Convention on the Elimination of All Forms of Discrimination Against Women has now been ratified by over 100 nations. In so doing, these nations have pledged to implement provisions giving women equal rights and fundamental freedoms. The 1993 United Nations Conference on Human Rights included all levels of abuse against women in their deliberations.

The task is enormous, since deeply embedded cultural mores, complex interpersonal relationships, sacred religious teachings, and subtle societal expectations must be altered. Nevertheless, nothing short of ensuring every woman's health and safety, providing her equal opportunity, and recognizing her full dignity will suffice.

SUMMARY

Violence, from war and revolution to sexual harassment and wife beating, prevents women from having the safety and security to actualize their potential. Military expenses subvert funds from health and human services so vital to improving women's status. The civil wars in Rwanda and the former Yugoslavia reveal patterns of rape, murder, and forced impregnation as a tactic of the conflict. Refugee camps of displaced women and children attest to the fact that women's lives, as they knew them, are destroyed by war. Cultural customs often incorporate a type of structural, normative violence against women; female genital mutilation is one such example. Domestic violence is a pervasive part of patriarchal families and is just starting to receive worldwide sanction. Women are harassed, raped, and beaten every hour, every day. Cultural myths and entrenched sexist attitudes frequently blame women for their own victimization. Efforts to stop violence against women require a two-pronged attack designed to promote peace and to advance women's status.

KEY WORDS
Apartheid
Colonialism
Companeras
Comfort stations
Comfort women
Dowry
Female sexual slavery
Forced impregnation
Ideology
Infibulation
International feminism
Lobola
Macro-level violence
Micro-level violence
Nationalism
Patriarchy
Peace
Sex-gender system
Sex tourism
Sunna circumcision
War crimes tribunals

Conclusions

Women's issues are remarkably similar worldwide, yet vary enough to make comparisons informative and useful for a feminist future. This book discusses and analyzes interrelated themes in women's lives, offering local or particular examples of many of the "critical areas of concern" identified at the Fourth World Women's Conference: family equality, sexual and reproductive rights, educational and work opportunities, good health care, and freedom from violence.

The complexities of viewing women's lives and challenges internationally are considerable. We want to acknowledge that there is a global economic and political hierarchy, and some women are privileged by their class, racial status, or age, while others may experience multiple oppression. We strive to respect the integrity and values of the cultures we discuss, yet we are committed to exposing practices that we believe are detrimental to women. We know that we frequently travel in controversial territory and that not all women experience gendered power relationships as a problem that has to be changed, nor are the recommended solutions always the same.

As communication and transportation technology advances, all parts of the world are more accessible and more subject to capitalist globalization. Feminism and the reaction to feminism is part of the globalization process. The exposure and diffusion of feminism means that women's rights are widely discussed and often accepted. This aspect of global feminism has the potential to make the commitment to women's equality a legitimate component of national and international institutions. Yet, there are no guarantees that a feminist future will easily unfold. Our own reservations defy convenient categories. We are concerned about the diverse, but ubiquitous, global backlash against feminists. We question the Western/Northern ethnocentrism inherent in current international feminist discourse. Will poor and third world women benefit from this liberal, capitalist orientation?

The realities of worldwide militarism, nationalism, poverty, and religion will undoubtedly shape ideas about women, men, and families. Conflict is certain over which theories and resulting policies are really in women's best interests.

BACKLASH/ROLLBACKS

Although worldwide feminism has entered the mainstream and feminist enthusiasm is alive and well in many corners of the world (maybe most particularly in developing regions), the movement is also plagued by violent opposition, disillusionment, and apathy. Women at the forefront of resistance are always susceptible to violent repression. We have witnessed examples of this in the beatings and murders of women, who have failed to follow Islamic dress and behavior codes, in Algeria, Iran, the Sudan, and Afghanistan; in India, where activists against so-called "dowry deaths" have, themselves, been threatened and raped; and in the United States, where women working in abortion clinics have been threatened and killed.

Feminism faces another type of backlash, which is equally disturbing. In many parts of the world, there is hostility and distrust of the feminist label. Conservative thinking that ascribes all social ills (e.g., poverty, divorce, overwork) to the women's movement attracts many women and men in Canada, the United States, and Western European countries. In Eastern Europe and Russia, there is a virulent effort to dislodge women from any employment gains they may have made under communist rule, although communism never actually lived up to its promise of sex equality. New laws and a new religious authority place women in a dependency role vis-à-vis men. Feminism carries a negative stereotype associated with the former totalitarian regime.

DIVERSITY AND SISTERHOOD

Despite common challenges, most women in wealthy countries and women of privileged status in all countries have very different realities from most women in poor countries and poor women in wealthy countries. Upper-class women depend on the services of poor women in their own country and share in the disproportionate international wealth maintained, in part, through the exploitation of women in developing countries. To overcome differences and join forces in international sisterhood, elite women need to understand and acknowledge how they and their governments contribute to the oppression of their disadvantaged sisters.

Other forms of diversity interfere with finding common ground. Women come from different races, ages, religions, ethnic backgrounds, and sexual orientations. Women with similar identities often form separate groups in order to be heard. Coalitions across these groups can begin to establish a common feminist cause.

WOMEN'S LEADERSHIP AND THE FUTURE

One of the greatest obstacles women face cross-nationally is the low number of women in official leadership positions. Leadership, in the traditional context, is about power and service to one's world and the ability to bring about progress for all. Women have always and will always be leaders, but they are often behind-the-scenes leaders. Those who become parliamentarians and heads of state have their style and agenda under scrutiny. The public and the press watch to see if they have the ability to survive in a tough masculine arena. We need equal female representation in official leadership positions as a simple matter of justice, as role models and as people who are personally connected to women's struggle for equality. We must also recognize the amazing accomplishments of women leaders on the local level within their own communities.

A BRIDGE TO THE FUTURE

Despite setbacks and stalled progress in some areas, the advances of women worldwide are worthy of applause. More and more women achieve success in higher education and emerge as doers in the public world, proving gender is no barrier to excellence. On the home front, women are striving for equal rights and greater respect, comprehensive health care, and an end to violence. Each gain creates other gains. For example, when a woman becomes literate, she teaches her children to read, and starts study groups in her community, thus many others become skilled, inspired, and confident.

We have the promise for a future in which women and men can work together and share decisions as the next millennium unfolds. The groundwork of the United Nations and nongovernmental agencies (NGOs) in galvanizing resources, forming networks, and brainstorming solutions is a strong beginning. International women's conferences and international conferences that include women's issues prove that we can transcend cultural, language, and governmental borders to understand and support each other. Perhaps most important is that women meeting globally have seen their issues in the broadest context and have articulated principles to ensure human rights (also women's rights), a sustainable environment, and peace in the world. The advancement of women means the progress and well-being of all humanity.

Notes

Introduction

1. The terms for various parts of the world present a dilemma. The designation of First World for developed democracies, Second World for formerly communist countries, and Third World for poor, exploited countries, often in the Southern hemisphere, appears awkward. Some object to the implicit hierarchy in the number system, yet others in poor countries say this classification calls attention to their plight.

2. Notable women speakers at the fourth women's conference included Rigoberta Menchu', Nobel Peace Prize winner; Prime Minister Benazir Bhutto of Pakistan; and First Lady Hillary Rodham Clinton of the United States.

Chapter 1

1. Collins, P. *Black Feminist Thought*, New York: Routledge, 1991; Garcia, A. The development of Chicana feminist discourse, *Gender and Society*, 3(2), 1986, pp. 217-238; Sanchez-Ayendez, Puerto Rican elderly women: Shared meanings and informed supportive networks. In J. Cole (Ed.), *All American Women: Lines That Divide, Ties That Bind*, New York: Free Press, 1986.

2. Skinner, B. *The Behavior of Organisms*, New York: Appleton-Century-Crofts, 1938; Bijou, S. *Child Development*, Englewood Cliffs, NJ: Prentice-Hall, 1976; Hoffman, L. Paris, S., Hall, E., and Schell, R., *Developmental Psychology Today*, New York: Random House, 1988.

3. Williams, C. The psychology of women, In J. Wetzel, M. Espenlaub, M. Hagan, A. McElhiney, and C. Williams, *Women's Studies: Thinking of Women*, Dubuque, IA: Kendall/Hunt Publishing Co., 1993; Lerner, H. *Women in Therapy*, New York: Harper & Row, 1988.

4. This young woman was interviewed on her way to the market outside the city of Oaxaca, Mexico, in October 1992.

5. See *Statistical Record of Women Worldwide*, edited by L. Schmittroth (1991), for a full description of worldwide life expectancies at birth. In some parts of the world, women's life expectancy is comparatively low (e.g., Angola, 46.1 years, Botswana, 59.7 years, and Cote d'Ivoire, 54.2 years), while in other areas women's life expectancy meets or exceeds 80 years (e.g., France and Switzerland).

6. Batezat, E. and Mwato, M. *Women in Zimbabwe*, Harare, Zimbabwe: Sapes, 1989; Kuper, A. *Wives for Cattle: Bride Wealth and Marriage in Southern Africa*, Boston: Routledge and Kegan Paul, 1982.

7. This was discussed in the *Government of Zimbabwe: Action Plan* (Government of Zimbabwe, 1986). In this document, an analysis of both the preindependence needs and the postindependence needs of Zimbabwe were made.

8. While interviewing nurses at a hospital in Bulaywo, a woman waiting to be seen for visible injuries to the face and arms was also interviewed. These comments represent how she explained her injuries and why she felt it necessary to stay within her present relationship (August 1993).

9. See Hughes, D.O. From bride-price to dowry in Mediterranean Europe. In M. Kaplan (Ed.), *The Marriage Bargain*, Binghamton, NY: The Haworth Press and the Institute for Research and History, 1985.

10. For greater explanations of European systems of dowry exchange, see Kaplan, 1985; and Collier, J. *Marriage and Inequality in Classless Societies*, Stanford, CA: Stanford University Press, 1988.

11. Kumari, R. *Brides Are Not for Burning: Dowry Victims in India*, New Delhi: Radiant Publishers, 1989; and Bennett, *Dangerous Wives and Sacred Sisters,* New York: Columbia University Press, 1983.

12. Nazzari, M. *Disappearance of the Dowry*, Stanford, CA: Stanford University Press, 1991; Kumari, R. *Brides Are Not for Burning*, 1989; Beatty, A. *Society and Exchange in Nias,* Oxford: Clarendon Press, 1992.

13. All the family and village neighbor women pay a rupee or two for the privilege of looking at the new bride's face, which had remained covered during most of the wedding ceremonies. For that small price they buy license to minutely examine and criticize the bride, her features, and the gifts sent with her by her parents (Bennett, *Dangerous Wives*, 1983).

14. July 1994 interview in Dakar, Senegal.

15. In traditional Korean marriages, this would be the last time a daughter would see her birth family until the birth of her first child. Thus, many daughters would cry through the second part of the ceremony as they grieved the loss of their family. Source: interview, January 1995, Korean married woman.

16. Jumping the broom is based on a slavery tradition of jumping the broom to symbolize a marriage that was not legally permitted among Africans held in slavery. This tradition was popularized by *Roots*, written by Alex Haley, and is incorporated in some African-American contemporary weddings. Source: interview, 1996, African-American young woman, recently married.

17. A Hindu woman recalls the significance of her marriage during an interview in September 1994. She recalled memories that testified to both the beauty of her marriage and the contradictions of being on display for all to observe.

18. Maclean, M. *Surviving Divorce: Women's Resources After Separation,* Washington Square, NY: New York University Press, 1991; Parkman, A. *No-Fault Divorce: What Went Wrong?* Boulder, CO: Westview Press, 1992; Robinson, M. *Family Transformation Through Divorce and Remarriage: A Systematic Approach*, London: Routledge, 1991; Gibson, C. *Dissolving Wedlock*, London: Routledge, 1994; Phillips, R. *Divorce in New Zealand*, Aukland, New Zealand: Oxford University Press, 1981.

19. Parkman, *No-Fault Divorce,* 1992; Gibson, *Dissolving Wedlock,* 1994; Dillon, M. *Debating Divorce: Moral Conflict in Ireland,* Lexington, KY: University Press of Kentucky, 1993; Maclean, *Surviving Divorce,* 1991.

20. Robinson, *Family Transformation,* 1991; Arendell, T. *Mothers and Divorce: Legal, Economic, and Social Dilemmas,* Berkeley: University of California Press, 1986.

21. Gibson, *Dissolving Wedlock,* 1994; Phillips, R. *Putting Asunder,* Cambridge, MA: Cambridge University Press, 1988.

22. Phillips, *Putting Asunder,* 1988; Robinson, *Family Transformation,* 1991.

23. See November 26, 1996, *The New York Times,* "Irish Vote to End the Divorce Ban by a Tiny Margin," Clarity, J.

24. Gibson, *Dissolving Wedlock,* 1994; Dillon, *Debating Divorce,* 1993; Robinson, *Family Transformation,* 1991.

25. See Phillips, *Putting Asunder,* 1988, for a discussion of the bitter and unsuccessful earlier attempts.

26. A judicial separation allows the person to not live with his or her spouse, but the two are still legally married. However, the Family Law Reform of 1989 allows property to be divided at separation.

27. Some recognition was always given to foreign divorce. If either spouse lives in a country where a divorce is granted, Ireland will recognize the divorce.

28. Before overturning the ban on divorce, the civil court could annul a marriage if a significant reason was presented. The lack of consent of a minor or a person who was actually legally married are two examples. Once annulment occurs, persons are treated as unmarried. Few judicial annulments were ever granted.

29. These were more common than civil annulment. They were granted by the Catholic church. These annulments can be granted for three reasons: (1) due to extreme impediment, previous valid marriage, impotence, etc; (2) due to improper procedures during the marriage ceremony; and (3) due to defective consent. After an ecclesiastical annulment, both parties are free to remarry in the church.

30. Interviewed during the Global Summit for Women in Dublin, Ireland, 1992.

31. Bascom, W. *The Yoruba of Southwestern Nigeria,* New York: Holt, Reinhart, and Winston, 1969; Beatty, *Society and Exchange,* 1992.

Chapter 2

1. Thorne, B. and Yalom, M., *Rethinking the Family,* Boston, MA: Northeastern University Press, 1992; Ward, M., *A World Full of Women,* Boston, MA: Allyn and Bacon, 1996.

2. hooks, b. *Ain't I a Woman: Black Women and Feminism,* Boston: South End Press, 1981; Baca Zinn, M. *Women of Color in the United States,* Philadelphia, PA: Temple University Press, 1994.

3. United Nations, "Changes in the Size of Households in Selected Developed Countries," *Report on the World Social Situation,* New York: United Nations, 1990. In this report, similar increases are noted in one-person households within England/ Wales, France, Germany, Sweden, and Switzerland. By the late 1980s, these countries' percentage of one-person households ranged from 22 percent to 33 percent.

4. The percentage of women's wages to men's wages varies tremendously. By 1989/1990, women's wages in Iceland were 90 percent of men's; women's wages in France, 89 percent of men's; in the United Kingdom, 70 percent; in Korea, 59 percent; and in Japan, 52 percent. *Yearbook of Labor Statistics, 1986-1988*, Geneva: International Labor Office, 1992.

5. Senior, O. *Working Miracles: Women's Lives in English-Speaking Caribbean*, London: James Curry, 1991; Gopaul-McNicol, S. *Working with West Indian Families*. New York: The Guilford Press, 1993.

6. Senior, *Working Miracles*, 1991; Gopaul-McNicol, *Working with West Indian Families*, 1993; Garcia, A. Development of Chicana feminist discourse, *Gender and Society*, 3(2), 1986: 217-238; Phoenix, A., The Afro-Caribbean myth, *New Society*, 82, 1988: 10-13; Powell, D. Caribbean women and their responses to familial experiences, *Social and Economic Studies*, 35, 1986: 83-130.

7. Polyandry is a multiple marriage pattern in which a woman is married to more than one male. A typical form is fraternal polyandry: a woman is married to a set of brothers.

8. Brody, E. Parent care as a normative family stress, *The Gerontologist*, 25(1), 1985: 19-29; Conway-Turner, K. and Karasik, R. Adult daughters' anticipation of caregiving responsibilities, *Journal of Women and Aging*, 5(1), 1993: 99-114.

9. Senior, *Working Miracles*, 1991; Gopaul-McNicol, *Working with West Indian Families*, 1993.

10. Gibson, C. *Dissolving Wedlock*, London: Routledge, 1994; Maclean, M. *Surviving Divorce: Women's Resources After Separation*. Washington Square, NY: New York University Press, 1991; Phillips, R. *Divorce in New Zealand*. Aukland, New Zealand: Oxford University Press, 1981.

11. Knox, D. *Choices in Relationships*. Minneapolis/St. Paul: West Publishing Co., 1994; Schwartz, M.A. and Scott, B. *Marriages and Families: Diversity and Change*, Englewood Cliffs, NJ: Prentice-Hall, 1994.

12. Swidler, A. *Homosexuality and World Religions*. Valley Forge, PA: Trinity Press International, 1993; Butler, B. *Ceremonies of the Heart: Celebrating Lesbian Unions*. Seattle, WA: The Seal Press, 1990; Katz, J. *Gay American History*. NY: Crowell, 1976; Faderman, L. *Surpassing the Love of Men: Romantic Friendships and Love Between Women from the Renaissance to the Present*. New York: William Morris and Co., 1981. See also Radcliffe Hall (1928), *The Well of Loneliness*, New York: Avon Books, 1956, as the first published piece on lesbianism that attempts to center lesbianism as an alternate lifestyle. Faderman, *Surpassing the Love of Men*, 1981, discussed the complexity of lesbian lifestyles and introduced a discussion that was new in the family literature.

13. Butler, *Ceremonies of the Heart*, 1990; and *The News Journal*, "New Law Lets Swedish Gays Marry," January 1995, p. 6.

14. *Connexions*, Global lesbianism 2, 1981b, critically explores the context for lesbians in many parts of the world.

15. See *Connexions* issues Global Lesbianism and Global Lesbianism 2, 1981a, b; and Schwartz and Scott, *Marriage and Families*, 1994.

16. Johnson, W. and Warren, D. *Inside the Mixed Marriage,* New York: University Press of America, 1993; Lee, R. *Mixed and Matched: Interreligious Courtship and Marriage in Northern Ireland,* New York: University Press of America, 1994; Knox, *Choices in Relationships,* 1994; Richard, M. *Ethnic Groups and Marital Choices,* Vancouver: UBC Press, 1991; Romano, P. *Intercultural Marriage: Promises and Pitfalls.* Yarmouth, ME: Intercultural Press, 1988.

17. Romano, P. *Promises and Pitfalls,* 1988; Johnson, W. and Warren, D. *Inside the Mixed Marriage,* 1993: Barbara, A. *Marriage Across Frontiers.* Philadelphia, PA: Multilingual Matters Ltd., 1989.

18. Barbara, A. *Marriage Across Frontiers,* 1989; Romano, P. *Promises and Pitfalls,* 1988; Johnson, W. and Warren, D. *Inside the Mixed Marriage,* 1993.

19. Embry, J. *Mormon Polygamous Families: Life in Principle,* Salt Lake City: University of Utah Press, 1987; Kilbride, P. *Plural Marriages for Our Times: A Reinvented Option,* Westport, CT: Greenwood Publishing Corporation, 1994; Bohannan, P. *All the Happy Families,* New York: McGraw-Hill Books, 1985.

20. Maillu, D. *Our Kind of Polygamy,* 1988; Levine, N., *The Dynamics of Polyandry: Kinship, Domesticity, and Population on Tibetan Border,* Chicago: University of Chicago Press, 1988; Bascom, W. *The Yoruba of Southwestern Nigeria,* New York: Holt, Reinhart and Winston, 1969.

21. Crouter, A. *Harem: The World Behind the Veil,* New York: Abbeville Press, 1989; Embry, J. *Mormon Polygamous Families,* 1987; Bohannan, P. *All the Happy Families,* 1985, Kilbride, *Plural Marriages,* 1994.

22. Bascom, W. *The Yoruba,* 1969; Levine, N. *The Dynamics of Polyandry,* 1988.

23. McAdoo, H. (Ed.), *Family Ethnicity: Strength in Diversity,* Newbury Park, CA: Sage, 1993; Staples, R. and Johnson, L., *Black Families at the Crossroads,* San Francisco: Jossey-Bass, 1992; Williams, N. *The Mexican American Family: Tradition and Change.* Dix Hills, NY: General Hall, Inc., 1990.

Chapter 3

1. Sanger, M. Birth control—A parent's problem or woman's? In A. Rossi (Ed.), *The Feminist Papers.* New York: Bantam Books, 1973: 533.

2. Sadik, N. *The State of the World Population.* New York: UNFPA/United Nations Population Fund, 1991: 10.

3. See Simon, J. and Kahn, H. (Eds.), *The Resourceful Earth: A Response to Global 2000,* Oxford, England: Basil Blackwell, Inc., 1984; or Kasun J. *The War Against Population,* San Francisco, CA: Ignatius Press, 1988, for a counterperspective to those concerned about the negative impact of high world population.

4. Weeks, J. *Population,* 1992; Jamison, E. and Hobbs, F., *World Population Profile: 1994,* Washington, DC: U.S. Department of Commerce, Economics, and Statistics Administration, Bureau of Census, 1994.

5. Pooler (1991) reports that in surveys asking U.S. college students "If you could only have one child, which one would you prefer?" 80 percent of males said they would want a boy, but a majority of female students (54 percent in 1985, and 58 percent in 1988) said they would want a girl.

6. Interview, 1994, eighteen-year-old woman, Granada, Spain.

7. Interview, 1994, eighteen-year-old woman, Vienna, Austria.

8. Interview, 1994, forty-four-year-old woman reflecting on the norms in Sichuan, China.

9. Agreement on a woman's sexual rights was not easy. One notable omission was the right to pursue a lesbian relationship.

10. Interview conducted by Ezeh, A., The influence of spouses, 1993: 171.

11. Interview conducted October 6, 1994, Wilmington, Delaware.

12. HIV infection is no longer a primarily male disease. Women are increasingly becoming infected with the virus. They are becoming infected at a significantly younger age than men, with many teenagers and women in their twenties in this category. The highest proportions of infected women at the present time are in sub-Saharan Africa. Studies suggest that the younger the age of intercourse and first pregnancy, the higher the incidence of HIV infection. The remedy to this urgent problem is intricately connected with the same measures that will reduce women's fertility and other sexually transmitted diseases—sex education for all young people and the empowerment of women to make informed choices. The ability of young women to protect themselves relies on the restructuring of power relations between men and women. If sexual intercourse is to take place, condoms provide the best protection against HIV infection, requiring the cooperation of both partners. (See Chapter 5 for further discussion of STDs and AIDS.)

13. During the fall of 1996, *The New York Times* ran a series of articles about Taliban policies. See: Burns, J., "Stoning of Afghan Adulterers: Some Go to Take Part, Others Just to Watch." *The New York Times,* November 3, 1996: 18; and Sciolino, E., "The Many Faces of Islamic Law." *The New York Times,* October 13, 1996: 4E.

14. Emma Goldman was born in Lithuania in 1869, and emigrated to the United States. She was jailed twice, once for giving public instruction in birth control. She was deported to Russia in 1919, became disenchanted with the Soviet experiment, and spent the rest of her life traveling, writing, and lecturing (Rossi, 1973; Ruth, 1990).

15. The U.S. delegation to the Mexico City Population Conference was headed by conservative, pro-life delegate James L. Buckley. He delivered a message from the Reagan administration concerning a reversal in U.S. policy toward world population that sent shock waves through the meeting. He announced that population growth per se was no longer considered an obstacle to economic growth; in fact, under certain conditions it might be beneficial. The U.S. goal was to create worldwide free markets and individual initiative (Dixon-Mueller, 1993b; Weeks, 1992).

16. Nafis Sadik grew up in India and Pakistan in the 1930s and 1940s. She battled against gender stereotypes to obtain an education and a career. As an obstetrician-gynecologist, she became interested in family planning while working with women in the rural villages of Pakistan. During her rise from advisor to the UNFPA in 1971 to executive director of the agency in 1987, she has fought to give women control of their own lives (Connors, 1994).

17. Many moderate Muslims and Catholics around the world did support the major goals of the population conference. During the conference, Catholic groups took out a one-page "open letter" to Pope John Paul II, in which they disagreed with the Vatican's position on contraception.

18. See Iwao, S. *The Japanese Woman: Traditional Image and Changing Realities*, New York: Free Press, 1993; WuDunn, S. "Japan May Approve the Pill, but Women May Not," *The New York Times,* November 27, 1996: A1, A10; Kristoff, N., "Baby May Make Three, but in Japan That's Not Enough," *The New York Times,* October 6, 1996: 3.

19. In 1969, President Nixon appointed a commission on Population and the American Future. In its final report of 1972, the commission's recommendations included: ZPG (zero population growth); family planning services regardless of age or marital status; and legal abortion and the adoption of the Equal Rights Amendment to the U.S. Constitution. Nixon effectively repudiated the report and condemned it to inaction. (Dixon-Mueller, 1993b; Weeks, 1992).

20. Betsy Hartmann, in *Reproductive Rights and Wrongs: The Global Politics of Population Control* (1995), questions the urgency of population control, exposes racist and sexist underpinnings of the population establishment, and criticizes the "top down" fashion in which birth control is delivered to poor women.

21. Keller, B. "Zimbabwe Takes a Lead Promoting Contraceptives," *The New York Times,* September 4, 1994: 16. One of the factors inhibiting contraceptive use by women is a fear about safety and long-term health consequences. Depo-Provera is one of the approved technologies that has raised controversy. See, for example, Bunkle, P. Calling the shots? The international politics of Depo-Provera. In Harding, S. (Ed.), *The Racial Economy of Science*, Indianapolis: Indiana University Press, 1993.

Chapter 4

1. International Wages for Housework Campaign. (November 1992).

2. See Laurie Bell, *Good Girls/Bad Girls: Feminists and Sex Trade Workers Face to Face,* Seattle, WA: Seal Press, 1987, for documentation of a Canadian conference face-off in which sex workers defended their jobs and their self-respect, while feminists listened, questioned, and reflected.

3. Gallin, R. Women and the export industry in Taiwan: The muting of class consciousness. In K. Ward (Ed.), *Women Workers and Global Restructuring,* Ithaca, NY: Cornell University, 1990; Aptheker, B. *Tapestries of Life: Women's Work, Women's Consciousness, and the Meaning of Daily Experience,* Amherst: University of Massachusetts Press, 1989; Bookman, A. and Morgen, S. *Women and the Politics of Empowerment,* Philadelphia, PA: Temple University Press, 1988.

4. Stockard, J. and Johnson, M. *Sex and Gender in Society,* Englewood Cliffs, NJ: Prentice Hall, 1992; Stoper, E. (Ed.), *Women, Power, and Policy: Toward the Year 2000.* New York: Pergamon Press, 1988.

Chapter 5

1. Stern, P. *Women, Health, and Culture*, New York: Hemisphere Publishing Corporation, 1986; Mangay-Maglacas, A. and Pizurki, H. *The Traditional Birth Attendant in Seven Countries: A Case Study in Utilization and Training*, Geneva: World Health Organization, 1981.

2. Turshen, M. *Women and Health in Africa*, Trenton, NJ: Africa World Press, 1991a; United Nations Development Programme. *Young Women: Silence, Susceptibility, and the HIV Epidemic*, New York: United Nations, 1993.

3. The World Bank. *A New Agenda for Women's Health and Nutrition.* Washington, DC: The World Bank Publications, 1994; World Health Organization. *Women's Health: Across Age and Frontier*, Geneva: World Health Organization, 1992; Smyke, P. *Women and Health*, Atlantic Highlands, NJ: Zed Books, Ltd, 1991.

4. Turshen, *Women and Health*, 1991a; Koblinsky, M., Timyan, J., and Gay, J. *The Health of Women, A Global Perspective*, Boulder, CO: Westview Press, 1993.

5. Turshen, M. *Women and Health*, 1991a: Koblinsky, M., Timyan, J., and Gay, J. *The Health of Women*, 1993.

6. Fee, E. (Ed.), *Women and Health: The Politics of Sex in Medicine*, New York: Baywood Publishing, Co., 1983; Wilkinson, S. and Kitzinger, C. (Eds.), *Women and Health: Feminist Perspectives*. London: Taylor and Francis, 1994.

7. World Health Organization. *Women's Health*, 1992; Peto, R., Boreham, J., Thun, M., and Heath, C. *Mortality from Smoking in Developed Countries 1950-2000*, New York: Oxford University Press, 1994.

8. Wilkinson and Kitzinger, *Women and Health: Feminist Perspectives*, 1994; Smyke, *Women and Health*, 1991.

9. The multiple ways that breast cancer impacts the lives of women is a popular point of discussion within the popular media, chat lines on the Web, and documentary production. Also see Wilkinson and Kitzinger, *Women and Health: Feminist Perspectives*, 1991.

10. Although official research on breast cancer connects risk factors to late childbirth and not having children, cancer activists seek to expose the influence of environmental contamination. "In Israel, PCB levels in the breast of women with cancer were three times higher than those of women without breast cancer. And in Sweden, women with high levels of lindane in their tissues were ten times more likely to develop breast cancer" (Steingraber, 1993, pg. 196). Also, the United States federal government finally restricted DDT and other chlorinated pesticides known to be carcinogens (cancer causing), but laws allow chemical companies to export these substances to the third world (Steingraber, 1993). Before she died of breast cancer in 1998, feminist activist and former U.S. congresswoman Bella Abzug helped found WEDO (Women's Environment and Development Organization). This organization is dedicated to exploring globally the link between pollutants and diseases of the reproductive system (Abzug, 1995).

11. This information was gathered by interviewing ministers of health in Harare, Zimbabwe, July 1991. This was part of a larger exploration of global health care.

12. The four too's have been adopted as a health slogan used by nurses, doctors, community workers, and midwives. This slogan underscores the relationship between contraceptive practices and infant mortality rates and is used widely for health education. Also see Turshen, 1991a.

13. Governmental documents specifically define the levels of health care provision and divide the country into provinces. The eight provinces are Matabeland South, Matabeland North, Midlands, Masvingo, Mashonaland West, Mashonaland East, Mashonaland Central, and Manicaland.

14. Interviewed Matabeland South, summer 1993.

15. Village community workers are trained for three months. This training includes: structure of health services; primary health care; interpersonal skills aiding in how to approach persons/families; prevention of illness; six killer diseases; guidelines for appropriate nutrition; information about referring parents to the well-baby clinics; appropriate sanitation practices; control of burns and proper use of mud stoves; breast-feeding promotion; and water purification.

16. Several district nurses were interviewed in southern Zimbabwe in 1992 and 1993. One nurse captured the sentiment of most by expressing the importance of working with the women within the family to impart health information. The women seen by nurses as the most helpful in this process were the young women who were of childbearing age.

17. Rate as of November 1992: $1Z = $.20 USA. All dollar values are referring to the Zimbabwe dollar (Z).

18. Mr. M. was interviewed in southern Zimbabwe, summer of 1993. He discussed the importance of the role of the village community worker but saw this role as not a full-time job/occupation, but as a part-time service to the community. This impression ran counter to the reality of the experience for women in this role. The village community workers reported both long hours and a full-time and deep commitment to their jobs.

19. This figure of $70(Z) a month was only a fraction of the salary received by supervisors, who reported receiving $600-$700 a month. This supervisory position entailed no overtime and was considered full-time.

20. Mhloyi, M. Perceptions on communications and sexuality in marriage in Zimbabwe, *Women and Therapy*, 10, 1990: 61-73; Mhloyi, M. *Issues on Women's Health in Zimbabwe*, Dublin, Ireland: Global Forum of Women, 1992.

21. Mangay-Maglacas, A. and Pizurki, H. *The Traditional Birth Attendant in Seven Countries*, 1981; Stern, P. *Women, Health, and Culture*, New York: Hemisphere Publishing Corporation, 1986.

22. Information is based on interviews with sixty-one traditional midwives in Matabeland South, November 1992. The quotes in the following material are from these interviews, unless otherwise noted.

23. Payment varied from village to village. In a few villages, trained midwives commanded a greater payment, but even in those cases, it would be a small amount $3 (Z) or two pieces of soap.

24. Traditional healers were interviewed in the Matabeland South Province in November 1992. Three male healers and one female healer were interviewed. District nurses were key informants in understanding the role of traditional healers.

25. Some large, urban area health stations have specialists housed at the local facility.

26. Dahl, E. Inequality in health and the class position of women: The Norwegian experience, *Sociology of Health and Illness,* 13, 1991; Maseide, P. Health and social inequity in Norway, *Social Science Medicine,* 11(3), 1990.

27. Malterud, K. Illness and disease in female patients. *Scandanavian Journal of Primary Health Care,* 5, 1987: 205-209; Malterud, K. Strategies for empowering women's voices in the medical culture, *Fifth International Congress on Women's Health Issues.* Kobenhaven, 1992b.

28. Family doctors were interviewed, in January 1992, as part of a health delegation with Global Exchange exploring Cuban health care.

29. Interview of a family doctor, Havana, Cuba, 1992.

30. Interviewed in Havana, Cuba, spring 1992.

31. Kuntz, D. "U.S. Embargo Threatens Cuban Public Health." *WFPHA Report,* Washington, DC: American Public Health Association Publications, 1993; Golden, T. "Health Care, Pride of Cuba Is Falling on Tough Times," *The New York Times,* October 30, 1994, p. 1; Lane, C., "Castro's Long, Long Goodbye," *The New Republic,* October 3, 1994, pp. 15-25.

32. The cause of this disease is not known, but it appeared on the island in 1991 and has spread widely; it creates serious visual damage.

33. Corrosive esophagitis results from the ingestion of caustics. Since soap is now rationed due to inability to import in large amounts, people are making their own soap from lye. Inhalation of fumes (often occuring to women) and the drinking of lye mixture (seen more frequently by children) are implicated in corrosive esophagitis.

34. Kuntz, D. "U.S. Embargo Threatens Cuban Public Health," *WFPHA Report,* 1993; Golden, T. "Health Care, Pride of Cuba Is Falling on Tough Times," 1994.

35. Wilson, D., Lavelle, S., Greenspan, G., and Wilson, C. Psychological predictors of HIV—Preventive behavior among Zimbabwean students, *The Journal of Social Psychology,* 13(2), 1990; Bruyn, M. Women and AIDS in developing countries, *Social Science Medicine,* 34, 1992.

36. Rao, A. *Women's Studies International: Nairobi and Beyond,* New York: The Feminist Press at the City University of New York, 1991; Ward, M. *A World Full of Women,* Boston: Allyn and Bacon, 1996.

37. Stern, P. *Women, Health and Culture,* 1986; Bruyn, M. Women and AIDS in developing countries, 1992.

Chapter 6

1. Nairobi Forward Looking Strategies for the Advancement of Women. In *Report of the World Conference to Review and Appraise the Achievements of the (United Nations) Decade for Women,* 1985.

2. This discussion of violence against women worldwide assumes an explicitly feminist perspective, assuming that force, injury, and the murder of women are wrong, regardless of culture. For an analysis of the debate between feminists and anthropologists on sex and violence, see Harvey, P. and Gow, P. *Sex and Violence: Issues in Representation and Experience,* New York: Routledge, 1994.

3. Reardon, B. *Sexism and the War System.* New York: World Policy Institute, 1983; Stiehm, J. The protected, the protector, the defender, *Women's Studies International Forum,* 5, 1982: 367-376.

4. See Chapter 4 for a discussion of prostitution as work. Barbara Sullivan has written an excellent article summarizing the debate about prostitution: Sullivan, B. Rethinking prostitution, In B. Caine and R. Pringle (Eds.), *Transitions: New Australian Feminisms,* New York: St. Martin's Press, 1995: 184-197.

5. French, M. "The Open Wound," *The Washington Post,* November, 1992: F1, F4; The United States passed legislation introduced by Representative Patricia Schroeder that makes the practice of FGM in the United States illegal. Both the United States and Canada have granted asylum to women who fled their countries to escape the ritual procedure.

6. Although Salem Mekuria doesn't dispute the need to eradicate FGM, she does accuse American scholars of sensationalism and focusing solely on this issue without presenting a broader context. See Mekuria, S. Female genital mutilation in Africa: Some African views, *Bulletin of Association of Concerned African Scholars,* Winter/Spring, 44(45), 1995: 2-6.

7. Madhu Kishwar argues that dowry is not the cause but a symptom of female oppression. The answer is to ensure daughters have money and inheritance in their own right. (From Manushi. "Dowry Calculation." September/October 1993.)

Glossary

acute care: a medical intervention in response to diseases that are characterized by being severe and of relatively short duration.

Agency for International Development (AID): this agency was established by the United States to fund foreign development. It distributes funds to international organizations for family planning.

antinatalist policy: a policy that includes governmental rewards and sanctions intended to decrease the national birth rate.

apartheid: South Africa's governmental policy of compulsory and systematic racial segregation, including the creation of independent "homelands." The policy was officially abolished in 1992.

birthrate: annual number of births per 1,000 population.

bride-price/bride wealth: a price or gift given to the family of the bride in exchange for allowing the bride to marry into their family.

colonialism: control by one power over another nation, area, or people.

comfort stations: a euphemism for prostitution camps set up by Japan during World War II, where women were held captive and forced to provide sex to Japanese troops.

comfort women: a translation of the Japanese term *jugan ianfu* (military comfort women), refers to women of various ethnic and national backgrounds and social circumstances who became sex laborers (forced prostitutes) for Japanese troops before and during WWII.

companeras: poor Guatemalan Indian women living in rural communities.

conjoint marriage: a marriage pattern that is both polygynous and polyandrous, as when fraternal polyandrous brothers marry jointly a second wife.

cottage industry: an industry whose labor force consists of individuals working at home with their own equipment.

cultural diffusion: the spread of cultural elements from one culture to another.

cultural imperialism: the extension or imposition of one's culture over another; examples include gender norms, gender roles, and preferred family forms.

cultural relativism: an appreciation of cultural differences and a recognition that a culture cannot be arbitrarily judged by the standards of another.

death rate: annual number of deaths per 1,000 population.

demographic transition theory: the assumption that industrialization will be sufficient to slow population growth.

demography: the science of population.

dowry: money, goods, or real estate that a bride brings into her marriage; the custom is often seen as a transfer of resources from the family of the bride to the family of the groom.

economically active: the term used to classify "productive" labor. The concept is problematic because it does not include unpaid labor.

ethnocentrism: the tendency to judge other people and cultures by the standards of one's own culture.

export processing zones (EPZs): tax-free areas designed to attract multinational corporations.

family of orientation: the family an individual is born into as established by the parental lines.

family of procreation: the family a woman marries into, in which she presumably will have children—procreate.

fecundity: the number of children a woman is capable of having.

female sexual slavery: a situation in which women and girls are subject to sexual exploitation and cannot change their circumstances.

femininity: a set of traits and behaviors commonly associated with females; these traits are based on the cultural patterns of female behavior within a particular society, often characterized by nurturance and care.

feminism(s): includes a number of perspectives which are guided by the belief that women are equal to men and that their experiences are as important as men's experiences.

feminization of poverty: the majority of those in poverty worldwide are women and their dependent children.

fertility: the actual number of children a woman bears.

fictive kin: a nonbiological (blood) relationship that operates as a part of an individual's kinship group; examples are a beloved older woman being considered an aunt or a beloved neighbor boy being considered a son.

forced impregnation: form of sexual torture in ethnic wars when women are raped and intentionally impregnated by men of the enemy group.

formal health sector: the part of health care services that consists of highly skilled and educated health personnel, facilities, and equipment that requires training, expertise, and financial commitment to develop.

fraternal polyandry: the marriage of a woman to a set of brothers at the same time.

global assembly line: a factory production system in which workers assemble parts or components of particular products. Eighty to ninety percent of light-weight assembly workers are female, thus the term is closely associated with women's roles and the status of women within the global economy.

global carrying capacity: the maximum human population that the earth can support indefinitely on a specific resource base, at a specific level of technology.

globalization: the trend toward a worldwide system of political, economic, and social networks; treating the whole world as a continuous sphere.

gross national product (GNP): the total value of goods and services produced. It includes only goods and services exchanged for money.

home-based production: work performed at home for cash; although many home-based businesses are self-employment, there is an increasing tendency for businesses to subcontract work in this way.

horizontally complex families: families that define their family as consisting of multiple individuals for a generation, such as siblings in a specific generation, usually existing within the same household.

ideology: a set of beliefs that explain and justify some actual or potential social arrangement.

infibulation: a procedure in which all external genitalia are removed and the two sides are stitched together with an opening just small enough to permit the passage of urine and menses.

informal health sector: the part of health care that includes providers of health care and services who are usually not formally educated or trained through institutions of higher education or professional schools, but who learn their trade through informal apprenticeships, observation, and practice; examples include traditional healers and traditional midwives.

international feminism: a perspective that views women's oppression as a global phenomenon and supports research and activism that seek to understand and unify women worldwide.

International Labor Office (ILO): United Nations umbrella agency that keeps statistics and makes recommendations on the work people do worldwide.

International Monetary Fund (IMF): this fund was established after World War II to facilitate international development, expansion, and trade. Loans made by IMF influence national economies and employment.

International Wages for Housework Campaign (IWFH): coalition movement to require governments to remunerate women for their domestic labor and to count this labor in their national statistics.

liberal feminism: a perspective grounded in the belief that sex inequality is rooted in discriminatory practices and can be eliminated through policies of educational, economic, and political reform.

lobola: a bride-price used in the southern parts of Africa.

machismo: the masculine ideal of aggression, courage, honor, and sexual prowess, prevalent in Latin America.

macro-level violence: large-scale violence supported by a government or by a resistance movement.

marianisma: the feminine ideal of obedience, moral superiority, stoicism, and glorification of motherhood, prevalent in Latin America.

marriage pool: the group of available marriage partners based on the criteria set by the individual and/or the family.

Marxist feminism: a perspective that views gender inequality as an aspect of class inequality within Capitalism. The remedy is to replace capitalism with socialism and integrate women and men in the economy.

masculinity: a set of traits and behaviors commonly associated with males; these traits are based on cultural patterns of male behavior within a particular society, often characterized by instrumentality.

maximalist perspective: a perspective which holds that women and men are essentially different.

micro-level violence: interpersonal violence (e.g., spousal abuse, sexual harassment).

midwife: an individual who assists in the birth of children and who has formal medical training in normal and problem births.

migration rate: the annual number of intercountry movers per 1,000.

minimalist perspective: a perspective which holds that, except for reproductive biology, women and men are similar.

morbidity: rate of disease seen within a particular population; usually reported by disease per 1,000 persons per year.

mortality: rate of deaths seen within a particular population; usually reported as deaths per 100,000 per year.

multinational or transnational corporations (TNCs): corporations headquartered in one country but having subsidiaries in other countries.

nationalism: a commitment to fostering beliefs and policies that permit a nation to control its own destiny.

natural fertility planning (NFP): a form of birth control without use of artificial contraceptives, based on the assumption that if intercourse takes place only during a woman's nonfertile days, she will not become pregnant.

no-fault divorce: a marital dissolution that does not assign blame to either party.

North American Free Trade Agreement (NAFTA): the U.S., Canadian, and Mexican convention on free trade in North America. Critics fear that it will further exploit women workers.

palimony: term popularized during the 1960s; relates to settlement of money or goods after the dissolution of a long-standing cohabitation relationship.

patriarchy: a system of norms and traditions that gives males (particularly husbands and fathers) authority over females (particularly wives and daughters).

peace: not only the absence of war or violence and hostilities at the national and international levels, but also the enjoyment of economic and social justice, equality of human rights, and fundamental freedoms within society.

polyandry: the marriage of a woman to multiple men at the same time.

polygamy: the marriage of one woman or one man concurrently to more than one husband or wife, also called plural marriage.

polygyny: the marriage of a man to more than one woman at the same time.

population explosion: the unprecedented increase in world population that has been occurring in the last 150 to 200 years. The trend is alarming because of its consequences in human misery, due to resource depletion and environmental destruction.

population growth rate: an annual measure of population increase calculated worldwide by births minus deaths, usually expressed as a percentage of the total population (e.g., 2 percent per year).

preventive medicine: medical practices that serve to avert the development of disease states.

pronatalist policy: a policy that includes governmental rewards and sanctions intended to increase the national birthrate.

radical feminism: this perspective sees women's oppression as a model of other oppressions. Radical feminists believe that inequality is rooted in patriarchal and heterosexual relations.

sex-gender system: a system in which biological sex roles are intertwined with socially constructed gender roles in a structured set of relationships.

sex-segregated work: the tendency for women to work in occupations where most of the other workers are women, likewise with male workers.

sex tourism: a section of the tourist industry that encourages men to travel to third world countries to purchase the sexual services of local women.

Socialist feminism: a perspective which argues that gender inequality is a product of both capitalism and the patriarchy; a belief that production and reproduction are interconnected and that race, class, and gender intersect to form multiple oppressions.

sunna circumcision: a procedure involving the excision of the prepuce of the clitoris and partial or total excision of the clitoris itself (clitoridectomy).

traditional healer: an individual who heals others by evoking healing knowledge from past generations or spiritual experiences, or who has unknown sources of healing power.

traditional midwife (TM): an individual who assists in the birth of children and who has learned the trade primarily through experience.

United System of National Accounts (UNSNA): the collection of statistics on "productivity" of all nations. This data is used to identify areas in need of economic assistance.

vertically complex families: families that define their family as multiple generations, usually existing within the same household.

wage gap: refers to the fact that men are paid more in every country of the world. Women's average pay is calculated as a percentage of men's average pay.

war crimes tribunals: an international judicial system established to prosecute crimes against humanity, which now includes sex-specific offenses.

The World Bank: an international banking establishment created in the aftermath of World War II to assist reconstruction; the present policies influence funding and employment worldwide.

Bibliography

AAUW (American Association of University Women) Report. *How Schools Short-change Girls.* Wellesley, MA: AAUW Educational Foundation developed by the Wellesley College Center for Research on Women, 1992.

Abzug, B. Women and the environment. *Women: Looking Beyond 2000.* New York: United Nations, 1995.

African countries lead misery index. *Africa News,* 36(2), May 1992: 1.

Aird, J. *Slaughter of the Innocents.* Washington, DC: The AEI Press, 1990.

Alberdi, I. and Alberdi I. Spain. In M. Wilson (Ed.), *Girls and Young Women in Education: A European Perspective.* Oxford: Pergamon Press, 1991: 153-170.

"Algerian Forces Report Killing Five Islamic Rebels." *The New York Times,* February 19, 1995: Sec. 1, p. 10.

American Health Association. *The Politics of Suffering: The Impact of the U.S. Embargo on the Health of the Cuban People.* Washington, DC: American Public Health Association, 1993.

Amir, M. *Patterns of Forcible Rape.* Chicago: University of Chicago Press, 1971.

Amnesty International. Killed for not wearing a veil: Human rights are women's rights. *Amnesty International* (pamphlet). New York: Amnesty International, 1995

Andersen, M. *Thinking About Women.* New York: Macmillan Publishing Company, 1993.

Aptheker, B. *Tapestries of Life: Women's Work, Women's Consciousness, and the Meaning of Daily Experience.* Amherst: University of Massachusetts Press, 1989.

Arab Women at Work. New York: United Nations Development Programme, 1991.

Arendell, T. *Mothers and Divorce: Legal, Economic, and Social Dilemmas.* Berkeley: University of California Press, 1986.

Aron, A., Corne, S., Fursland, A., and Zelwer, B. The gender-specific terror of El Salvador and Guatemala. *Women's Studies International Forum,* 14, 1991: 37-47.

Baca Zinn, M. *Women of Color in the United States.* Philadelphia, PA: Temple University Press, 1994.

Barbara, A. *Marriage Across Frontiers.* Philadelphia, PA: Multilingual Matters Ltd., 1989.

Barnet, R. and Cavanaugh, J. *Global Dreams.* New York: Simon and Schuster, 1994.

Barry, K. *Female Sexual Slavery.* Englewood Cliffs, NJ: Prentice-Hall, 1979.

Barry, K. Social etiology of crimes against women. *Victimology: An International Journal,* 10, 1985: 164-173.

Bascom, W. *The Yoruba of Southwestern Nigeria.* New York: Holt, Reinhart, and Winston, 1969.

Batezat, E. and Mwato, M. *Women in Zimbabwe.* Harare, Zimbabwe: Sapes, 1989.

Beatty, A. *Society and Exchange in Nias.* Oxford: Clarendon Press, 1992.

Begum, K., Anstorp, T., Dalgare, O., and Serensen, T. Social network stimulation: Health promotion in a high risk group of middle aged women. *Acta Psychiatry Scandinavica. Supplement,* 76, 1987: 33-41.

Bell, L. *Good Girls/Bad Girls: Feminists and Sex Trade Workers Face to Face.* Seattle, WA: Seal Press, 1987.

Benallegue, N. Algerian women in the struggle for independence and reconstruction. *International Social Science Journal,* 13, October 1983: 703-717.

Bennett, L. *Dangerous Wives and Sacred Sisters.* New York: Columbia University Press, 1983.

Berger, M. and Buvinic, M. (Eds.), *Women's Ventures.* West Hartford, CT: Kumarian Press, 1989.

Bernard, J. *The Female World from a Global Perspective.* Indianapolis: Indiana University Press, 1987.

Bernstein, G. Haruko's work. In C. Brettell and C. Sargent (Eds.), *Gender in Crosscultural Perspective.* Englewood Cliffs, NJ: Prentice-Hall, 1993: 225-234.

Bijou, S. *Child Development.* Englewood Cliffs, NJ: Prentice-Hall, 1976.

Blackwood, E. Sexuality and gender in certain Native American tribes: The case of cross gender females. *Signs: The Journal of Women in Culture and Society,* 10, 1984: 27-42.

Blau, F. and Winkler, A. Women in the labor force: An overview. In J. Freeman (Ed.), *Women, A Feminist Perspective.* Mountain View, CA: Mayfield, 1989: 265-286.

Bohannan, P. *All the Happy Families.* New York: McGraw-Hill Books, 1985.

Bollag, B. Battling fundamentalism. *The Chronicle of Higher Education,* 40, February 1994: A42.

Bookman, A. and Morgen, S. *Women and the Politics of Empowerment.* Philadelphia, PA: Temple University Press, 1988.

Brinton, M. Gender stratification in contemporary urban Japan. In P. Burstein (Ed.), *Equal Employment Opportunity.* New York: Aldine DeGruyter, 1994: 349-355.

Brody, E. Parent care as a normative family stress. *The Gerontologist,* 25(1), 1985: 19-29.

Browner, C. The politics of reproduction in a Mexican village. In C. Brettell and C. Sargent (Eds.), *Gender in Cross-Cultural Perspective.* Englewood Cliffs, NJ: Prentice-Hall, 1993: 385-395.

Brownmiller, S. *Against Our Will.* New York: Bantam Books, 1975.

Bruyn, M. Women and AIDS in developing countries. *Social Science Medicine,* 34, 1992: 249-262.

Brydon, L. and Chant, S. *Women in the Third World.* New Brunswick, NJ: Rutgers University Press, 1989.

Bunkle, P. Calling the shots: The international politics of Depo-Provera. In S. Harding (Ed.), *The Racial Economy of Science.* Indianapolis: Indiana University Press, 1993: 287-302.

Burns, J. "Bangladesh, Still Poor, Cuts Birth Rate Sharply." *The New York Times,* September 13, 1994: A10.

Burns, J. "Stoning of Afghan Adulterers: Some Go to Take Part, Others Just to Watch," *The New York Times,* November 3, 1996: 18.

Bussey, G. and Tims, M. (Eds.), *Pioneers for Peace.* Oxford: Alden Press, 1980.

Butler, B. *Ceremonies of the Heart: Celebrating Lesbian Unions.* Seattle, WA: The Seal Press, 1990.

Buxrud, E. Are the health services a good working place for female physicians? *Tidsskr Nor Laegeforen.* Oslo, Norway: 1993.

Cagatay, N., Grown, C., and Santiago, A. The Nairobi Women's Conference: Toward a global feminism. *Feminist Studies,* 12, 1986: 401-411.

Cantor, D. and Bernay, T. *Women in Power.* New York: Houghton Mifflin Company, 1992.

Carmody, D. *Women and World Religions.* Englewood Cliffs, NJ: Prentice-Hall, 1989.

Carr, I. Women's voices grow stronger: Politics and feminism in Latin America. *National Women's Studies Association Journal,* 2(3), Summer 1990: 450-463.

Catasus, S. *Cuban Women: Changing Roles and Population Trends.* Geneva: UNFPA, International Labor Office, 1988.

The Centre for Development and Population Activities (CEDPA). *The CEDPA Experience: A Success Story for Women.* Washington, DC: CEDPA Training Program, 1994.

Charles, F. France. In M. Wilson (Ed.), *Girls and Young Women in Education: A European Perspective.* Oxford: Pergamon Press, 1991: 67-89.

Chin, J. Current and future dimensions of the HIV/AIDS pandemic in women and children. *The Lancet,* 36, 1990: 221-224.

Clarity, J. "Irish Vote to End Divorce Ban by a Tiny Margin." *The New York Times,* November 26, 1996:1.

Clarity, J. "As Law Takes Effect, Irish Embrace Divorce at Arms's Length," *The New York Times,* February 28, 1997: A5.

Cock, J. *Maids and Madams.* Scranton, PA: Salem House Publishers, 1990.

Collier, J. *Marriage and Inequality in Classless Societies.* Stanford, CA: Stanford University Press, 1988.

Collins, P. *Black Feminist Thought.* New York: Routledge, 1991.

Comaroff, J. *The Meaning of Marriage Payments.* London: Academic Press, 1980.

Comas-Diaz, L. *Women of Color.* New York: Guilford Press, 1994.

Connexions. Global lesbianism. *Connexions: An International Women's Quarterly,* 1981a.

Connexions. Global lesbianism 2. *Connexions: An International Women's Quarterly,* 1981b.

Connexions. Forum '85 Nairobi, Kenya. *Connexions: An International Woman's Quarterly,* Summer/Fall, 1985.

Connexions. Pregnancy police. *Connexions: An International Woman's Quarterly,* 31, 1989: 6-7.

Connexions. Sovereign state, sovereign selves: The impact of NAFTA on Mexican women. *Connexions: An International Women's Quarterly,* Winter, 1994: 35.

Connors, L. Nafis Sadik aiming for consensus on the royaling issue of population control. *The Los Angeles Times,* September 4, 1994: M3.

Conway-Turner, K. Old Skills and New Knowledge: Midwifery in Contemporary Zimbabwe. *Health Care for Women International,* 18, 1997: 565-574.

Conway-Turner, K. and Karasik, R. Adult daughters' anticipation of care-giving responsibilities. *Journal of Women and Aging,* 5(1), 1993: 99-114.

Croll, E., Davine, D., and Kane, P. (Eds.), *China's One-Child Family Policy.* New York: St. Martin's Press, 1985.

Crouter, A. *Harem: The World Behind the Veil.* New York: Abbeville Press, 1989.

Dahl, E. Inequality in health and the class position of women: The Norwegian experience. *Sociology of Health and Illness,* 13, 1991: 492-505.

Daly, M. Indian suttee: The ultimate consummation of marriage. In L. Richardson and V. Taylor (Eds.), *Feminist Frontiers.* New York: Random House, 1983: 189-191.

Davies, M. (Ed.), *Third World—Second Sex.* Atlantic Highlands, NJ: Zed Books Ltd., 1983.

Davis, E. *The First Sex.* Baltimore, MD: Penguin Books, 1972.

Davis, G. and Murch, M. *Grounds for Divorce.* Oxford: Clarendon Press, 1988.

Department for Economic and Social Information and Policy Analysis. *Report on the World Social Situation 1997.* New York: United Nations, 1997.

Dillon, M. *Debating Divorce: Moral Conflict in Ireland.* Lexington: University Press of Kentucky, 1993.

Dixon-Mueller, R. The sexuality connection in reproductive health. *Studies in Family Planning,* 24, 1993a: 269-282.

Dixon-Mueller, R. *Population Policy and Women's Rights.* Westport, CT: Praeger, 1993b.

Dobash, R. and Dobash, R. Violence against women. In L. O'Toole and J. Schiffman (Eds.), *Gender Violence,* New York: New York University Press, 1997: 266-278.

Duncan, M., Tibaux, G., Pelzer, A., Reimann, K., Pentherer, J.F., Simmonds, P., Young, H., Jamie, Y., and Daroughar, S. First coitus before menarche and risk of sexually transmitted diseases. *Lancet,* 335, 1990: 338-340.

Dworkin, A. Genocide: Chinese footbinding. In L. Richardson and V. Taylor (Eds.), *Feminist Frontiers.* New York: Random House, 1983: 178-187.

Dynes, W. and Donaldson, S. *Studies in Homosexuality: Lesbianism.* New York: Garland Publishing, 1992.

Earth Negotiations Bulletin. A Summary of the International Conference on Population and Development (ICPD). International Institute for Sustainable Development, 1994. New York: United Nations.

Eaton, M. Lesbians and the law. In S. Stone (Ed.), *Lesbians in Canada.* Toronto: Between the Lines, 1990: 109-132.

Edwards, W. *Modern Japan Through Its Weddings: Gender, Person, and Society in Ritual Portrayal.* Stanford, CA: Stanford University Press, 1989.

Ehrlich, P. and Ehrlich, A. *The Population Explosion.* New York: Simon and Schuster, 1990.

Eichenbaum, L. and Orbach, S. *Understanding Women.* New York: Basic Books, 1983.

Embry, J. *Mormon Polygamous Families: Life in Principle.* Salt Lake City: University of Utah Press, 1987.

Engles, F. The origin of the family, private property, and the state. In S. Ruth (Ed.), *Issues in Feminism.* Mt. View, CA: Mayfield Publishing Co., 1990: 179-186.

Enloe, C. *Bananas, Bases, and Beaches.* Los Angeles: University of California Press, 1989.

Eshleman, J. *The Family.* Fourth Edition. Boston: Allyn and Bacon, 1991.

Eshleman, J. *The Family.* Sixth Edition. Boston: Allyn and Bacon, 1994.

Eshleman, J. *The Family.* Eighth Edition. Boston: Allyn and Bacon, 1997.

Estioko-Griffin, A. and Griffin, P. Woman the hunter: The Agta. In C. Brettell and C. Sargent (Eds.), *Gender in Cross-Cultural Perspective.* Englewood Cliffs, NJ: Prentice-Hall, 1993: 206-215.

Ettore, E. What can she depend on? Substance use and women's health. In S. Wilkinson and C. Kitzinger (Eds.), *Women and Health: Feminist Perspectives.* London: Taylor and Francis, 1994.

Ezeh, A. The influence of spouses over each other's contraceptive attitudes in Ghana. *Studies in Family Planning,* 24, 1993: 163-173.

Faderman, L. *Surpassing the Love of Men: Romantic Friendship and Love Between Women from the Renaissance to the Present.* New York: William Morris and Co., 1981.

Farley, J. *Sociology.* Englewood Cliffs, NJ: Prentice-Hall, 1994.

Fee, E. (Ed.), *Women and Health: The Policies of Sex in Medicine.* New York: Baywood Publishing Co., 1983.

Fernandez-Kelly, P. *Women, Men, and the International Division of Labor.* Albany, NY: State University of New York Press, 1983.

Franklin, D. and Sweeny, J. Women and corporate power. In E. Boneparth and E. Stoper (Eds.), *Women, Power, and Policy.* New York: Pergamon Press, 1988:48-65.

French, M. "The Open Wound." *The Washington Post,* November 27, 1992: F1, F4.

Fuentes, A. and Ehrenreich, B. *Women in the Global Factory.* Boston: South End Press, 1984.

Gallin, R. Women and the export industry in Taiwan: The muting of class consciousness. In K. Ward (Ed.), *Women Workers and Global Restructuring.* Ithaca, NY: Cornell University, 1990.

Garcia, A. The development of Chicana feminist discourse. *Gender and Society,* 3(2), 1986: 217-238.

Garcia, J. Caribbean migration to the mainland: A review of adaptive experiences. *Annals of the American Academy of Political and Social Science,* 48, 1986: 114-125.

Gelles, R. and Cornell, C. *International Perspectives on Family Violence.* Lexington, Toronto: Lexington Books, 1983.

Genovese, M. *Women as National Leaders.* Newbury Park, CA: Sage Publications, 1993.

Gibson, C. *Dissolving Wedlock.* London: Routledge, 1994.

Global Forum of Women. *Global Forum of Women: New Visions of Leadership.* Volume 1. Dublin, Ireland: Global Forum of Women, 1992.

Goldberg, C. "Sex Slavery, Thailand to New York." *The New York Times,* September 11, 1995: B1.

Golden, T. "Health Care, Pride of Cuba Is Falling on Tough Times." *The New York Times,* October 30, 1994: 1.

Goldsmith, E. All in her mind! Stereotypic views and the psychologization of women's lives. In S. Wilkinson and C. Kitziner (Eds.), *Women and Health: Feminist Perspectives.* London: Taylor and Francis, 1994.

Goodman, E. "A World Too Small for Its People." *The News Journal,* September 13, 1994: A7.

Gopaul-McNicol, S. *Working with West Indian Families.* New York: The Guilford Press, 1993.

Government of Zimbabwe. *Government of Zimbabwe Action Plan.* Harare, Zimbabwe: Ministry of Health, 1986.

Graham, H. Surviving by smoking. In S. Wilkinson and C. Kitziner (Eds.), *Women and Health: Feminist Perspectives.* London: Taylor and Francis, 1994.

Gruenbaum, E. The movement against clitoridectomy and infibulation in Sudan: Public health policy and the women's movement. In C. Brettell and C. Sargent (Eds.), *Gender in Cross-Cultural Perspective.* Englewood Cliffs, NJ: Prentice-Hall, 1993: 411-422.

Guttman, J. *Divorce in Psychological Perspective.* Hillsdale, NJ: Lawrence Erlbaum Association, 1993.

Guyer, J. Women in the rural economy: Contemporary variations. In M. Hay and S. Stichter (Eds.), *African Women South of the Sahara.* Essex, United Kingdom: Longman Scientific and Technical, 1995: 23-43.

Haavio-Mannila, E. Inequalities in health and gender. *Social Science Medicine,* 22, 1986: 141-149.

Hafner, S. *Nice Girls Don't Drink.* New York: Bergen and Garvey, 1992.

Hall, R. *The Well of Loneliness.* New York: Avon Books, 1956.

Hart, N. *When Marriage Ends.* London: Tavistock Publications, 1976.

Hartman, B. *Reproductive Rights and Wrongs.* Boston, MA: South End Press, 1995.

Harvey, P. and Gow, P. *Sex and Violence: Issues in Representation and Experience.* New York: Routledge, 1994.

Hedges, C. "Everywhere in Saudi Arabia, Islam Is Watching." *The New York Times,* January 6, 1993a: A4.

Hedges, C. "Foreign Maids in Kuwait Fleeing by the Hundreds." *The New York Times,* February 24, 1993b: A3.

Heise, L. International Dimensions of Violence Against Women. *Response,* 12, 1989: 3-11.

Heise, L. "When Women Are Prey." *The Washington Post,* December 8, 1991: C1, C3.

Henshaw, S. and Van Hort, J., *Abortion Factbook.* New York: Alan Guttmacher Institute, 1992.

Hochschld, A. *The Second Shift: Working Parents and The Revolution at Home.* New York: Viking Press, 1989.

Hofferth, S., Rahn, J., and Baldwin, W. Premarital sexual activity among U.S. teenage women over the past three decades. *Family Planning Perspectives,* 19, March/April, 1987: 46-53.

Hoffman, L., Paris, S., Hall, E., and Schell, R. *Developmental Psychology Today.* New York: Random House, 1988.

hooks, b. *Ain't I a Woman: Black Women and Feminism.* Boston: South End Press, 1981.

Hughes, D.O. From bride-price to dowry in Mediterranean Europe. In M. Kaplan (Ed.), *The Marriage Bargain.* Binghamton, NY: Haworth Press and the Institute for Research and History, 1985: 13-58.

Hutter, M. *The Family Experience: A Reader in Cultural Diversity.* New York: MacMillan Publishing Co., 1991.

Informe Annual 1990. Republica de Cuba: Ministerio de Salus Publica, 1990.

Iwao, S. *The Japanese Woman: Traditional Image and Changing Realities.* New York: New York Free Press, 1993.

Jacobson, G. *Safe Motherhood in the SADCC Region: The Challenge for Survival.* New York: Family Health Care International, 1991.

Jacobson, J. Women's health: The price of poverty. In M. Koblinsky, J. Timyan, and J. Gay (Eds.), *The Health of Women, A Global Perspective.* Boulder, CO: Westview Press, 1993: 3-32.

Jamison, E. and Hobbs, F. *World Population Profile: 1994.* Washington, DC: U.S. Dept. of Commerce, Economics, and Statistics Administration, Bureau of the Census, 1994.

Johnson, W. and Warren, D. *Inside the Mixed Marriage.* New York: University Press of America, 1993.

Kaarsholm, P. *Cultural Struggle and Development in Southern Africa.* Harare, Zimbabwe: Baobab Books, 1991.

Kak, L.P. and Signer, M.B. The introduction of community-based family planning services in rural Mali: The Kibougou family health project. *Working Paper #2.* Washington, DC: CEDPA, 1993.

Kalish, S. Culturally sensitive family planning: Bangladesh's story suggests it can reduce family size. *Population Today,* 22(2), 1994: 5.

Kaplan, M. (Ed.), *The Marriage Bargain.* Binghamton, NY: The Haworth Press and the Institute for Research and History, 1985.

Kasun, J. *The War Against Population.* San Francisco, CA: Ignatius Press, 1988.

Katz, J. *Gay American History.* New York: Crowell, 1976.

Kelkar, G. Women and structural violence in India. *Women's Studies Quarterly,* XIII, Fall/Winter, 1985: 16-18.

Keller, B. "Zimbabwe Takes a Lead Promoting Contraceptives." *The New York Times,* September 4, 1994: 16.

Khan, N. *Setting the Record Straight.* Gulbert Lahore, Pakistan: ASR-Applied Socio-Economic Research, 1989.

Khotkina, Z. Women in the labour market: Yesterday, today, and tomorrow. In A. Posadskaya (Ed.), *Women in Russia: A New Era in Russian Feminism.* Moscow: Verso, 1994: 85-108.

Kilbride, P. *Plural Marriages for Our Times: A Reinvented Option.* Westport, CT: Greenwood Publishing Corporation, 1994.

Kimmel, D. *Adulthood and Aging.* New York: John Wiley and Sons, 1990.

Kishwar, M. Dowry calculations. *Manushi.* September/October, 78, 1993: 8-17.

Klein, K.G., Mayhew, P., Silber, E., and Stitzel, J. (Eds.), Women's studies administrators—Personal and professional intersections. *Women's Studies International Forum,* 9, 2, 1986: 111-112.

Knox, D. *Choices in Relationships.* Minneapolis/St. Paul: West Publishing Co., 1994.

Koblinsky, M., Campbell, O., and Harlow, S. Mother and more: A broader perspective on women's health. In M. Koblinsky, J. Timyan, and J. Gay (Eds.), *The Health of Women, A Global Perspective.* Boulder: Westview Press, 1993: 33-62.

Koblinsky, M., Timyan, J., and Gay, J. (Eds.), *The Health of Women, A Global Perspective.* Boulder: Westview Press, 1993.

Kolenda, P. *Caste in Contemporary India.* Prospects Heights, IL: Waveland Press, Inc., 1985.

Kontogiannopoulou-Polydorides, G. Greece. In M. Wilson (Ed.), *Girls and Young Women in Education: A European Perspective.* Oxford: Pergamon Press, 1991: 91-113.

Koss, M., Heise, L., and Russo, N. The global health burden of rape. In L. O'Toole and J. Schiffman (Eds.), *Gender Violence.* New York: New York University Press, 1997: 223-241.

Kristoff, N. "Baby May Make Three, but in Japan That's Not Enough." *The New York Times,* October 6, 1996: 3.

Kumari, R. *Brides Are Not for Burning: Dowry Victims in India.* New Delhi, India: Radiant Publishers, 1989.

Kuntz, D. U.S. embargo threatens Cuban public health. *WFPHA Report.* Washington, DC: American Public Health Association Publications, 1993.

Kuper, A. *Wives for Cattle: Bride Wealth and Marriage in Southern Africa.* Boston: Routledge and Kegan Paul, 1982.

Lane, C. "Castro's Long, Long Goodbye." *The New Republic,* October 3, 1994: 15-25.

Lederman, R. Looking back: The women's peace camps in perspective. In D.E.H. Russell (Ed.), *Exposing Nuclear Phallacies.* New York: Pergamon Press, 1989: 244-256.

Lee, R. *Mixed and Matched: Interreligious Courtship and Marriage in Northern Ireland.* New York: University Press of America, 1994.

Lenhart, S. and Bernstein, A. *The Psychodynamic Treatment of Women.* Washington, DC: American Psychiatric Press, 1993.

Lerner, G. An interview with Nawal El-Saadawi. *The Progressive,* 56(4), April, 1992: 32-35.

Lerner, H. *Women in Therapy.* New York: Harper & Row, 1988.

Levine, N. *The Dynamics of Polyandry: Kinship, Domesticity, and Population on the Tibetan Border.* Chicago: University of Chicago Press, 1988.

Levinson, D. *Family Violence in Cross-Cultural Perspective.* Newbury Park, CA: Sage Publications, 1989.

Levitan, S., Belous, R., and Gallo, F. *What's Happening to the American Family? Tensions, Hopes, Realities.* Baltimore, MD: Johns Hopkins University Press, 1988.

Library of Congress. End female genital mutilation in the United States—HR 941. Washington, DC: 104th Congress, First Session, 1995: 1-5.

Lim, L. *Foreign Direct Investment and Industrialization in Malaysia, Singapore, Taiwan, and Thailand.* Washington, DC: OECD Publications and Information Center, 1991.

Lindsey, L. *Gender Roles.* Englewood Cliffs, NJ: Prentice-Hall, 1994.

Lipman-Blumen, J. *Gender Roles and Power.* Englewood Cliffs, NJ: Prentice-Hall, 1984.

Lowenson, R. Harvests of disease: Women at work on Zimbabwean plantations. In M. Turshen (Ed.), *Women and Health in Africa.* Trenton: World Press, Inc., 1991: 35-40.

MacKinnon, C. Turning rape into pornography: Post-modern genocide. *Ms,* July/August, 1993: 24-30.

Maclean, M. *Surviving Divorce: Women's Resources After Separation.* Washington Square, NY: New York University Press, 1991.

Maillu, D. *Our Kind of Polygamy.* Nairobi: Keinemann Kenya, 1988.

Malterud, K. Illness and disease in female patients. *Scandinavian Journal of Primary Health Care,* 5, 1987: 205-209.

Malterud, K. Women's undefined disorders—A challenge for clinical communication. *Family Practice,* 9, 1992a: 299-303.

Malterud, K. Strategies for empowering women's voices in the medical culture. *Fifth International Congress on Women's Health Issues.* Kobenhaven, 1992b.

Malthus, T. *An Essay on Population.* New York: Augustus Kelley, 1798.

Mangay-Maglacas, A. and Pizurki, H. *The Traditional Birth Attendant in Seven Countries: A Case Study in Utilization and Training.* Geneva: World Health Organization, 1981.

Manz, B. *Refugees of a Hidden War.* New York: State University of New York Press, 1988.

Margolis, D. Women's movements around the world: Cross-cultural comparisons. *Gender and Society,* 7, 1993: 379-399.

Marshall, S. and Stokes, R. Tradition and the veil: Female status in Tunisia and Algeria. *The Journal of Modern African Studies,* 19, 1981: 625-646.

Martin, S. Sexual harassment: The link joining gender stratification, sexuality, and women's economic status. In J. Freeman (Ed.), *Women: A Feminist Perspective.* Mountain View, CA: Mayfield Publishing Company, 1989: 57-75.

Martin, S. *Refugee Women.* London: Zed Books, Ltd., 1992.

Maseide, P. Health and social inequity in Norway. *Social Science Medicine,* 11(3). 1990: 331-342.

Mason, M. Woman and shame: Kin in culture. In C. Bepko (Ed.), *Feminism and Addiction.* Binghamton, NY: The Haworth Press, 1991.

Matson, R. Nairobi—Where the end is the beginning. *The Humanist,* November/December, 1985: 12-16.

McAdoo, H. (Ed.), *Family Ethnicity: Strength in Diversity.* Newbury Park, CA: Sage, 1993.

McDonnell, N., Himunyanga-Phiri, T., and Tembo, A. Widening economic opportunities for women. In G. Young, V. Samarasinghe, and K. Kusterer (Eds.), *Women at the Center.* West Hartford, CT: Kumarian Press, 1993: 17-29.

McFarlane, G. Mixed marriages in Ballycuan, Northern Ireland. *Journal of Comparative Family Studies,* 10(2), 1979: 191-205.

Meeker-Lowry, S. Maquiladoras: A preview of free trade. *Peacework,* 31(2) April/May, 1993: 3-5.

Mekuria, S. Female genital mutilation in Africa: Some African views. *Bulletin of Concerned African Scholars,* 44(45), Winter/Spring, 1995: 2-6.

Menchu, R. *I, Rigoberta Menchu.* (A. Wright, Trans.) New York: Verso, 1992.

Mhloyi, M. Perceptions on communication and sexuality in marriage in Zimbabwe. *Women and Therapy,* 10, 1990: 61-73.

Mhloyi, M. *Issues on Women's Health in Zimbabwe.* Dublin, Ireland: Global Forum of Women, 1992.

Miles, R. *The Women's History of the World.* New York: Harper & Row, 1990.

Miller, B. Female infanticide and child neglect in rural north India. In C. Brettell and C. Sargent (Eds.), *Gender in Cross-Cultural Perspective.* Englewood Cliffs, NJ: Prentice-Hall, 1993.

Miller, J. "Women Regain a Kind of Security in Islam's Embrace." *The New York Times,* December 27, 1992: Sec. 4, p. 6.

Moghadam, V. *Modernizing Women.* Boulder and London: Lynne Rienner Publishers, 1993.

Moore, K., Nord, C., and Peterson, J. Nonvoluntary sexual activity among adolescents. *Family Planning Perspectives,* 21, 1989: 110-114.

Morello, T. Good, clean fun. *Far Eastern Economic Review,* December 2, 1993: 27-28.

Morgan, R. *Sisterhood Is Global.* New York: Anchor Books, 1984.

Morgan, R. *Sisterhood Is Global.* New York: The Feminist Press, 1996.

Morgan, R. and Steinem, G. The international crime of genital mutilation. In L. Richardson and V. Taylor (Eds.), *Feminist Frontiers.* New York: Random House, 1980: 191-195.

Nazzari, M. *Disappearance of the Dowry.* Stanford, CA: Stanford University Press, 1991.

Neft, N. and Levine, A. *Where Women Stand.* New York: Random House, 1997.

"New Law Lets Swedish Gays Marry." *The News Journal,* January 10, 1995: 6.

Newsom, D. and Carrell, B. *Silent Voices.* New York: University Press of America, 1995.

Nikolic-Ristanovic, V. War and violence against women. In J. Turpin and L. Lorentzen (Eds.), *The Gendered New World Order.* New York: Routledge, 1996: 195-211.

"No Apology for Victims." *The New York Times,* December 15, 1996:14.

O'Barr, J. Reflections on Forum '85 in Nairobi, Kenya: Voices from the international women's studies community. *Signs,* 11(3), 1986: 584-586.

Omran, A. *Family Planning in the Legacy of Islam.* New York: Routledge, 1992.

Otero, M. Solidarity group programs: A working methodology for enhancing economic activities of women in the informal sector. In M. Berger and M. Buvinic (Eds.), *Women's Ventures.* West Hartford, CT: Kumarian Press, 1989.

Parkman, A. *No-Fault Divorce: What Went Wrong?* Boulder, CO: Westview Press, 1992.

Perlez, J. "In Rwanda, Births Increase and the Problems Do, Too." *The New York Times,* May 31, 1992: 1, 12.

Perlez, J. "A Painful Case Tests Poland's Abortion Ban." *The New York Times,* April 2, 1995: 3.

Peterson, V. and Runyan, A. *Global Gender Issues.* Boulder, CO: Westview Press, 1993.

Peto, R., Lopes, A., Boreham, J., Thun, M., and Heath, C. *Mortality from Smoking in Developed Countries 1950-2000.* New York: Oxford University Press, 1994.

Petsalis, S. *Silent Power: Portrait of Nigerian Women.* Montreal: Meridian Press, 1990.

Phillips, R. *Divorce in New Zealand.* Aukland, New Zealand: Oxford University Press, 1981.

Phillips, R. *Putting Asunder.* Cambridge, MA: Cambridge University Press, 1988.

Phoenix, A. The Afro-Caribbean myth. *New Society,* 82, 1988: 10-13.

Pitts, M., Humphrey, M., and Wilson, P. Assessments of personal and general risks of HIV and AIDS in Harare, Zimbabwe. *Health Education Research,* 6(3), 1991: 307-311.

Pitts, M., McMaster, J., and Wilson, P. An investigation of preconditions necessary for the introduction of a campaign to promote breast self-examination amongst Zimbabwean women. *Journal of Community and Applied Social Psychology,* 1, 1991: 33-41.

Pooler, W. Sex of child preferences among college students. *Sex Roles,* 25, September, 1991: 569-576.

Portugal, A. Not even with a rose petal. In R. Morgan (Ed.), *Sisterhood Is Global.* New York: Anchor Books, 1984: 550-554.

Posadskaya, A. (Ed.), *Women in Russia: A New Era in Russian Feminism.* New York: Verso, 1994.

Powell, D. Caribbean women and their responses to familial experiences. *Social and Economic Studies,* 35, 1986: 83-130.

Prado, M. Working-class Mexican American women and volunteerism: We have to do it! In E. Higginbotham and M. Romero (Eds.), *Women and Work: Exploring Race, Ethnicity and Class.* Volume six. Newbury Park, CA: Sage Publications, 1997:197-215.

Preston, J. "A Woman's Shooting of Attacker Rivets Mexico." *The New York Times,* February 5, 1997: 193.

Randall, M. *Sardino's Daughters Revisited: Feminism in Nicaragua.* New Brunswick, NJ: Rutgers University Press, 1994.

Randall, M. Gathering rage: The failure of 20th century revolutions to develop a feminist agenda: The case of Nicaragua. In K. Conway-Turner, S. Cherrin, J. Schiffman, and K. Turkel (Eds.), *Women's Studies in Transition: The Pursuit of Interdisciplinarity.* Newark, DE: University of Delaware Press, 1998.

Rao, A. *Women's Studies International: Nairobi and Beyond.* New York: The Feminist Press at the City University of New York, 1991.

Rao, R. and Husain, S. Invisible hands: Women in home-based production in the garment export industry in Delhi. In A. Singh and K. Kelles-Viitanen (Eds.), *Invisible Hands.* Newbury Park, CA: Sage Publications, 1987: 56-57.

Reardon, B. *Sexism and the War System.* New York: World Policy Institute, 1983.

Richard, M. *Ethnic Groups and Marital Choices.* Vancouver: UBC Press, 1991.

Robertson, I. *Sociology.* New York: Worth Publishers, Inc., 1987.

Robinson, M. *Family Transformation Through Divorce and Remarriage: A Systematic Approach.* London: Routledge, 1991.

Romano, P. *Intercultural Marriage: Promises and Pitfalls.* Yarmouth, ME: Intercultural Press, 1988.

Roos, P. *Gender and Work: A Comparative Analysis of Industrial Societies.* Albany: State University of New York, 1985.

Rossi, A. (Ed.), *The Feminist Papers.* New York: Bantam Books, Inc., 1973.

Rothman, B. *Loving and Learning.* Lexington, KY: Lexington Books, 1990.

Rugh, A. *Family in Contemporary Egypt.* Syracuse, NY: Syracuse University Press, 1984.

Russell, D. *Lives of Courage.* New York: Basic Books, Inc., 1989.

Russell, D. and Van de Ven, N. *Crimes Against Women: Proceedings of the International Tribunal.* East Palo Alto, CA: Frog In The Well, 1984.

Ruth, S. *Issues in Feminism.* Mountain View, CA: Mayfield Publishing Co., 1990.

Ryerson, W. Population communications international: Its role in family planning soap operas. *Population and Environment: A Journal of Interdisciplinary Studies,* 15, 1994: 255-264.

Sadik, N. *The State of World Population.* New York: UNFPA/United Nations Population Fund, 1991.

Saint-Germain, M. Women in power in Nicaragua: Myth and reality. In M. Genovese (Ed.), *Women as National Leaders.* Newbury Park, CA: Sage Publications, 1993: 70-102.

Sanchez-Ayendez, M. Puerto Rican elderly women: Shared meanings and informal supportive networks. In J. Cole (Ed.), *All American Women: Lines That Divide, Ties That Bind.* New York: Free Press, 1986: 172-186.

Sanday, P.R. The socio-cultural context of rape: A cross-cultural study. In L.L. O'Toole and J.R. Schiffman (Eds.), *Gender Violence.* New York: New York University Press, 1997: 52-66.

Sanger, D. "History Scholar in Japan Exposes a Brutal Chapter." *The New York Times,* January 2, 1992: A4.

Sanger, M. Birth control—A Parent's problem or woman's? In A. Rossi (Ed.), *The Feminist Papers.* New York: Bantam Books, 1973.

Sanger, M. Women and the new race. In S. Ruth (Ed.), *Issues in Feminism.* Mountain View, CA: Mayfield Publishers, 1995: 506-510.

Saperstein, S. and Stutsman R. Sustainability: The global challenge. *ZPG Backgrounder,* Zero Population Growth, August, 1989.

Schechter, S. *Women and Male Violence.* Boston, MA: South End Press, 1982.

Schmidt, W. "Sweden Redefines Sexual Revolution." *The New York Times,* March 22, 1992: Sec. 4, p. 2.

Schmittroth, L. *Statistical Record of Women Worldwide.* Detroit: Gale Research, Inc., 1991.

Schuler, M. (Ed.), *Freedom from Violence: Women's Strategies from Around the World.* New York: UNIFEM Widbooks, 1992.

Schuler, S. *The Other Side of Polandry.* Boulder, CO: Westview Press, 1987.

Schwartz, M.A. and Scott, B. *Marriages and Families: Diversity and Change.* Englewood Cliffs, NJ: Prentice-Hall, 1994.

Sciolino, E. "The Many Faces of Islamic Law," *The New York Times,* October 13, 1996: 4E.

Senior, O. *Working Miracles: Women's Lives in English-Speaking Caribbean.* London: James Curry, 1991.

Shapiro, D. and Tambashe, B. The impact of women's employment and education on contraceptive use and abortion in Kinshasa, Zaire. *Studies in Family Planning,* 25(2), 1994: 96-110.

Sheffield, C. Sexual terrorism. In L. O'Toole and J. Schiffman (Eds.), *Gender Violence.* New York: New York University Press, 1997: 110-127.

Shenon, P. "China's Mania for Baby Boys Creates Surplus of Bachelors." *The New York Times,* August 4, 1994: A1, A8.

Shostak, M. Women and men in !Kung society. In B. Brettell and C. Sargent (Eds.), *Gender in Cross-Cultural Perspective.* Englewood Cliffs, NJ: Prentice-Hall, 1993: 154-162.

Sidel, R. *Women and Children Last.* New York: Penguin Books, 1987.

Siedlecky, S. and Wyndham, D. *Populate and Perish.* Sydney, Australia: Allen and Unwin, 1990.

Siem, H. *Choices for Health: An Introduction to Health Services in Norway.* Oslo, Norway: Universitetsforlaget As, 1986.

Simon, J. and Kahn, H. (Eds.), *The Resourceful Earth: A Response to Global 2000.* Oxford, England: Basil Blackwell, Inc., 1984.

Simons, M. "In Europe's Brothels, Women from the East." *The New York Times,* June 9, 1993: A1, A8.

Singh, A. and Kelles-Viitanen, K. (Eds.), *Invisible Hands.* Newbury Park, CA: Sage Publications, 1987.

Sivard, R. *World Military and Social Expenditures* 1996. Sixth Edition. Washington, DC: World Priorities, 1996.

Skinner, B. *The Behavior of Organisms.* New York: Appleton-Century-Crofts, 1938.

Smith, L. and Padula, A. *Sex and Revolution: Women in Socialist Cuba.* New York: Oxford University Press, 1996: 57-69.

Smyke, P. *Women and Health.* Atlantic Highlands, NJ: Zed Books, Ltd., 1991.

Soh, C. The Korean "comfort women": Movement for redress. *Asian Survey,* 36(12), 1996: 1226-1240.

Stack, C. *All Our Kin.* New York: Harper & Row, 1974.

Stanley, A. "Sexual Harassment Thrives in the New Russian Climate." *The New York Times,* April 17, 1994: 8.

Staples, R. and Johnson, L. *Black Families at the Crossroads.* San Francisco, CA: Jossey-Bass, 1992.

Staunton, I. *Mothers of the Revolution.* Bloomington, IN: Indiana University Press, 1990.

Steingraber, S. If I live to be 90 still wanting to say something: My search for Rachel Carson. In M. Stocker (Ed.), *Confronting Cancer, Constructing Change.* Chicago: Third Side Press, 1993: 181-199.

Stern, P. *Women, Health, and Culture.* New York: Hemisphere Publishing Corporation, 1986.

Stiehm, J. The protected, the protector, the defender. *Women's Studies International Forum,* 5, 1982: 367-376.

Stockard, J. and Johnson, M. *Sex and Gender in Society.* Englewood Cliffs, NJ: Prentice-Hall, 1992.

Stone, L. *Road to Divorce.* Oxford: Oxford University Press, 1990.

Stone, M. *When God Was a Woman,* New York: Harcourt Brace Jovanovich, 1976.

Stone, S. *Lesbians in Canada.* Toronto: Between the Lines, 1990.

Stoper, E. (Ed.), *Women, Power, and Policy: Toward the Year 2000.* New York: Pergamon Press, 1988.

Stopes, M. *Married Love.* New York: Eugenics Publishing Co., Inc., 1931.

Sullivan, B. Rethinking prostitution. In B. Caine and R. Principle (Eds.), *Transitions: New Australian Feminisms.* New York: St. Martin's Press, 1995: 184-197.

Sullivan, S. "Born Under a Bad Sign," *Newsweek,* September 23, 1996: 49-51.

Swidler, A. *Homosexuality and World Religions.* Valley Forge, PA: Trinity Press International, 1993.

Sykes, P. Women as national leaders: Patterns and prospects. In M. Genovese (Ed.), *Women as National Leaders.* Newbury Park, CA: Sage, 1993: 219-299.

Szydlowski, H. and Dudziak, G. Poland. In M. Wilson (Ed.), *Girls and Young Women in Education: A European Perspective.* Oxford: Pergamon Press, 1991.

Taeuber, C. *Statistical Handbook on Women in America.* Phoenix, AZ: Oryx Press, 1996.

Thompson, J. Women and war. *Women's Studies International Forum,* 14, 1991: 63-75.

Thorne, B. and Yalom, M. *Rethinking the Family.* Boston: Northeastern University Press, 1992.

Tiano, S. *Patriarchy on the Line: Labor, Gender, and Ideology in the Mexican Maquila Industry.* Philadelphia, PA: Temple University Press, 1994.

Travis, C. (Ed.), *Biologically Based Methods for Cancer Risk Assessment.* New York: Plenum Press, 1989.

Turshen, M. *Women and Health in Africa.* Trenton, NJ: Africa World Press, 1991a.

Turshen, M. Gender and health in Africa. In M. Turshen (Ed.), *Women and Health in Africa.* Trenton, NJ: Africa World Press, Inc., 1991b: 107-124.

Turshen, M. Taking women seriously: Toward democratic health care. In M. Turshen (Ed.), *Gender and Health in Africa.* Trenton, NJ: Africa World Press, Inc., 1991c: 205-220.

UNIFEM. *UNIFEM in Beijing and Beyond.* New York: United Nations Development Fund for Women (UNIFEM), 1996.

United Nations. *Nairobi Forward Looking Strategies for the Advancement of Women.* New York: United Nations, 1985: 32.

United Nations. Changes in the size of households in selected developed countries. *Report on the World Social Situation.* New York: United Nations, 1990: 154.

United Nations. *Women, Challenges to the Year 2000.* New York: United Nations Department of Public Information, 1991a.

United Nations. *World's Women 1970-1990.* Social statistics and indicators, Series K. No. 8. New York: United Nations, 1991b.

United Nations Development Programme. *Arab Women at Work.* New York: United Nations, 1991: 11.

United Nations Development Programme. *Young Women: Silence, Susceptibilty, and the HIV Epidemic.* New York: United Nations, 1993.

Villee, C. (Ed.), *Fallout from the Population Explosion.* New York: Paragon House Publishers, 1985.

Waldman, G. and Waldman, L. (Eds.), *Understanding Women: The Challenge of Cross-Cultural Perspective.* Columbus, OH: The Ohio State University Press, 1992.

Ward, M. *A World Full of Women.* Boston: Allyn and Bacon, 1996.

Waring, M. *If Women Counted.* San Francisco, CA: Harper, 1988.

Warren, C., Hiyari, F., Wingo, P., Abdel-Aziz, A., and Morris, L. Fertility and family planning in Jordan: Results from the 1985 Jordan husbands' fertility survey. *Studies in Family Planning,* 21, 1990: 33-39.

Weeks, J. *Population.* Belmont, CA: Wadsworth Publishing Co., 1992.

Wernersson, I. Sweden. In M. Wilson (Ed.), *Girls and Young Women in Education: A European Perspective.* Oxford: Pergamon Press, 1991.

Wilkerson, I. "Hard Life Is Getting Harder for South Africa's Domestics." *The New York Times,* October 10, 1994: A1.

Wilkinson, S. and Kitzinger, C. (Eds.), *Women and Health: Feminist Perspectives.* London: Taylor and Francis, 1994.

Will War Crimes Against Women Finally Count? *Ms,* May/June, 1996:24-25.

Williams, C. The psychology of women. In J. Wetzel, M. Espenlaub, M. Hagan, A. McElhiney, and C. Williams, *Women's Studies: Thinking of Women.* Dubuque, IA: Kendall/Hunt Publishing, 1993: 27-62.

Williams, N. *The Mexican American Family: Tradition and Change.* Dix Hills, NY: General Hall, Inc., 1990.

Wilson, D., Lavelle, S., Greenspan, G., and Wilson, C. Psychological predictors of HIV—Preventive behavior among Zimbabwean students. *The Journal of Social Psychology,* 13(2), 1990: 293-295.

Wilson, M. (Ed.), *Girls and Young Women in Education: A European Perspective.* Oxford: Pergamon Press, 1991.

Wiser, A. Women's peace caravan. In D.E.H. Russell (Ed.), *Exposing Nuclear Phallacies.* New York: Pergamon Press, 1989: 288-291.

Women and revolution. *Journal of the Spartacist League Central Committee Commission for Work among Women,* 44, Winter/Spring, 1995.

Women's World Banking. The credit guarantee mechanisms for improving women's access to bank loans. In M. Berger and M. Buvinic (Eds.), *Women's Ventures.* West Hartford, CT: Kumarian Press, 1989: 174-184.

Woolf, V. *Three Guineas.* New York: Harcourt, Brace and Company, 1938.

The World Bank. *A New Agenda for Women's Health and Nutrition.* Washington, DC: The World Bank Publications, 1994.

World Bank World Development Report: Investing in Health. New York: Oxford University Press, 1993.

World Health Organization (WHO). *Women's Health: Across Age and Frontier.* Geneva: WHO, 1992.

Wright, C. "Taslima Nasreen's Campaign Endangers Other Reformers." *The Christian Science Monitor,* August 8, 1994: 19.

WuDunn, S. "Japan May Approve the Pill, but Women May Not." *The New York Times,* November 27, 1996: A1, A10.

Yearbook of Labour Statistics 1986-1988. Geneva: International Labor Office, 1992.

Younis, N. and Zurayk, H. A community study of gynecological and related morbidities in rural Egypt. *Studies in Family Planning,* 24(3), 1993: 46-52.

Zabalza, A. and Tzannatoes, Z. The effects of Great Britain's antidiscrimination legislation on relative pay and employment. In P. Burstein (Ed.), *Equal Employment Opportunity.* New York: Aldine DeGruyter, 1994: 49-69.

Zurayk, H., Khattab, H., Younis, N., Kamal, O., and El-Helw, M. Comparing women's reports with medical diagnoses of reproductive morbidity conditions in rural Egypt. *Studies in Family Planning,* 26(1), 1995: 14-21.

Index

Page numbers followed by the letter "t" indicate tables.

Woolf, Virginia, 7
Work for wages, as "real work," 106
Workforce, women in, 38
Workplace
  gender stereotypes, 132
  and sexual harassment, 199
World Bank, 118
World Conference on Human Rights,
    Vienna (1993), 11
World Fertility Survey (WFS), 74
World Population Conference, Cairo
    (1994), 69,88-89
World Summit for Social
    Development, Copenhagen
    (1995), 11

Yoruban, and polygyny, 62

Zambia
  education in, 126
  women's enterprises, 133
Zia, Khaleda, 99
Zimbabwe
  facts concerning, 146t
  family planning efforts in, 100
  health care, 133-156
    formal system, 146
  prostitution in, 2
  remarriage in, 43
  sanitation in, 147
  women's minority status, 24
  women's work, 109

Order Your Own Copy of
This Important Book for Your Personal Library!

WOMEN, FAMILIES, AND FEMINIST POLITICS
A Global Exploration

_____ in hardbound at $49.95 (ISBN: 0-7890-0482-8)

_____ in softbound at $29.95 (ISBN: 1-56023-935-2)

COST OF BOOKS_____

OUTSIDE USA/CANADA/
MEXICO: ADD 20%_____

POSTAGE & HANDLING_____
*(US: $3.00 for first book & $1.25
for each additional book)
Outside US: $4.75 for first book
& $1.75 for each additional book)*

SUBTOTAL_____

IN CANADA: ADD 7% GST_____

STATE TAX_____
*(NY, OH & MN residents, please
add appropriate local sales tax)*

FINAL TOTAL_____
*(If paying in Canadian funds,
convert using the current
exchange rate. UNESCO
coupons welcome.)*

☐ **BILL ME LATER:** (\$5 service charge will be added)
(Bill-me option is good on US/Canada/Mexico orders only;
not good to jobbers, wholesalers, or subscription agencies.)

☐ Check here if billing address is different from
shipping address and attach purchase order and
billing address information.

Signature_____

☐ **PAYMENT ENCLOSED:** $_____

☐ **PLEASE CHARGE TO MY CREDIT CARD.**

☐ Visa   ☐ MasterCard   ☐ AmEx   ☐ Discover

Account #_____

Exp. Date_____

Signature_____

Prices in US dollars and subject to change without notice.

NAME_____

INSTITUTION_____

ADDRESS_____

CITY_____

STATE/ZIP_____

COUNTRY_____ COUNTY (NY residents only)_____

TEL_____ FAX_____

E-MAIL_____
May we use your e-mail address for confirmations and other types of information? ☐ Yes   ☐ No

Order From Your Local Bookstore or Directly From
The Haworth Press, Inc.
10 Alice Street, Binghamton, New York 13904-1580 • USA
TELEPHONE: 1-800-HAWORTH (1-800-429-6784) / Outside US/Canada: (607) 722-5857
FAX: 1-800-895-0582 / Outside US/Canada: (607) 772-6362
E-mail: getinfo@haworthpressinc.com
PLEASE PHOTOCOPY THIS FORM FOR YOUR PERSONAL USE.

BOF96